The Road to Growth

towards a thriving Church

'Bob Jackson's approach is straightforward – he studies the evidence, analyses it and then shows what we can do about it. Challenging and inspiring – this should be essential reading for every bishop, priest and lay person who wants the Church to grow.'

Dominic Walker
Bishop of Monmouth

'Once again Bob has produced some radical thinking which leaders of every part of the Church of England need to consider as they make their plans. This is not always an easy read for people who have been the policy makers, but it is certainly an essential read.'

Canon Dr Christina Baxter
Principal, St John's College Nottingham

'As with *Hope for the Church*, Bob Jackson here bases his critique of much current Church practice on *actual research*. He helps us to see what does or doesn't make a spiritually healthy and growing Church. He challenges many parochial and diocesan sacred cows – including the Parish Share. He describes and affirms pluriform good practice. This book ought to be debated at every Bishop's Staff Meeting and in every Deanery.'

Christopher Hill
Bishop of Guildford

The Road to Growth

towards a thriving Church

CHURCH HOUSE
PUBLISHING

Bob Jackson

Church House Publishing
Church House
Great Smith Street
London SW1P 3NZ
Tel: 020 7898 1451
Fax: 020 7898 1449

ISBN 0 7151 4073 6

Published 2005 by Church House Publishing

Bible quotations are from the New Revised Standard version of the Bible copyright © 1989 by the Division of Christian Education of the National Council of the Churches in the USA. All rights reserved.

The opinions expressed in this book are those of the author and do not necessarily reflect the official policy of the General Synod of The Archbishops' Council of the Church of England.

Cover design by Andy Stonehouse

Typeset in Rotis Semi Sans by RefineCatch Ltd, Bungay, Suffolk

Printed in England by The Cromwell Press Ltd, Trowbridge, Wiltshire

Contents

Contents

List of tables

List of figures

List of figures

Preface

The widespread, positive reaction to my first book on church growth (*Hope for the Church*, Church House Publishing, 2002) encouraged me not just as an author but as an Anglican. It showed me that our denomination is now ready to engage with the issue of its own survival and future. Over the two years following publication I continued researching the causes of church growth and decline, until at the end of 2004 I was invited to try applying the lessons learnt as Archdeacon of Walsall and Growth Officer in the Diocese of Lichfield. This new book has emerged both out of the research years and the early months of my descent into venerability.

The purpose of the book is not simply to report a new set of important research findings. It is to show how a diocese, both out in the parishes and in its human resource and financial functions, can overturn its old cycle of decline and begin a new cycle of growth. There is no doubt that we live in a more challenging world for the growth of the Christian Church in the early twenty-first century but, equally, there is no doubt that, in the providence of God, growth is entirely possible for those who intelligently apply the lessons of the evidence marshalled in this book and elsewhere.

So my hope is that readers will not only find stimulation from the book but will actually put some of its conclusions into practice – please use it as a practical tool rather than an academic talking point.

As always, I am enormously grateful to a large number of people who have helped with the gestation of this book. Everything in it of any value results not from blue skies pipe dreaming but from observation of what God is doing in churches all around the country, and of how so many heroes of the faith are doing it with him. We live in exciting times, the Holy Spirit is on the move, the Church of England is changing fast, we are becoming a missionary church, and my thanks go to hundreds of quiet pioneers whom I have spotted making this happen on the ground.

Special thanks go to my wife and children who maintain, with some truth, that I am once more simply the editor of a family effort. Chapter 9, for example, is in large part the work of my daughter, the Revd Ruth Jackson. My special thanks go also to Canon Robert Warren, my *Springboard* friend and colleague, for his mentoring and encouragement and to Kathryn Pritchard, my long-suffering editor, who is responsible for the very important 'Explorations' series from Church House Publishing. However, all the errors, dodgy reasoning and subjective conclusions that you, dear reader, may spot are entirely of my own making.

Foreword

When I read this book in typescript, I found it a stimulating aid to self examination and also repentence for certain aspects of my own practice as a bishop over the past decade. I imagine that mine will not be a unique experience.

Looking back over more than 30 years in ordained ministry, I can see the landscape littered with the remains of many bright ideas. Instead, however, of experiencing the salutary pain of discovering that they were not all very good ideas, what has most commonly happened is that the Church has moved on to embrace a new enthusiasm before properly evaluating the effectiveness, in terms of the growth of the Church at every level, of yesterday's favoured strategy.

In consequence as we face in the London region the challenge of substantial population increase, major new housing developments in a number of places and an ever more diverse multi-ethnic mix, we are looking urgently for candid assessments of previous responses to similar conditions in order to make better informed decisions. There is remarkably little such material available and this is where Bob Jackson's new book is so very valuable.

The Road to Growth is an evidence based review of what has worked and what has not in contributing to the growth of a thriving Church. Several of yesterday's sacred cows are slain along the way while a score of useful new areas for research are opened up.

One of the many things I found helpful was the evidence collected to show that church growth tended to happen between years five and twelve of an incumbency and that able clergy were sometimes moved too soon. I imagine that may diocesan staff meetings, clergy chapters and gatherings of lay leaders will want to work through the implications of the evidence collected by Bob Jackson for their own practice.

Without minimizing the effects of social and cultural change *The Road to Growth* is a liberating piece of work because it shows that at least some of the factors hobbling the Church can yield to determined and clear sighted change in policies at the parish and diocesan levels. This energizing book also affirms something which we do not need to employ McKinsey's to tell us, which is that if any church is to thrive it must be full of the joy and laughter which comes from life in the Spirit of Christ.

✠ Richard Londin

Part 1

The present situation and how we got here

The heart of this book is about how local churches can thrive and grow in the early twenty-first century. Here in Part 1, I set the scene by describing some of the current realities, showing how numerical decline and growth is not so much the automatic result of social change as the consequence of internal church leadership and policies. Part 2 describes how churches are already finding ways of growing in numerical and ministry strength. Parts 3 and 4 describe how the right human and financial resources can best be provided to enable this resurgence of the local churches. If many of the causes of past decline are self-inflicted, then future growth is possible for a reforming Church.

1

Building hope

Hope does not disappoint us. (Romans 5.5 NRSV)

From hope to growth

This is a book about the growth of the Church of England. It shows how the Church in places is already growing and how it can grow nationally in the future. My aim is for it to be practical and realistic, containing hard-won lessons mined from the coalface of parishes up and down the land. In *Hope for the Church*[1] I laid out the grounds for hope for the future growth of the Church. Here, I suggest how the different parts and forces of the Church of England can in practice be marshalled together to give momentum to the growing Church. I hope it will be a source of inspiration and help for church members and leaders in the parishes as well as those with wider responsibilities. We are all increasingly aware that the growth of the Church will not come about as a result of one or two star players or influential leaders. It depends on the collective effort of the whole people of God following the promptings of God to build the kingdom of God.

The Road to Growth is not about glib, short-term solutions promising quick results. The Church of England in its present state will not be capturing the postmodern culture sometime soon. We have to walk before we can run. The quality of instrument in the hand of God that is the Church of England today makes national transformation a rather ambitious target. But the Church *is* ready to grow as a counter-cultural force within post-Christian society. And once the Church has had some solid years of growth under its belt, then greater things are possible. As the Israelites had to grow in number (and spiritual stature) in the wilderness before they could conquer the Promised Land, so must the Church grow before its influence can be strong enough to transform English society.

First, time for a quick update and some background to this book:

3

Change of role

I spent two years following the writing of *Hope for the Church* as a 'Spring-board' Missioner, working for the Archbishops, researching church growth and disseminating the findings. Increasingly, I found myself giving consultancy advice to churches and dioceses. I had achieved every Christian's secret ambition – to continue serving the Lord fervently, but in a purely advisory capacity! However, all good things come to an end and the time came to attempt the much harder job – not just telling other people what to do but actually trying to do it myself. After a lifetime of praying 'Lord I'll do anything for you, except be an archdeacon; Lord I'll go anywhere for you except the West Midlands', the inevitable happened. When I first told someone that I was to be Archdeacon of Walsall, the answer came, 'beautiful country, Poland'. But I am now happily settled among the warm hearts and ready wits of the West Midlands, not only as archdeacon but also as Bishop's Growth Officer. Most congregations appear to be led by people whose hearts are truly in the new diocesan strategy, entitled 'Going for growth'. Attendance and membership in the Diocese of Lichfield have been in decline for years but in the providence of God we believe the time has now come to reverse that.

Signs of hope

Hope for the Church has certainly been widely read and, increasingly, I find that many of its suggestions are being implemented. Some groups of churches we have worked with most intensively at Springboard do seem to have started to grow. There are now a number of large pockets of attendance growth around the Church of England. London is the largest, but in recent months I have discovered pockets of growth in Essex and in Cambridge, and there are clearly a number of others. When the 2003 October count figures were published, there were more dioceses where numbers of adults had gone up than had gone down. The Diocese of London added 3,000 people to its average weekly attendance in October 2002 compared with 2001, and a further 5,000 in October 2003 compared with 2002, a gain of 8,000 (11 per cent) in just two years. That sort of growth spread around the country would totally transform the Church of England and, eventually, England itself. National adult attendance in October 2003 was 2 per cent up on 2002. Easter and Christmas attendance was also up 2 per cent.

I have no idea how much any of this was helped by *Hope for the Church* or Springboard, but these are both part of the wider movement in the Church that has been changing the culture of 'acceptance of decline' into a new culture of 'going for growth'. There are signs it is beginning to work.

Nevertheless, the other indicator of the numbers of people in church – usual Sunday attendance (uSa) – continues to show declining numbers. This is a more stable, steady indicator than the October count and has been collected for many years. However, it has its own limitations: it is collected differently in different dioceses, and it includes only congregations that meet on Sundays. In 2003 the national uSa of adults fell 1 per cent, and of children, 4 per cent.

At the time of writing, the messages are mixed and we are not sure whether the actual numbers of people meeting for worship in the Church of England are going up or down. A period of mixed messages is certainly a great improvement on the recent past. However, even if we are collectively turning things round, we are only just starting.

So the goal of this book is to help transform fragile signs of hope for the Church into a solid road to growth.

I believe there are workable strategies to make this possible. The next chapter outlines the challenges facing us, together with the main growth strategies I will be outlining in the rest of the book.

2

The genesis of the exodus of numbers

I alone am left. (1 Kings 19.14 NRSV)

A disappointing decade

The average Church of England diocese in 1994 had a usual Sunday attendance (uSa) of about 20,000 adults and 4,500 children. It paid 240 clergy. Its diocesan budget was fixed by first estimating the cost of maintaining the existing operation and workforce, then deducting expected 'other' income from the Church Commissioners and historic resources, and so producing a residual requirement of 'parish quota' to fill the gap.

However, by 2004 the average diocese had a Sunday attendance of only 17,000 adults left to pay the bills, plus 3,200 children. At some time in the intervening years the increases in quota (now called 'parish share') needed to maintain the workforce had become unrealistic. Quota arrears mounted and budget deficits reared their ugly heads. So the diocese was forced to change the way it put its budget together. Now it fixes the parish share rise, at least in part, on the basis of what the parishes can afford to pay. This means that the residual item becomes the amount of money the diocese can afford to spend without eating into its reserves. Most of this is spent on its paid workforce so, in some dioceses, the number of parochial clergy 'employed' has become determined by the diocesan budget forecast. By 2004 the average diocese had reduced its number of employed clergy from 240 to 200.

If these long-term trends continue, then, by sometime in the middle of the century, each diocese will end up with its own Elijah, probably the cathedral dean, lamenting 'I am the only one left'. We believe these trends may already be turning round, but the dragon of decline has not yet been slain.

Not every church and diocese is in the grip of this decline cycle. A vicar of a growing church, having consulted his colleague, Ron, informed me that 'The Genesis of the Exodus of Numbers is not due to Ron or me'. However, my starting point is the world in which many Anglicans are still living – where the strains and stresses of diminishing attendance, deteriorating finances and a decreasing paid workforce put us in the grip of a spiral of decline that we may have learned to manage but not to reverse. Fewer people in the pews means, other things being equal, less income to the diocese and fewer potential ordinands. A diocesan budget under pressure means, other things being equal, fewer clergy can be employed in the parishes and congregations feel squeezed by financial demands. Fewer clergy in the parishes means, other things being equal, fewer people in the pews and less desire to pay in to a diocese that is providing less and less ministry in return.

Figure 2.1 The cycle of decline – contributing factors

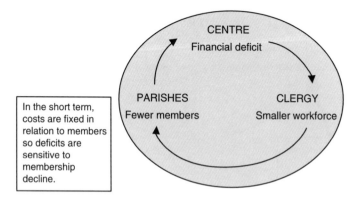

In the commercial world: make a loss → downsize → lose customers → make a loss

These links are not inevitable in every case, for instance, sometimes congregations grow when they lose their own vicar. There are many other factors at work as well as the three central factors of smaller congregations, fewer paid clergy and more financial constraints. Sometimes these mask the impact of the decline spiral: for instance, more generous giving has meant that diocesan incomes have risen despite smaller church attendance. Other factors that tend to accelerate the cycle are depicted in Figure 2.2 on page 8.

Outside factors

1 The supply of clergy

The increasingly elderly age profile of clergy means that more are retiring each year. The average number of retirements in the five years 1990–1994 was 338. For 1998–2002, it was 360 – out of a smaller total. In the early 1990s, 3 per cent of the clergy retired each year; by the early 2000s, this had gone up to 4 per cent.

Figure 2.2 The cycle of decline – additional contributing factors

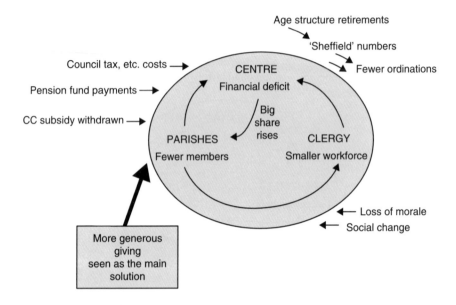

At the same time, as fewer people have come forward, fewer stipendiary clergy have been ordained. In the early 1990s, ordinations averaged 335, for 1998–2002, the average was 282 (though with the upsurge in 2003 shown in Table 2.1 below). In addition, the net loss of clergy for reasons other than death or retirement has also increased. This is harder to estimate, because of transfers both ways between parochial and chaplaincy ministries, and those who have left over the ordination of women. However, it seems that the net loss has about tripled since 1995.

Table 2.1 Recommendations for training for stipendiary ministry

Age group	1983	1993	2003
20–29	200	102	78
30–39	74	108	109
40–49	27	37	109
50–59	2	2	28
Total	303	249	324

Table 2.1 shows up the other major problem with ordinations – the increasing age of the ordinands. In 20 years, the number of recommendations of people under 30 has gone down 61 per cent and that of people aged over 40 has gone up 372 per cent. The serious missiological consequences of this are outlined in Chapter 3.

2 The morale of clergy and churches

This increase in the number of clergy apparently leaving the profession may have something to do with the next external factor – loss of morale. As the work of leading churches becomes more stressful, as clergy workloads increase as numbers go down, as congregations continue to dwindle, as the media image of the Church deteriorates, and as dioceses pressurize clergy to deliver more and more parish share each year, the morale of some clergy has sunk very low. That more are not leaving the profession despite low morale may simply be because clergy feel trapped in their tied housing and unskilled for other jobs. However, evidence about morale is mixed and it is hard to generalize – the report *Generosity and Sacrifice*[1] reported high job satisfaction rates among clergy. The increasing number of self-supporting (NSM) clergy hardly indicates a general loss of heart or confidence in the value of the ordained ministry.

Sometimes it is low morale among parishes that is contributing to the decline cycle. Typically this arises when parishes perceive that the diocese is demanding more and more money from fewer and fewer church members who are getting less and less back in terms of the provision of ministry. The diocesan centre becomes mistrusted and parishes become disgruntled.

3 The deployment of clergy

The size of the clergy workforce is possibly not the main determinant of its effectiveness. Chapter 3 will cover four specific factors in the management of the clergy workforce that have impeded growth: the creation of team ministries, the discouragement of young ordinands, encouraging clergy to leave posts too early, and leaving posts vacant for too long.

4 Social change

The complex societal reasons for declining church attendance are the subject of lively debate that it is not necessary to rehearse at this point. Yet clearly much of the decline in church attendance is against the backdrop of factors external to the life of the Church, factors that can be heroically summarized in the phrase 'social change'. It is the contention of this book that internal church failings and weaknesses are surprisingly important causes of attendance loss. But this is, clearly, in a context of social change that has made people less likely anyway to attend church out of habit, duty, social convention, or communal religious belief. Whereas people once belonged to churches 'automatically', irrespective of the quality of what was on offer, now churches have to work hard to attract and hold people. So, external social change is a major engine helping to turn the wheel of the cycle of decline.

5 Loss of central subsidy

Thanks to greater personal generosity from individual church members, the financial problems of dioceses do not begin with dwindling congregations. What smaller congregations have meant is that payments have not risen as fast as they would have if congregations had been growing, and so the generosity of the people has not been able to compensate fully for the loss of central subsidy faced by the dioceses. Parish ministry and mission support from the Church Commissioners is the money left over once other, statutory and priority, expenditure has been deducted from the Commissioners' income. The main categories of this are clergy pensions, and the financial support of bishops and cathedrals. As a result, parish ministry support from the Commissioners fell from £57 million in 1993 to £26 million in 2003, a drop of more than a half even before making allowance for inflation. Our average diocese, therefore, lost £720,000 in income from the Commissioners, a big hole in a turnover of £10 million or so per annum.

6 Other cost inflation

The stipends of the clergy have risen in recent years by the rate of inflation or a little more, but the cost of other items, such as pension contributions, council tax payments and the central church levy, has been rising much faster. In addition, most dioceses have not been able to reduce their support and supervisory workforce in line with the reductions in the parish clergy. The costs of archdeacons, diocesan secretaries and so on have therefore loomed a little larger within a workforce that is shrinking overall.

7 Parish share increases

Dioceses have been asking for more generous giving in order to finance parish share increases large enough to pay all the existing clergy, in order to maintain the levels of ministry necessary to sustain the congregations to pay the parish share! This solution has worked to some extent, but in some dioceses its limits have been reached and downsizing has begun. Moreover, the drive for parish share has generated its own problems. Some larger churches have been able to pay the increases demanded only by dispensing with their own assistant staff, and so leaving themselves open to numerical decline. Other churches have felt pushed into becoming organizations whose main purpose in life is to raise money. When the major items on the PCC agenda and in church life are fund-raising events and initiatives, then a church has forgotten its main purpose in life and is unlikely to be attracting new people to the free grace and unconditional love of God in Christ. The result is that large increases in parish share can themselves directly cause a further reduction in church attendance and membership.

The downsizing diocese

The net result of all this, as illustrated in Figure 2.2, is that many dioceses are caught in a continuous process of downsizing, from which there appears to be no easy escape. It is the equivalent to the business world's company that loses customers, so it makes a loss, so it reduces its workforce and activities, so it loses further customers, so it makes another loss, so it downsizes further, and so on until it eventually disappears. Such is the cycle of decline facing some dioceses.

It is important to note here that the falling number of paid clergy is not only a result of tighter finances – the national workforce of paid clergy has been going down (by around 1 per cent pa) at the same time as the capacity to pay for them. Some dioceses have cut their clergy numbers for financial reasons, others because their allocation out of a reducing national total has gone down.

Interestingly, too, although the falling number of paid clergy is clearly a part of the general decline cycle that many dioceses face, Chapter 10 will show that fewer paid clergy does not always mean fewer people in the pews.

This membership–workforce–finances downsizing cycle exists side by side with all the signs of new growth and new ways of being church that we see today. The Church of England is a great glorious mixture of decay and delight, bereavement and new birth, sadness and hope. What is needed is a strategy for generating a new cycle of growth in which delight, new birth and hope begin to take over.

A strategic response

In the book of Acts, it would seem that God the Holy Spirit had a strategy for the growth of the Church. This involved the Church at Antioch adopting an appropriate church growth policy – church planting. It also involved appropriate human resource selection and preparation – Barnabas and Paul.

It doubtless also involved appropriate financial support, though as usual this was probably the first thing to go wrong and Paul had to be bailed out by the Philippians.

Sometimes Christian leaders are wary of the concept of adopting a strategy for the Church because they think this means imposing some uniform behaviour patterns on all churches or church members. Nothing should be further from the truth. Barnabas and Paul went to Cyprus but Niger, Lucius and Manaen stayed at home. The Church at Antioch sent missionaries, but the church at Joppa did not.

'Strategy' here means the coordination of a set of policies around a strategic aim, the same aim as in Acts – to grow the Christian Church. A diocese with a strategy for growth will be encouraging and resourcing its parish churches to find good practices, appropriate changes, fresh expressions and renewed spirituality for their own growth, and it will be coordinating its own financial and human resources policies to provide a helpful framework within which growth can occur in the local churches. It is essential that the thinking is joined up and that every parish and element in the diocese is involved in the strategic effort, otherwise positive moves can be cancelled out. For example, it is no good the bishop urging churches to reorder their interiors to make them more user friendly if the diocesan advisory committee is going to turn down the faculty applications. It is no good the parishes looking for new incumbents in their thirties if the vocations directors are telling candidates in their twenties to go away and get some experience of life. It is no good the diocesan missioner trying to set up a network of youth and young adult con-gregations if the diocesan board of finance has no budget heading for such initiatives. If genuine momentum is to be gathered, then the brakes have to be pulled off all the way round the cycle of growth that is illustrated in Figure 2.3. Each of the main headings on the diagram helping to push round the growth cycle in the right direction is the subject of its own chapter – here we are simply introducing them and showing how they fit together to form a strategy.

Working round the cycle

In the remainder of the book, I will work around the factors that generate the cycle of growth, starting with the growth of the local church as the key to everything else. I shall then move on to issues of human resources, with a fresh look at the way we use and value both lay and ordained members of our churches. Finally, the focus will move to how financial resources can be provided to fuel and sustain the growth of the Church.

My hope is that this agenda will provide a blueprint for effective cooperation between parish and diocese for the turning round of the Church. Only a

Figure 2.3 The cycle of growth

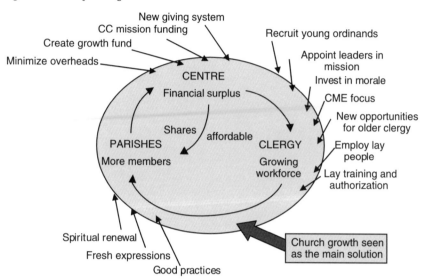

Increase sales → make a profit → invest in production → increase sales

coordinated strategy involving all the main aspects is likely to succeed in delivering significant future growth. However, this is not to suggest that just one or two changes or policies will never give a helpful push in the right direction. We live in an imperfect world and we should not despair if every aspect of a growth strategy is not in place. Perhaps the God of grace will honour the attempt even if it is not very successful in human terms.

However, before that, in Chapter 3 I set out to demonstrate that much of the impetus for decline is coming from the Church of England's own uncertainty about how to manage its life effectively in a changing world. It is not the inevitable result of outside forces about which nothing can be done. It is the direct result of internal weakness and policies that can be reversed. Many individual churches and some whole streams and dioceses are in fact growing numerically in today's changing world because of the quality and relevance of what they are doing. What is being achieved by some is open to all.

To the extent that this 'internal weaknesses' explanation of the decline cycle and key to the growth cycle is true, it may lead to a sense of depression about the quality of organization that the Church of England really is. What it should lead to is new hope and optimism, for, if the causes are internal, then the remedies are as well. It is actually within the power of the Church to dismantle its own decline cycle and erect a growth cycle in its place. Sociologists of the death of religion may call this thesis naive, but the detailed evidence from within the woof and warp of real church life says it cannot be dismissed lightly. The construction materials for the road to growth are already known and many of them are in place. So long as God the Builder has construction teams across the nation, the Church of England will grow and flourish in wonderful new ways over the coming years.

3

Self-inflicted wounds

Let the elders who rule well be considered worthy of double honour.
(1 Timothy 5.17 NRSV)

Corporate and individual responsibility

It is not an easy job to lead a local church well. It is even harder to lead a diocese or denomination well. During the times when the pace of social and ecclesiastical change was slower, when active hands-on management of the affairs of the Church was less important, leaders could often get away with simply occupying a position and devoting energies to wider concerns. Today it is widely understood that church leaders at every level must take active steps to manage, lead and inspire the Church well if it is to survive and prosper. It is therefore interesting to note Paul's ruling (above) that elders who direct the affairs of the Church are worthy of double honour not automatically by virtue of their position but conditionally by virtue of their performance.

The evidence for the impact of honourable but misguided policies offered in this chapter should not be used as an excuse to blame individual leaders for the decline of the Church. It is a general culture of evidence-based decision-making that has been lacking. We have all sometimes been content to rely on anecdote, hunch, speculative theology, personal preference, or force of personality – for what else has there been to go on? We are not in the business of playing the blame game with our chosen scapegoats. Rather, the appropriate Christian response is corporate repentance, defined as a humble, contrite shared determination to live and lead in a new and better way in the future.

We can shape our own future

Sociologists, statisticians, media commentators and others sometimes suggest the decline of the Church is inevitable in the postmodern world. But the truth is that decline is neither universal nor irreversible. Many churches, some dioceses and one or two denominations have learnt how to grow again in a postmodern world. Others can learn from their example.

One reason why so many churches are finding ways of growing today is that there are many positives for church growth in the emerging post-modern culture. People are on spirituality searches and many who discover Christian spirituality will find their holy grail. People are looking for some-thing 'that will work for me'. Those who meet Christians able to explain why their faith works for them are likely to give Jesus a try. People are increasingly desperate to find community and belonging in a dislocated world, and churches that offer this will attract. A post-Christian society that essentially believes in nothing will increasingly contain people who cannot live in that moral and spiritual vacuum. They may have to get over the labelling, rejection and fear that such a society has of people who believe in some-thing, anything. A non-believing society sometimes marginalizes, even demonizes, its Christians with its stereotype labelling – 'fundamentalist', 'moralizer', 'do-gooder', 'intolerant', 'narrow-minded' – but not everyone is taken in by this.

So people uncomfortable with the new correctness of non-believing may well be attracted by the newly counter-cultural Church. In the short term, this may not mean the Church will recapture the centre ground of the culture, but it may well mean that it grows as a counter-cultural force. If it is true that the capital city is in the forefront of social change, it may be no coincidence that (as shown in Chapter 8) in London today the Church of England is a fast-growing force. What is happening in the churches in London today might be a capital city one-off, but it might just be a foretaste of what will happen in the whole country tomorrow.

If the social conditions do not preclude a resurgent Church, then we in the Church have a chance of shaping our own future. Whether the Church dies or grows will be determined by the way in which we face our contem-porary challenges. Good leadership and good practices can grow the Church. Poor leadership and practices shrink it. The truth of this is evidenced by the fact that much of the recent decline of the Church is actually the result of internal culture rather than external inevitabilities. The follow-ing examples of practices and policies that have actually shrunk the Church illustrate the importance of internal reform as part of the road to growth.

1 Team ministries

There was a widespread move through the 1970s and 80s towards the creation of team ministries. A team rector was appointed to have supervision over several parishes, and team vicars were appointed with oversight of single parishes within the team. In part the team parishes were a response to the problem of the isolation of the clergy. Qualitative arguments were deployed to do with mutual support, the sharing of gifts, clergy career paths, and the benefits to the parishes of having access to a team of clergy instead of just one. However, pilot teams were not set up and monitored to discover whether and how they worked and what the snags were. Dioceses simply thought teams were a bright idea and created large numbers of them. The incidence of teams in different dioceses varies enormously, depending mainly on whether a diocese had, in this period, a 'teams enthusiast' among its senior staff. Once large numbers of teams were up and running it does not seem that there was any systematic attempt to monitor or assess their progress.

However, stories of dysfunctional teams began to circulate. It gradually became clear that teams often created more problems than they solved, and dioceses stopped setting them up. One or two dioceses (e.g. London) have in recent years dissolved their teams, but most continue with them if only for the usual reason that it is hard work to abolish legal creations, even quite recent ones.

In a number of dioceses where I have looked at the attendance trends of team parishes I have found them to be significantly worse than those of traditional 'single-vicar' parishes. Examples are given below:

Figure 3.1 Percentage change in adult attendance in team ministries and other parishes, Chichester, 1990–2001

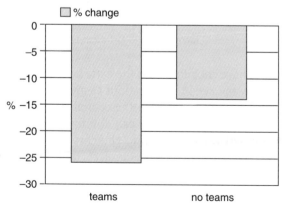

Figure 3.2 Diocese of Lichfield usual Sunday attendance (uSa) of adults in teams and non-teams 1995–2000

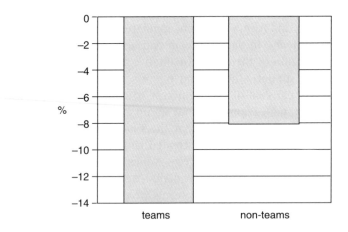

Figure 3.3 Diocese of Chester change in total uSa in teams and non-teams 1999–2002

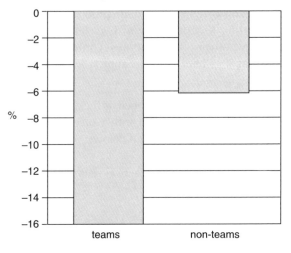

One problem teams have encountered is the extra layer of administration and meetings imposed by the need for the various clergy and parishes to relate to each other. These take time away from the central task of functioning well as ministering Christian churches. They can also focus the churches inwards (relating to each other) whereas growing churches need to focus outwards (relating to the world). Local Ecumenical Projects (LEPs) can suffer from the same problem.

Some teams have been bedevilled by conflicts and personality clashes within them. Some clergy, especially of the old school, have not found it easy to share responsibility and compromise on ideas. This is grist to the mill of the old jibe that clergy are like manure – spread them around evenly and they do some good, pile them up in one place and they just create a stink. Moreover, the clergy have not been helped by the ambiguity of relationships embodied in the team setup. Who is in charge of the team vicar's parish – the team vicar who lives in the vicarage and appears to be responsible for the church or the team rector who has legal charge and may feel entitled to tell the team vicar what to do?

In many teams the clergy are on comparatively short contracts (five to seven years), and the evidence suggests that church growth is likely to happen best somewhere between the fifth and twelfth years of a ministry. In one diocese, the average length of stay of incumbent-vicars was 9.5 years and of team vicars 5.9 years. So team vicars are leaving just as they are entering their most productive years in post when the groundwork has been laid, their people have learned to trust them, and they have grown to know the church and area well. The review process by which other members of the team and certain church members have a say in whether licences are renewed at the end of each fixed term adds an extra stress on to clergy life, and can lead to pro-longed periods of uncertainty. 'Will the team rector's licence be renewed?' Then, if it is not, 'How long will the rector linger on, a lame duck, before finding another post?' followed by 'How long will we have to wait for a new team rector?' That whole period of uncertainty can take several years.

Because team posts tend to come vacant more often than others, the problem of long vacancies leading to attendance loss (see point 4 below) looms larger in team parishes. In some dioceses there may also be a feeling that team posts can safely be left vacant for longer than single-incumbent parishes (because the rest of the team can cover for them), thus adding to the attendance loss.

One advantage of having a team of clergy rather than just one is that, between them, they can deploy a fuller range of gifts and abilities for the benefit of the whole parish. However, this very strength may also disempower some lay people. A vulnerable vicar with obvious gaps in his or her ability or gifting range may leave more room for the growing of lay ministry than an omnicompetent team able to turn its collective hand to anything. Finally, dioceses can view team parishes as soft targets for cuts in posts. It is easier, legally and practically, to remove one post from a team than to amalgamate two independent parishes.

So it is that the creation of team parishes appears to have made a modest but noticeable contribution to the decline in attendance in the Church of England. This is not necessarily to argue that traditional single-vicar parishes should not be tampered with, nor even that teams should be abolished. It may be that more radical solutions than teams are needed, or that teams can be made to work by addressing the problems identified above. The point for now is that they are one of the self-inflicted wounds from which the Church has been bleeding.

2 Short incumbencies

It is time to tell the sad story of the Very Active Archdeacon. It began when he noticed that the patron was having difficulty finding a new vicar for St A, one of the larger churches in the diocese. The Very Active Archdeacon realized that Smith, vicar of St B, would fit the bill. Smith was a bright young first incumbent, doing a good job, who had been at St B for five years and had not really thought of moving on yet. But he was flattered to be asked to take on St A, and accepted. The Very Active Archdeacon felt good about himself. He then realized that St B no longer had a vicar, so he rang Jones, vicar of SS C, D, E and F in the rural part of the diocese. Jones had only been there for three years, but all that dashing around between C, D, E and F was doing her head in. She accepted with alacrity. The Very Active Archdeacon, who had become awfully busy filling vacancies right across the diocese, realized with a sigh that it was probably his moral responsibility to find a new vicar for SS C, D, E and F. Now whom could he ring?

The Very Active Archdeacon thought that he was managing the affairs of the diocese rather well. In a way he was. But he was also contributing to its decline. All the evidence shows that parishes lose people during vacancies, and that it is normally better to have longer incumbencies than shorter ones. Before the Very Active Archdeacon stepped in, St B had been looking forward to a period of growth. Now it faced decline. The Archdeacon had looked only at the good he could do for the parish whose vacancy he was trying to fill. He failed to look at the harm he was doing to the parish he was prematurely robbing of its vicar.

This is not to say that archdeacons and others should not try to fill vacancies. It is important that this is done promptly, as shown below. It is simply that a premature reshuffling of the pack is a very damaging way of doing it, turning stability into unexpected upheaval in parishes across the diocese. Better to advertise vacancies and so allow only those looking for a move to apply. With luck, the successful candidate will come from another diocese, meaning that SS B, C, D E and F can be left alone for a few years, quietly to grow with Smith and Jones, and the Very Active Archdeacon can put his feet up for a while!

3 Discouraging the young ordinands

The statistical evidence shows that, on average, younger clergy are more likely to be associated with church growth than are their older colleagues. In Wakefield between 1996 and 2000, incumbents aged under 40 added on average 9 per cent to their Sunday attendance, incumbents aged 40 to 55 lost 2 per cent and incumbents aged over 55 lost 10 per cent.

Figure 3.4 Diocese of Wakefield uSa change by age group of incumbent 1996–2000

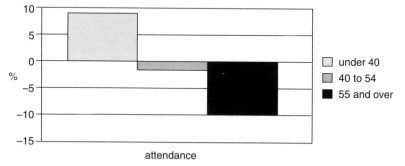

Data from surveys in Church in Wales dioceses reveals similar patterns to those in England. In Monmouth between 2002 and 2004, incumbents aged under 45 added on average 12 per cent to their congregations, clergy aged 45 to 54 added 3 per cent and clergy aged over 55 lost 2 per cent. Similarly, most of the church growth in St Asaph was in churches with an incumbent or priest in charge aged under 45.

Figure 3.5 Diocese of Monmouth uSa change by age group of incumbent 2002–2004

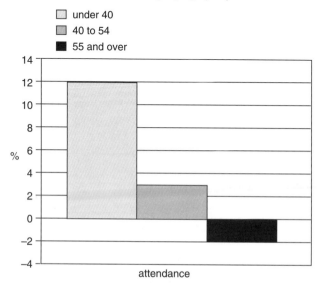

Figure 3.6 Diocese of St Asaph uSa change by age group of incumbent 2003–2004

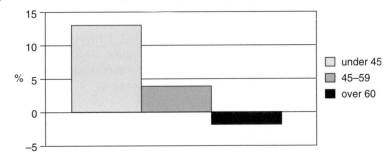

In London, the electoral rolls in parishes with an incumbent aged under 45 grew 21 per cent between 1996 and 2002. There was only 7 per cent growth in parishes with older incumbents.

Figure 3.7 Diocese of London change in electoral rolls by age group of incumbent 1996–2002

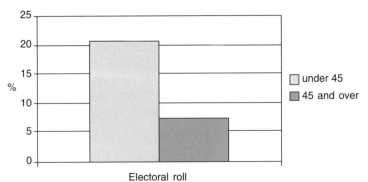

Among a sample of New Wine churches, an Anglican stream with overall growing attendances, from 2001 to 2003 attendance grew on average by 4 per cent in churches where the incumbent was over 45 and by 19 per cent where the incumbent was under 45.

Figure 3.8 New Wine Networks churches attendance change by age of incumbent 2001–2003

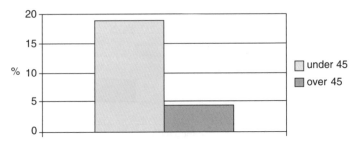

This pattern is linked with the average age of congregations – younger clergy tend to have younger congregations and it is younger congregations that tend to grow. For example, in Monmouth on average 26 per cent of the adults in the younger clergy's congregations were aged under 45. The average for the diocese is only 17 per cent. Though their total congregational attendance rose 12 per cent from 2002 to 2004, the number of children increased 21 per cent and adults just 10 per cent. Among New Wine churches with incumbents aged under 45, attendance of adults rose between 2001 and 2003 by 15 per cent and attendance of children rose by 34 per cent.

Figure 3.9 New Wine Networks churches uSa by age group of incumbent 2001–2003

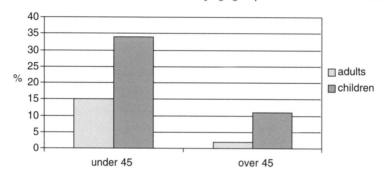

In the really fast-growing churches in the Kensington Episcopal Area of London – those with young incumbents – the attendance of adults rose 41 per cent between 2001 and 2003, but that of children by 58 per cent. The younger clergy, often with families of their own, are clearly attracting families and younger adults to their churches.

Figure 3.10 Kensington Episcopal Area attendance change in fast-growing churches with incumbents under 45, 2001–2003

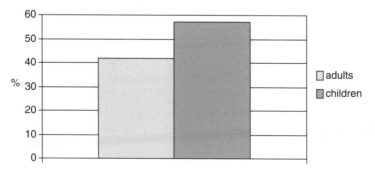

The English Church Census[1] data suggests that the average age of Anglicans has risen in the last 25 years from around 37 to 47. The attraction of the young is the key growth dynamic required to turn churches round in the future. The key people to do this are young clergy.

Yet the average age of the clergy has been rising strongly. It is currently around 52. The main reason for this is that the average age of people accepted for ordination training has also been rising. In 1967, 70 per cent of those accepted for ordination training were under 30. By 2001, this had fallen to 14 per cent. In 1993, the average age of those accepted for training (including non-stipendiaries) was 38, in 2000 it was 42 and in 2002 it was 43. Someone accepted for training at the age of 43 will, on average, be around 49 or 50 before beginning a first incumbency. Table 3.1 shows the age structure of full-time stipendiary curates at 31 December 2002. Their average age was 41, a little lower than suggested above by the average age of training-acceptance, which includes non-stipendiaries.

Table 3.1 Age of full-time stipendiary curates at 31 December 2002

Age group	men	women
Under 25	4	1
25–29	117	24
30–34	223	52
35–39	231	64
40–44	211	93
45–49	98	95
50–54	78	78
55–59	49	41
60 plus	24	11

The point to all this is that the ageing of the clergy through the ageing of the ordinands has not come about primarily through the drying up of the supply of young adults. It has been the result of a deliberate change in policy or ethos. From sometime in the 1970s, the idea developed that it was better for potential ordinands to have had some experience of 'the real world' before training for the ministry. Young candidates were told to go away and come back in a few years' time. Some did, others found another career and responsibilities, and never did. The green young curate doing the youth work gradually became a species almost extinct. That there are still significant numbers of young people and young adults prepared to offer themselves for full-time ministry in the Church of England is proven by the rise of the Centre for Youth Ministry in several of the colleges.[2] Once again, in the last four or five years, they have attracted people in their late teens and early twenties, the difference being that the professional ministry for which they are training does not involve ordination. The policy of the Church of England's Ministry Division is, again, to encourage young ordinands, but, in the absence of active recruitment policies and of role models, very few come forward of their own volition.

Having spent the last few years looking into the anatomy and causes of the decline of the Church of England, it seems clear to me that this deliberate change in culture to exclude the young from ordination is the gravest self-inflicted wound of all. The fields are still white ready to harvest – families and teenagers clearly respond readily to churches offering appropriate leadership, relationships, values and culture – but the labourers in the 25–45 generation are too few to reap the harvest.

4 Lengthy vacancies

If the exclusion of young ordinands has been the deepest self-inflicted wound from the late twentieth century, the deepest new wounds today are being made by the lengthening of vacancies between incumbencies. This problem is so acute that in some dioceses it looks as though most or all of the net attendance loss is happening in parishes that are vacant. This is a self-inflicted wound for two reasons: one is the culture of taking things slowly when a vacancy is about to arise, the other is the deliberate policy brought in by some dioceses in recent years of extending vacancies 'in order to save money'.

There is no objective reason why the process of finding a replacement should not start the moment a vicar announces her or his resignation. This is the normal procedure in other walks of life. But the culture of the Church per-suades us it is normal to wait until the previous incumbent has left. Similarly, it is sensible to keep reducing the number of posts nationally in line with the falling number of stipendiary clergy. But reluctance to grasp nettles means there are too many posts chasing too few clergy. Less desirable posts in the North and Midlands can take years to attract even a single candidate. The policy of extending vacancies to save money is another example of a change brought about without any consideration of the evidence either a priori or ex post. Research was not undertaken to discover what the experience of churches with long vacancies in the recent past had been, and monitoring has not normally been undertaken to ascertain the impact of the long vacancies dictated by the new policy. A tight financial corner, a brave speech and a reassuring anecdote have sometimes been considered sufficient justification for *assuming* the damage caused by long vacancies will be small.

However, staff in four dioceses have been able to compile the information needed to help me measure the attendance trends in parishes during and after vacancies of differing lengths over recent years. The basic technique is to follow through 'usual Sunday attendance of adults' (uSa) statistics in the year before a vacancy, the year or years of a vacancy, and up to the first full year following the vacancy. Groups of churches with similar vacancy lengths have had their attendances added together to produce an average experience. This is shown in Figure 3.11:

Figure 3.11 Change in adult uSa in four dioceses during and after vacancies

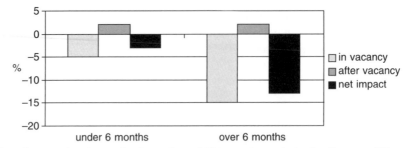

Data from 55 churches under 6 months and 232 over 6 months in the dioceses of Chester, Lichfield, Monmouth and Chelmsford

It is clear that there is very little loss of attendance in short vacancies but a large loss in long ones.

In the Diocese of Lichfield, the experience of 154 different churches in vacancy since 1998 has been charted in rather more detail. The preponderance of long vacancies is only partly the result of policy – it is also because some parishes are difficult to fill, and because sometimes the weighty processes just take a very long time to get through. The results are as follows:

Table 3.2 Attendance change during vacancy in 154 churches in Diocese of Lichfield since 1998

Vacancy length	Attendance change to end of vacancy	Bounce back in first full year	Net impact	Number of churches
0–6 months	−3%	+2%	−1%	27
6–9 months	−12%	+1%	−11%	51
9–12 months	−16%	+4%	−13%	32
over 12 months	−21%	+2%	−19%	44

Just as striking as the large loss of attendance during a long vacancy is the failure of attendance to recover during the first year of the new incumbent. The net impact column of Table 3.2 measures the 'permanent' loss of attendance associated with the vacancy. The total net loss in the 154 vacancy parishes was around 1,400, which represents about 60 per cent of the total loss of attendance in the period. However, full data was not available in a large number of other vacancies not included in the 154. Allowing for these

Figure 3.12 Change in uSa during and after a vacancy since 1998 (sample of 154 churches)

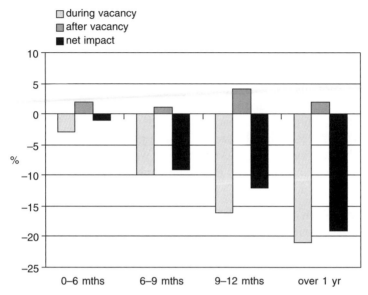

Figure 3.13 Attendance trend at a typical larger church with eight-year incumbencies and one-year vacancies

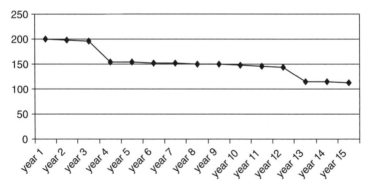

suggests that most of the diocesan attendance loss in the period happened during vacancies of over six months. The implication of the experience of the 27 parishes with short vacancies is that, if all vacancies had been kept under six months, this diocese would not have been in significant numerical decline.

An average parish with a vicar for eight years and a congregation of 200 would, therefore, go down to 160 as a result of a twelve-month vacancy. Slipping slowly to 145 for the next eight years, it would go down to 115 during the next vacancy, and so on. That is how the churches are shrinking.

In the Diocese of Chester, the attendance loss in 25 parishes, almost all with vacancies over six months, was 21 per cent, with a 2 per cent bounce back in the first full year of the new incumbent. The net loss was, therefore, 19 per cent. Once again, this is sufficiently large to account for the majority of total attendance decline in the diocese.

In the Diocese of Monmouth in recent years, the policy has been to keep vacancies short in order to avoid congregational loss. However, it has not always been possible to arrange for a vacancy to be filled within six months. Twenty-four churches had a vacancy of under six months. They lost 4 per cent of attendance during the vacancy and a further 2 per cent in the first full year of the new incumbent. Eleven churches with vacancies over six months lost 19 per cent in the vacancy and a further 3 per cent in the first full year after it.

It can be seen that the results from all three dioceses are almost identical: longer vacancies are associated with the permanent loss of nearly 20 per cent of the congregation.

The Diocese of Chelmsford had a policy of extending vacancies to save money on stipends until it was noticed that parish share payments fell off substantially in a number of parishes in vacancy. There was then a change of policy. In the most recent years, the aim has been to fill vacancies quickly because it is felt the presence of a vicar encourages the parish to pay its share. However, during the period 1996 to 2003, the average vacancy length seems to be longer than in any of the other three dioceses studied, although the net loss of attendance in longer vacancies is less:

Table 3.3 Attendance trend in vacant churches in Diocese of Chelmsford 1996–2003

Vacancy length	Attendance change to end of vacancy	Bounce back in first full year	Net impact	Number of churches
under 6 months	−11%	+15%	+2%	4
6–11 months	−6%	+2%	−4%	30
12 months & over	−16%	+10%	−8%	39

The sample size of churches with short vacancies is too small for conclusions to be drawn. However, the churches with long vacancies show a similar attendance drop while the vacancy is happening, but a stronger bounce back once the new incumbent is in place. The net impact is a permanent loss of 'only' 8 per cent. This may be less than half the size of impact in the other three dioceses, but it still leads to significant attendance loss.

There is a discussion in Chapter 10 of the causes of attendance loss in vacancies and of what can be done to prevent them. It has been sufficient for this chapter to show that the combination of a general culture of accepting long vacancies, together with deliberate but naive economy measures, has been probably the major single cause of Anglican church attendance loss in recent years.

Living without self-harm

Rector and vicar teams, short incumbencies, lack of young clergy, destructive financial regimes, and long vacancies may all be self-inflicted wounds, but the Church bleeds from them nevertheless. However, the fact that much of the Church's decline is due not to external change but to internal failings does mean that better-informed management of the Church's own affairs should yield church-growth fruit. It should not be imagined it is easy to change an inherited culture and familiar patterns, but we know it is possible because it is already being done. The Diocese of London has unravelled its team parishes. The average age of its deacons is 35. The Diocese of Monmouth is keeping most of its vacancies short. It has a few adults in its congregations so it is planning a new teens–students–young adults church in order to nurture a new generation of leaders. Slowly we are learning to make policy decisions that are based on evidence, the impact of which will be monitored. We can heal our self-inflicted wounds if we are determined to do so.

Part 2

Delivering church growth in the parishes

In the diagram depicting the cycle of growth in Chapter 2, 'Church growth' was labelled as the main solution. The five chapters in Part 2 set out ways in which church growth in the parishes can be generated, and in fact is already happening. This is the heart and content of what it means to be a resurgent, thriving church. Parts 3 and 4 will then set out how the human and financial resources can be deployed to support and sustain this growth of the local churches across the land.

4

Church growth – the main solution

> They broke bread at home and ate their food with glad and generous hearts, praising God and having the goodwill of all the people. And day by day the Lord added to their number those who were being saved. (Acts 2.46-47 NRSV)

Growing the Church and kingdom

There has long been a debate or division between those in the Church who see the Church's own growth as a proper and significant object of the Church's own attention, and those who do not. Arguments against focusing on the growth or numerical size of the Church include the contention that it is the kingdom that matters, not the Church; that what counts is quality not quantity; that small is often beautiful; and that we are called to be the Church for others, not for ourselves.

But numbers matter because of what they represent: growth is often a sign of quality not an alternative to it. It suggests that people are finding a Christian faith and a place in the Christian community. It is *their* transformation we seek, rather than *our* growth, but the two are part of the same process. Also, the numbers involved in the life of the Church determine the capacity of the Church to do good in the world – to be an agent of the kingdom of heaven. A growing, confident, secure community is likely to have the vision, the opportunity and the human resources to be salt in society and make the world a better place. Finally, the Church's message will only gain respect and credence in society if it is seen to come from a growing Church. Against a background of decline the instinct of the media is to mock and belittle. Against a background of growth the spokespeople for the Church have a chance of a fairer hearing.

In this chapter I argue that it is important to concentrate on the growth of the Church for another reason as well – the very practical one that the Church of England is in a cycle of decline from which only its numerical growth can release it. It is 'grow or die' time. The fixation on financial solutions alone (a mix of cost-cutting and parish share increases) is suicidal. Working for the growth of the kingdom through the growth of the Church, however, has a chance of fixing the finances as well. Jesus himself put it best of all in concluding his exhortation not to be preoccupied with or to worry about money: 'Seek first his kingdom and his righteousness and all these things will be given to you as well.'[1] This is a promise to God's people collectively as well as individually: if we find health and strength in our kingdom business then all these money things will be added to us as well.

Congregation size

This may seem an obvious and unexceptional statement: the more people there are to contribute to the parish share, the bigger the amount is likely to be. However, it can prove surprisingly difficult to convince diocesan boards and committees of such a simple truth. Their experience is that the payment of share depends much more on the attitude of the parish and the rigour with which the diocese itself pursues its money. The unspoken assumptions include: that the church in decline is losing only its fringe members, who didn't contribute a lot of money anyway; that many parishes have deep reserves out of which to pay the share; and that the gap between what the regulars should give and actually do give is so huge that greater generosity can easily balance the books. They are suspicious of the reliability of statistics of attendance decline anyway. What is more, dioceses do not seek evidence for the relationship between congregation trends and parish share paid, and do not provide information for others to test the relationship. The result is that a matter that should be settled by reference to the objective evidence is done so by qualitative argument and force of personality.

So let us look at some objective evidence to see if we can find a correlation. In the Diocese of Bradford, there were 20 churches that experienced significant attendance loss in 2002 and 20 that experienced a significant gain. 'Significant' is defined as plus or minus 10 per cent.

Table 4.1 Churches gaining and losing adult attendance 2001–2002, Diocese of Bradford

	Adult uSa	Share paid
20 gainers	+15%	+6%
20 losers	−22%	−5%

Total share paid in the diocese rose 3 per cent in 2002; but it fell by 5 per cent from churches in significant numerical decline and rose by 6 per cent from churches in significant numerical growth. Moreover, the faster the growth or decline in attendance, the greater the contrast in share paid. The *ten* fastest declining churches dropped 9 per cent of their share payments, and the *ten* fastest growing added 15 per cent.

When it comes to share arrears, half the 20 declining churches fell behind in 2002, by a total of £61,000 arrears. Of the 20 growing churches, only four fell into arrears, three of them just marginally. The total arrears were £19,000, almost all from one large church that was facing very rapid rises in its share demand.

It is indeed true that the contrast in payments between the growing and declining churches is not as great as that in their attendance trends. Factors such as use of reserves do indeed come into play. However, it is also true that there is a significant difference in parish share performance between the two groups. Declining churches paid 5 per cent less share and ran up deficits of £61,000 between them. Growing churches paid 6 per cent more share and ran up deficits of only £19,000. A diocese of declining churches has severe financial problems, a diocese of growing churches is in financial heaven.

Balancing the books – the real solution

Another diocese, facing cuts in 'other' income and in reserves, calculated how much parish share it would need per head in order to sustain its present ministry and expenditure on three different scenarios:

1. That attendance would continue to decline at the same rate as the recent past.
2. That attendance would be stable over the next few years.
3. That adult attendance would rise by an average of 1 person per church per annum.

Under scenario 1, the break even parish share needed per head rose from £300 in 2002 to £440 in 2008 in real terms at 2002 prices. This was deemed completely impractical. Large cuts in costs and clergy would be inevitable. Under scenario 2, the increase needed per head was from £300 to £380. This was still an increase in real terms of 27 per cent over six years, plus what would be needed for inflation, and still impractical. Under scenario 3, however, no per capita increase was needed at all – the growing costs would be paid for by the growing congregations.

How can such a modest growth as one person per church per annum make such a difference? Part of the answer to this is that larger congregations often do not result in larger costs to churches. Churches have high fixed costs and low marginal costs. So most of the extra giving from the extra people can go

Figure 4.1 Chelmsford's 'stewardship' alternatives

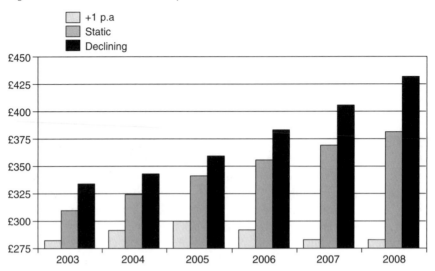

straight into parish share. By the same token, falling congregations are still faced with many of the same bills, and so their parish share capacity can be rapidly eroded, at least in the long term once reserves have been used up and the remaining members are giving realistically. Another part of the answer is that, in many dioceses, over half the churches have an adult attendance of under 50, so a net gain of only six people in six years is adding a helpful 10 to 15 per cent to the congregation of the average church.

The conclusion to this is that the cycle of decline can only be defeated by church growth. Initial church growth is the route to the financial prosperity and growing paid workforce that will provide the financial and human resources for the next phase of growth. This is not the only, or even the main, motive for attending to evangelism and church growth: the main motive is a missionary response to the Great Commission of Jesus to share the good news in all the world – but it is an additional motive.

The focus of diocesan and parish life, therefore, needs a shift from 'gathering in the share' to 'growing the Church'. Only if the church is grown will the costs be met and the mission be developed.

The right policy objective

How can such a shift in policy focus be realized? The annual budgets and accounts will still present themselves, and the clergy will still expect to be paid. A diocese that stops worrying about money and instead adopts a number of expensive growth strategies will soon hit the reality buffers. Neither is it any use giving one group of people in a diocese the objective of balancing the books and another group the objective of growing the Church and expecting them to work in semi-isolation from each other. Thinking and strategy need to be joined together. Probably the best way to do this is to develop a new measure to act as the policy variable the diocese is trying to control. Such a measure would enable the diocese to refocus on the growth of the Church while at the same time maintaining its financial discipline.

The fundamental financial relationship in a diocese is between the number of people available to pay employment costs and the number of people employed. This is a relatively new fundamental relationship because, in times past, most of the costs were paid for centrally. We have now entered an era where the costs have to be met locally. So the number of church members or attenders per person employed is what determines the long-term stability and direction of the labour force. This number is affected by generosity (giving per head), by overheads (costs other than the employment costs of the workforce), and by the terms and conditions of employment (pension contributions, housing policies, etc.). But more and more church members are already giving realistically towards the recommended 5 per cent of income level and some dioceses are saying that there is no longer much more scope for increases in real per capita giving. Overheads and employment cost changes may make a modest difference, but the core employment costs form the major item.

It should, therefore, be possible for any diocese to estimate a target figure for 'membership or attendance per person on the payroll' that will provide long-term financial health and stability. This target will differ between dioceses according to giving levels, the amount of 'other' income, and the weight of overheads.

The point is that this measure can be changed either by reducing the number of people on the payroll or by increasing the number of people available to pay for them. Church growth and financial prudence are brought together in one policy objective around which everyone in the diocese can unite. 'Our aim is to increase the number of church members per person on the payroll from the present 95 to 120. We'll achieve as much of this as possible by increasing the number of members, and do the rest by reducing the payroll.'

Dioceses compared

It is instructive to take a look at the actual figures around the dioceses because there are dramatic differences between them. By and large, dioceses with higher numbers of members per employee are those with lesser financial headaches. Those adopting the more draconian economy measures are those at the bottom of this particular league table. We here use adult usual Sunday attendance as the membership measure simply because it is a reliable and stable series that has been collected for a very long time. The number of lay employees in dioceses is not something that is published so we here use data only on the clergy, which is published. Further work would therefore need to be done on these figures before starting to use them for operational purposes, but the table below at least gives an interesting first view.

Table 4.2 Adult attendance per stipendiary employed 2002: diocesan league table for the Church of England

1	Guildford	106	26	Sodor & Man	79
2	Gloucester	105	26	Worcester	79
3	Salisbury	104	28	Sheffield	78
4	Chester	103	28	Southwark	78
5	Canterbury	98	30	Bradford	77
5	Oxford	98	31	Lichfield	76
5	Portsmouth	98	31	Ripon & Leeds	76
8	Chichester	97	33	Derby	75
9	Winchester	96	33	Leicester	75
10	St Eds & Ips	95	35	Birmingham	74
11	Rochester	92	35	Manchester	74
12	Bath & Wells	90	37	Chelmsford	73
12	Blackburn	90	37	Wakefield	73
12	Liverpool	90	39	Carlisle	72
12	Peterborough	90	39	Lincoln	72
16	Coventry	89	41	Southwell	71
16	St Albans	89	42	Newcastle	70
18	Bristol	87	43	Durham	68
18	Ely	87			
20	Hereford	86			
21	London	84			
21	Norwich	84			
23	Exeter	83			
23	Truro	83			
25	York	81			

A diocese with an attendance of over 100 per stipendiary will clearly find it much easier to pay the clergy than one with only 68.

Reducing the number of stipendiary clergy releases vicarages for sale and so produces a new income stream out of which remaining clergy can be paid. However, the prospect of a few clergy surviving through living off the sale of the homes of the others, while ministering to ever dwindling congregations does not exactly bring a warm glow of expectation. The way to avoid this scenario is for the Church to grow.

In this chapter we have shown up the limitations of concentrating only on the financial side of the decline cycle – of making higher shares and clergy cuts the main response. Rather, the main solution to the decline cycle has to be the growth of the Church. For all sorts of reasons more important than that of turning round the institution of the Church before it dies, but for that reason as well, we have to focus our energies and efforts on growing local churches. The next four chapters consider ways of growing the local church that are being effective today.

5

Church growth through good practices

And I, when I am lifted up from the earth, will draw all people to myself.
(John 12.32 NRSV)

God is the grower of the Church

The most important good practice for the growth of the Church is to allow
God to do his work. Jesus will draw all manner of people to himself through
being lifted up on a cross. It may be folly to some and a stumbling block to
others, but to those whom God has called, it is the power and wisdom of God.
Churches that promote and advertise themselves, while keeping Jesus in the
background for fear he will put people off, or because they are not quite sure
of him themselves, or because the buildings, the music and the traditions
form the limit of their interest, have got the whole thing the wrong way
round. Usually it is Jesus who attracts people and the Church that puts them
off.

Jesus says of Peter, 'On this rock I will build my church'[1] – the building
materials may be human but the master builder is Jesus himself. Paul says of
himself, the church planter, and Apollos, the church leader, 'I planted, Apollos
watered, but God gave the growth'.[2] So the picture emerges that it is indeed
God's job to grow his Church, but he has chosen to rely on his human agents
to ensure delivery – lifting him up rather than ourselves; growing a Jesus
movement rather than a human institution; being the living stones he quar-
ries for the building of his Church; and acting as the under-gardeners doing
the master gardener's bidding.

So the good practices described here work in churches that genuinely desire
to see Jesus lifted up, and are working out how best they can help in this
rather than get in the way. I do not know how churches that have lost touch
with the living Jesus, or have no agenda for sharing the good news about
him, can grow at all. I suspect their days are numbered. For who will keep
shopping every week for a tin that promises the earth on the label but is
empty inside?

This chapter is not suggesting that good practices are an adequate substitute for a crucified Saviour, but rather that their effectiveness is largely limited to churches that wish to exalt him. For some churches the prior question is Ezekiel's 'Can these dry bones live?' Yes, because God is the God of resurrection, but the Spirit of Jesus will need to rattle them into life first of all before the following good practices become relevant and effective.

Methodology – identifying the good practices

In *Hope for the Church*[3] I identified a number of good practices for the growth of the Church, the evidence for which comes partly from the English Church Census data gathered in 1989 and 1998.[4] Rather than repeat any of that, this chapter reports the results of several surveys of Anglican churches in different dioceses and streams in the period since 2002 when *Hope for the Church* was published. In particular, I would like to thank clergy from the dioceses of London (Willesden and Kensington areas), Winchester, Lichfield, Llandaff, Monmouth, St Asaph, Cashel and Ossory, and the New Wine network for completing a total of nearly 600 of my questionnaires designed to identify those good practices that are associated with church growth in ordinary parishes today. Churches in a number of other dioceses and situations have also contributed to the patterns described and conclusions reached here. A typical questionnaire is reproduced in Appendix 1. It is designed both to check the evidence on good practices (such as process evangelism courses) that have been previously identified, and to give the respondents opportunity to list the changes and factors they themselves see as significant for their own church's story. Typically, all churches, not just growing ones, were surveyed in a diocese or area so factors associated with decline emerge along with those associated with growth.

1 Characteristics of the clergy

The first set of good practices uncovered relates to the recruiting, appointing and keeping of the clergy. Three significant relationships emerge from the data: long-stay incumbents are more likely to have declining churches, while women incumbents and younger incumbents are more likely to have growing churches. The ideal candidate profile for a church that wishes to grow would appear to be young, female and willing to stay in post for ten to twelve years!

The age of the clergy

Younger clergy – and their young families – attract younger congregations. This is an aspect of the general truth that clergy tend to attract people about ten years either side of them in age. Younger clergy, as well as being able to relate more naturally to the younger generations, also tend to have more energy and not to have lost their drive and ambition. They are less tied to traditional forms, more likely to try new things, and more likely to have an accurate instinct for what will draw postmoderns to God through the Church. They are more likely to see themselves not as parish pastors but as leaders in mission. Their perspective is more likely to be that the old 'Christendom' order is dead or dying. They are less likely to see the State Church as part of the Establishment, of the official governance and organization of society. Younger clergy are more likely to believe that they are leading a missionary Church in a post-Christian society. They are less likely to see themselves as pillars of society and servants of an institution and more likely to see themselves as leaders of a counter-cultural movement. So their churches are more likely to grow (see Chapter 2).

By 'Christendom' is meant a situation in which the Church of England has a privileged position in society as of right, where it is assumed that all citizens are Christians and that the job of the Church is to give spiritual nurture, pastoral care and moral leadership.

All this does not mean that the older clergy are to be written off, and they should certainly not use this finding as an excuse for putting their feet up prematurely. Rather, attention needs to be given to helping them rediscover their joy, energy, vision and direction as the years roll by (see Chapter 10).

How long clergy stay

The finding that long-stay clergy are more likely to have declining congregations is also associated with age, as clergy that have stayed a long time in one place are likely to be older on average than those that have just arrived. It seems that churches need a fresh incumbent every so often to lead them into new growth, but not too often. Clergy in post for 5 to 12 years are more likely to be associated with growth than either clergy recently arrived (learning the area, gaining trust) or clergy who have been there a long time (settled down, no fresh vision).[5] The evidence from some recent surveys is summarized below. In each case the 'medium stay' category is either 5–10 or 5–12 years. It is clear from every one of these surveys that long-stay clergy are more likely to have shrinking congregations, but the evidence about whether new incumbents are achieving quick turnarounds is more mixed. A quick turn-around may be more likely if the church had reached a low ebb under the previous incumbent, and if the area is one of rapid population turnover (such as Kensington). A settled population has long memories, a mobile one responds to the here and now.

Table 5.1 Percentage change in uSa in six dioceses

Diocese	% Change in Sunday attendance		
	short–stay	medium–stay	long–stay
Chester 1999–2002	−9	−2	−9
London 1996–2002 (ER)	+2	+21	+2
Cashel & Ossory 2002–2004	0	−3	−8
Monmouth 2002–2004	7	4	−1
St Asaph 2002–2004	9	0	−4
Kensington 2002–2004	25	14	5

One implication of these findings is that churches with a different 'curate-in-charge' every three years may have particular problems growing in a sustained way; another is that short-term contracts (e.g. team vicars for five years) may be bad for church growth. Similarly, it is not clear that a 'freehold for life' is a very sensible option. In other words, the two common patterns today (indefinite freeholds and short-term contracts) are problematic for the growth of the Church. Better to give clergy a ten- or twelve-year perspective on what needs to be done – perhaps with a ten- or twelve-year contract. Similarly, clergy and their parishes could think in and work for such ten- to twelve-year perspectives themselves, whatever arrangements are made for them from above.

Women incumbents

The evidence gathered from these surveys relating to women incumbents is summarized in the table below. This evidence may not be decisive, because there is attendance trend information on only 75 parishes with women incumbents, and mostly over fairly short periods. More evidence would be helpful, but it is striking that the trend for women incumbents is worse than that for men in only one of the nine surveys. Even in London, the churches with women incumbents are still growing significantly. So, although it seems important to keep gathering information on parishes with women incumbents, it does increasingly seem as though women are, on average, leading growing churches and being rather more successful in this than men.

A paper from the Welsh National Centre for Religious Education compares attendance trends between 1994 and 2000 in dioceses with few women incumbents with those having a larger number.[6] No difference was found, but this is not surprising when so many other powerful factors are involved in attendance trends in dioceses. For the first time, here is a large sample of real parish data, which is clearly what is needed for the question to be answered properly.

Table 5.2 Attendance change in parishes with a woman incumbent

Diocese	No. of women incumbents	Attendance change when incumbent is	
		Female	Male
Wakefield 2000–2001	15	+16%	−3%
Chester 1999–2002	8	+9%	−8%
Llandaff 2002–2003	12	(50–50–0)	(29–56–17)*
New Wine 2001–2003	4	+10%	+8%
London 2001–3 or 2002–4	10	+5%	+12%
Lichfield 2002–2003	2	0%	0%
Monmouth 2002–2004	10	+6%	+3%
St Asaph 2002–2004	11	+9%	+3%
Cashel & Ossory 2002–2004	3	+4%	−2%
Total	75	+9%	+2%

* These figures relate to the percentage of clergy who reported 'rising-steady-falling' congregations. So, for example, 6 of the 12 women (50 %) reported rising congregations and 6 steady.

Such findings do not of themselves affect the theological arguments for and against the ordination of women, although there may be a certain force in the 'by their fruits ye shall know them' argument. However, they do begin to answer the practical worries that churches with women priests would not thrive because their ministry would not be accepted, or would be in some way limited by their gender. In view of the sensitivity and controversial nature of this particular issue, a broader study than this, looking at the health and growth of churches with women incumbents, would seem now to be overdue – which PhD student will grasp this nettle?

Of the 75 women incumbents above, 47 appear to have had growing congregations in the period indicated. There are a number of possible theories about why women incumbents appear to be so much more likely to have growing churches than men. Perhaps women priests of the first generation have had to be particularly able and determined to achieve their goal, and they are not going to let their opportunity pass. Perhaps they have usually been given only the smaller and less well regarded livings, and so have found it easier to grow churches from a smaller base. Perhaps women are more naturally relational-leaders than some of the men, who may more naturally deal in policies and programmes – an approach that might grow businesses but is less likely to grow communities. There is still much to discover about the value of women's ministry to the Church, but there would appear already to be much to rejoice over, for the historic opening up of the priesthood to women is already bearing its church growth first-fruits.

Short vacancies

It was shown in Chapter 2, from a detailed study of parish records, that churches shrink in long vacancies, and in Chapter 10 is a discussion of what can be done to shorten the vacancies in order to stop churches shrinking. It is just worth noting for completeness here that the ideal young, female incumbent who stays for ten years should be replaced when she leaves within six months.

2 The age structure of the congregation

The evidence from the surveys reinforces the finding reported in *Hope for the Church* that younger congregations are more likely to see numerical growth.[7] Around the country the age structure of congregations varies a great deal, but the universal finding is that the younger congregations are less likely to be shrinking and more likely to be growing. The key question is what percentage of the adult congregation is aged under 45:

Table 5.3 Attendance change in younger and older congregations

	Cashel	St Asaph	Monmouth	Willesden	Kensington	New Wine
Younger congregations	−2%	8%	8%	10%	26%	11%
Older congregations	−6%	−1%	−2%	4%	10%	−2%

'Younger' churches are defined differently in different dioceses in order to even up the numbers in each half. I have defined the 'younger' churches in Cashel as those having at least 25 per cent of their adults aged under 45; in St Asaph (where congregations are especially elderly) as those where at least 10 per cent of the adults are aged under 45; in Monmouth 15 per cent, New Wine churches 25 per cent, and the Willesden and Kensington churches 50 per cent.

In every diocese there is a concomitant truth to the above, which is that churches are shrinking older and growing younger. This is shown by the fact that shrinking churches are losing children faster than adults, while growing churches are gaining children faster than adults. In total over the last five years the Church of England has been losing adults from usual Sunday attendance at the rate of about 1 per cent per annum but children at about

3 per cent per annum. Yet where churches are growing the number of children is rising faster than the adults. The three main groups of growing churches in the recent surveys are in Willesden, Kensington and the New Wine network:

Table 5.4 Attendance change of adults and children where churches are growing

Churches	Adult attendance	Child attendance
Willesden 2002–2003	+6%	+10%
Kensington 2002–2004	+16%	+24%
New Wine 2001–2003	+10%	+17%

This general background truth – that growth normally comes through attracting younger adults and children – comes to life during the analysis of the specific changes and factors associated with growth identified by the churches themselves. Many of these involve initiatives with children, young people and families, and these seem to be the key to new growth in many places. It is clear, though, from the growth rates achieved by the three whole groups of churches above (each sample representing 50 to 100 churches) that it is indeed possible in postmodern Britain to attract the young back to the churches, because in these places it is already happening.

3 Process evangelism courses

The evidence in *Hope for the Church* drawn from the English Church Census data was that churches running courses did not have a different attendance trend from other churches until they had run them for at least three years.[8] After that there was a steadily building significant growth trend. There was no difference in the trend between parishes using Alpha and those using a different course. The question asked in the diocesan surveys does not distinguish between churches that have used a course for several years as an integral part of an evangelism and incorporation strategy and those that just tried a course once. The results, however, do confirm the perhaps surprising lack of correlation between the use of courses and church growth:

Table 5.5 Attendance change in churches using courses

Diocese or area	Alpha churches	Other courses	No courses used
St Asaph	+3%	+6%	+3%
Monmouth	+6%	+6%	−1%
Cashel	−6%	−6%	−2%
Kensington	+12%	+13%	+41%
Willesden	+6%	+3%	0%

Only in Monmouth and Willesden did the courses appear to be associated with a better attendance trend, and the result in Kensington, the heart of 'Alpha-land', appears to be particularly striking. Perhaps in this area it is particularly difficult to compete with Holy Trinity Brompton itself in the provision of Alpha courses. Other, much smaller, churches have found other ways in which to do their evangelism and incorporation. The 'welcome–friendship–child provision' route into church life does not need a course in place. New members might then join a home group, cell or other small group for their learning and nurture, so bypassing the courses completely.

Nobody can doubt the enormous value and impact of Alpha, Emmaus and the other courses and, where they are used, they are often highly effective. However, the evidence suggests that they are by no means essential for church growth to happen. Churches mention other factors more frequently and strongly when it comes to explaining their growth. Perhaps the truth is that there are no 'off the peg' guaranteed techniques of doing evangelism and securing church growth. On the one hand the nature of some churches and communities can render them immune to the best ideas and endeavours, and on the other hand the Spirit of God can work in unique ways in each unique situation. Perhaps God's gentle correction to well-meaning enthusiasts asserting that 'the only way' to reach the nation today is through Alpha courses or cell structures or some other latest happening idea is the taxidermist's conclusion that there is more than one way to skin a cat. This may not only be due to God's own infinite creativity coupled with his baffling tendency to be always on the move doing new things. It may also be because God may honour our honest endeavours at communicating the faith and growing the Church whichever routes we choose. It may be more effective to try something, anything, now than to spend ages looking for just the right technique to turn up. And it is usually more effective to seek the route that is more relevant to today's world than to cling to the one that worked yesterday.

4 Provision for teenagers

How well a church provides for teenagers is both a litmus test of its ability to nurture new adult Christians and a principal determinant of the size of its work with children of all ages. It also helps determine how many adults will attend the church. Churches that make provision for children but not for teenagers ('because we don't have any' or 'because we don't have the leaders') are thereby telling their children that they should leave the church as they enter puberty. The same situation faces the children as it would the adults in a church where people were not allowed to attend the groups and activities once they had retired. Such a church would not have many members over 65.

In general, churches fall into three groups:

- those that make little or no provision for teenagers;
- those with youth groups of one sort or another;
- those with a youth-minister and/or specialist youth worship provision.

Where there is an organized group, numbers are greater and the trend is better than where there is none. Where there is a paid worker, then the numbers are much greater and the trend better than where there is a group run by volunteers. In the dioceses of Chester and St Albans, churches with youth ministers have rising numbers of under 16s, and the other churches have rapidly falling numbers. In Chichester, a number of churches all happened to appoint a youth minister or worker for the first time around 1997–8. Prior to this, their attendance trends of under 16s had been downward, but afterwards the trends were reversed. Other churches continued to lose the children:

Table 5.6 Child attendance changes in churches that gained a youth minister around 1998, compared with those that did not (Diocese of Chichester)

Worker?	uSa 1990	uSa 1998	uSa 2001	% change 1998–2001
Yes	1173	718	899	+25
No	7001	5487	4727	−14

Hardly any churches in St Asaph or Monmouth had youth ministers, but even the provision of volunteer-led groups made a decisive difference:

Table 5.7 Numbers of under-18s attending church on Sundays 2002–2004

	No youth provision	Youth groups
St Asaph	9 to 8	12 to 14
Monmouth	8 to 7	13 to 20

In Cashel, only nine groups of parishes made significant provision for young people, and their numbers rose slightly between 2002 and 2004, whereas numbers of under 18s in the other churches went down 7 per cent.

The exceptional growth in child numbers in churches with no youth provision in Kensington is associated with a number of churches that have grown rapidly with young families – youth provision will need to follow if the growth is to be maintained.

Table 5.8 Average child attendance in churches making different levels of provision for children

	No teen provision	Youth groups	Youth minister
Willesden	22 to 24	26 to 27	69 to 81
Kensington	17 to 25	28 to 34	68 to 80

Attendance of under-16s relates to 2001–3 in Willesden, and to 2002–4 in Kensington.

Also, churches that already have large numbers of children are more likely to appoint paid workers or ministers for them. However, it is still clear that numbers follow quality of provision. Where the churches are making good provision the children and young people are growing in numbers. The fields are indeed white ready to harvest. It is just that the labourers are few – too few churches so far are providing groups and paid leadership to halt the national trends. However, if and when more churches do so, then the national trend will be reversed, perhaps dramatically. In the smaller churches of the Kensington area (under 100 adults on a Sunday) the number of children in church on a Sunday has gone up by 50 per cent in only two years, between 2002 and 2004. As shown earlier in this chapter, growing churches grow younger – when churches start to grow again, the number of children rises faster than the number of adults. So we reach the interesting conclusion that we in the Church already know how to attract growing numbers of children and young people – through finding volunteer and paid leaders for their groups and worship events, and in fact through adopting any good practice for the growth of the Church. If we do this in more places then overall numbers will rise again.

5 Service times

Suppose the Church of England is an old-fashioned metal bucket, and the people are the water in the bucket. God is still pouring water in from the top but the overall level inside is gradually going down because water is leaking out of several holes in the bottom slightly faster. The art of growing the Church may be less about attempting to tip God's elbow so that more water flows in, and more about identifying and mending the major leakages. Major holes identified through this book include larger churches, long vacancies, churches that do not change, children, certain dioceses and, here, Sunday evenings and early communions. On balance, church attendance is going down at early Sunday Communion, and on Sunday evenings, but steady or rising at main Sunday morning services and at weekday services. This appears to be true for all dioceses, though the following table is compiled from forms returned from Cashel, Monmouth, Llandaff, St Asaph, Kensington and Willesden. The subsets from each of these disparate dioceses tells the same story as the total below:

Table 5.9 Attendance trends at different services times (numbers of churches, usually in 2004)

	Rising	Steady	Falling	Rising–Falling
Early communion	20	168	30	−10
Main morning	203	280	79	+124
Sunday evening	33	140	75	−44
Weekday	86	199	33	+53

In general, the respondents are slightly more optimistic about trends in these surveys than they are when filling in the official forms that result in the published figures. Even bearing that in mind, however, the results are clear-cut. There is a small balance of decline at early communion, although total numbers are usually small. The main decline is on Sunday evenings, a process many people think began in the late 1960s when *The Forsyte Saga* was first shown on television early on Sunday evenings! This process is clearly still continuing. Although many evening services have now been closed (only half the churches surveyed above still had one) the remainder have a clear balance of decline. It is also clear from the data what the difference is between the shrinking and the growing Sunday evening congregations. In general, the shrinking congregations are at fairly traditional style evening services – evening prayer, evensong, etc. Very few people now go to church twice on a Sunday, and fewer and fewer of the older people are happy to turn out in the dark for badly attended services in cold buildings. The growing congregations are at churches that have targeted the two main natural Sunday evening churchgoing groups: teenagers and young adults without children. Many teenagers are in bed all through Sunday mornings, but are ready to go out at night. They do not wish to worship in the same family service as the small children and be made to behave in childish ways. Young adults without children, whether single or married, are all likely to be in work during the week, meaning there is pressure on the weekend for household chores as well as socializing. Sunday evening may suit them best.

Perhaps the most surprising finding from these surveys is the huge balance of growing congregations reported at main Sunday morning service times. The sample does include many churches from the growing Diocese of London, so the national picture in England will not be as positive as this. However, it is clear that this is not only when most of the people come to church, it is also where most of the church growth is. It is probably a true generalization that the growing congregations in this time-slot tend to be in services that are modernizing and making good provision for children – see below.

However, there is also a large positive balance of churches reporting rising weekday congregations. The national totals in the published data are showing a small annual decline, but it may be that this will start to turn round because there are two clear trends beneath the headline figures. Traditional 'Prayer Book Wednesday Communion' type services targeted at retired people are probably in overall numerical decline. But a range of new 'fresh expressions' style events is developing, and modest but growing numbers of people are attending them. The age group at these newer events is clearly younger than the others – the number of children attending church midweek is now rising in the Church of England even though the number of adults is falling slightly.

The church growth conclusions from this data seem fairly clear: churches that wish to attract new people, to hold their existing people, and to grow should concentrate their efforts at the main Sunday morning services (especially with families), on trying new things during the week, and perhaps on Sunday evening for teenagers and young adults. This does not, of course, mean they can abandon the older folk at early Sunday and midweek communion but rather that the Church's developmental programme will probably bear greater fruit at other times.

In recent years I have come across a number of churches that conducted a parish survey as part of their preparation for planting a new congregation, often in an area where there is no easily accessible local church at the moment. They have asked the local residents a question something like this: 'If we were to start a new church congregation in your local area, what time and day would be most likely to attract you to come?' Sometimes, rather than conduct a survey, the vicar has simply asked around at the school gate. In every case the answers obtained were amazingly consistent and nothing like the normal service times that we stick to for largely historic reasons! The community response in each case was that the service time most likely to attract would be between 4 p.m. and 5 p.m. on either Saturday or Sunday. This allows people both to continue with their busy lives during the day at the weekend and to go out in the evening. Early teatime is especially favoured by parents because the children are freer from other activities, and may be getting a little difficult to handle by that time of day. Usually people would like the service to last less than an hour so they can go home for tea and still have an evening. Other churches may wish to be guided by these findings, or, better, be provoked into conducting their own local surveys to find what might work best in their own local area.

One vicar wanted to move the service to what he thought would be a more accessible and attractive time for newcomers. He asked the older members why the present time had been fixed as it was in the last change some years ago. 'Because it fitted in with the bus timetable,' came the answer. 'But the buses don't run any more!' retorted the vicar, thinking he had won the argument. 'Yes but we've got used to this time now' came the response.

Existing congregations are usually reluctant to move their service time to suit potential newcomers. This is not only because the people for whom the present time is convenient are the ones who are actually coming, but also because the comfort of familiar routines is powerful. In some cases it may be easier to start a new service than to shift the existing congregation from its ingrained habits. If a congregation will change, however, it is surprising how quickly the new time will become the hallowed tradition to be defended against future tinkering vicars.

6 The church notice-board

In a multicultural world, churches that are multicultural in their own expression are likely to reach more people than those that are not. There used to be an Anglican culture. The future lies with multicultural Anglicanism. A Radio 1 church will reach Radio 1 people, a Radio 3 church Radio 3 people, a multichannel church most people. If the distinctive feature of Anglicanism is that we are here for everybody, then sticking within one tight worshipping tradition is not being very Anglican. Larger churches that adopt multi-congregation models of church life are likely to grow through attracting a coalition of different types of people. Smaller churches may benefit from sorting out their specialisms between them in order to ensure a range of provision in the local area. The selection of service times designed to suit the different target groups of a multi-congregation church would seem to be an important matter. Questionnaire analysis and a large number of individual church stories probably suggests the following guidelines when reviewing service patterns and repainting the notice-board:

Older people and traditional Anglicans:
Early Sunday morning but not too early – 9 a.m. is better than 8 a.m. – and any mid-Sunday morning time.

Families/carers with younger children:

Mid Sunday morning or Saturday or Sunday around 4.30 p.m.

Young people and young adults without children:

Saturday or Sunday evenings, probably 7 p.m. rather than 6.30 p.m.

People with no churchgoing background:

Mid morning on a Sunday or a tailor-made event at a range of times during the week, including midweek evenings.

Some churches attempt to cater for variety in worshipping aspirations and music culture by having a range of service styles at the same service time. St Everywhere's is a case in point:

Figure 5.1 St Everywhere's notice-board

Welcome to St Everywhere

- 1st Sunday   Family Service with Sandpit
- 2nd Sunday   Solemn High Mass
- 3rd Sunday   'Old Hymns' Songs of Praise
- 4th Sunday   Extra-loud Eucharist with rock band 'Terminal Explosion'
- 5th Sunday   Outdoors in the graveyard

Come every week!

St Everywhere's slogan may be 'Come every week!' but in practice most people will self-select. The congregation on the first Sunday will be markedly different from that on the second. The spread of such variety at the same service time may be a contributory factor to the trend to less frequent attendance. People are much more regular at services that are themselves regular and always reliably somewhere around their own cultural preference.

The issue of whether church members attend less frequently than they used to was covered in *Hope for the Church.*[9] The conclusion was that there was actually no evidence from the available data that people were coming less often, but perhaps that was because the former every-week regulars who now go twice a month have been balanced out by the four times a year people who now never come at all. The average remains the same but everyone is sliding down the frequency scale. It is how some people leave the church. However, there is a rather neat mathematical way of testing the declining frequency theory, and maybe there is one reader who will rise to the challenge. The numerically challenged have my permission to skip the following paragraph. I promise you it is an isolated case!

Not for the mathematically faint-hearted

If you assume randomness in the incidence of attendance, then the attendance figures each week will form a normal distribution over the year. If 100 people each come every week and there are no visitors, then attendance is always 100, and the standard deviation is zero. But the more irregular is each individual, the greater the standard deviation, which can be normalized for congregation size by translating into a coefficient of variation. The greater the coefficient of variation, the more irregular each individual congregation member is, or, put the other way, the greater the number of individuals who figure in the attendance statistics with a given mean. All that is needed for charting changes in attendance frequency is attendance data per week for the latest year plus a past year for a number of churches. In churches where the coefficient of variation has increased, then attendance has become less frequent. There now, that wasn't too difficult, was it? If anyone understood that and would like a sabbatical project or an MA in church statistics, away you go! On the other hand, if some mathematical genius sees a flaw in my clever dodge, then please don't tell me because I'm feeling rather pleased with it!

St Wooldyed's problem is the opposite to that of St Everywhere.

It offers three different service times, but only one service type. It is trying to attract the same segment of the population three times over and is likely to remain rather small. This seems such a waste of the church's ability to put on services at three different times on a Sunday. Better to have three target groups than one.

Figure 5.2 St Wooldyed's notice-board

Welcome to St Wooldyed

Come to St Wooldyed's for reverence and tradition:

8.00 Early Mass
10.30 Morning Mass
6.30 Evening Mass

We always use the proper Prayer Book at St Wooldyed

Three similar services – one type of person

The Upper Creek Group has a slightly different problem.

Figure 5.3 Upper Creek Group's notice-board

THE UPPER CREEK GROUP OF PARISHES

Our services are as follows:

St Without's 9.30am alternate Sundays

St Paddle's 11am Family Service 1st & 3rd Sundays, otherwise Eucharist

Little Snoring 8am Holy Communion (1st Sunday) 6.30 (2nd & 4th Sundays)

Great Creek 9am (summertime) 11am (wintertime) – see church noticeboard for local variations

Joint Services 5th Sundays and other feast days – location varies

Come and join us!

The vicar and reader are trying to fit the pattern around their ability to get from one place to the next on the principle that they have to be present. The resultant confusion means that the challenge to 'Come and join us' needs to have added to it the words 'If you can find us'. It is very hard to build continuity and community with anything other than a regular weekly, reliable event. This should probably be the priority and guiding principle in every situation. It is sometimes argued that people come less often, so we can get them all together by having a service only once or twice a month. They will then organize their diaries around the church services. But most people will still not do this – they will not book their holidays or family visits to suit the church. People with a weekly service may come only every fortnight, but the same people offered fortnightly worship will only come every month.

In general, it is probably true that rural groups where the clergy and readers whizz round on a giant rota like a Methodist circuit are causing problems and decline potential for themselves. Every week it can feel as though the service is taken by a visiting preacher. There is no continuity of ministry and pastoral care. Most small congregations thrive best when there is one focal-point person for leadership, continuity and pastoral care. The rural group tends to work best when the incumbent concentrates on just one or two congregations (perhaps the ones with the most potential rather than the largest) and offers oversight to the rest while ensuring each one has its own recognized leader – a reader, retired priest, OLM, NSM, churchwarden or whoever. Each leader can be absent from her or his own congregation in order to visit others one week a month. Otherwise, leaders should build and lead at their own base.

All Saints' notice-board (*opposite*) gives a clear indication of the nature of each of the four Sunday services. Each service, hopefully, will do what it says on the tin. Four different types of people will be attracted by four different types of service offered at appropriate times and at the same timing and in the same style every week. All Saints may wish to consider how to develop services midweek but it appears to have adopted some good practices for Sundays.

It is surprising how many church notice-boards are actually out of date or misleading or keep quiet about one or more services on offer, perhaps because they are new or midweek. This may be partly because of the painting problem – it is a major task to repaint the notice-board, especially if you suspect that there may be further changes soon after you have done the job. Some churches say 'We all know what we do anyway, and we never get newcomers so what's the point?' The point is that they never will get newcomers if they meet in secret. In the present world where continuous change is here to stay, notice-boards should not be painted at all. Boards should be

Figure 5.4 All Saints' notice-board

Welcome to All Saints

Our services every week are:

- 9.30   Holy Eucharist with Choir
- 11.00   Family Service with groups for children
- 4.00   Service in Urdu
- 7.00   Contemporary Praise

Four distinct services – four types of people

designed so that they can be altered quickly and easily as changes occur and experiments are tried.

To conclude, this chapter has presented some good practices that lead to church growth. But good practices are useless without good attitudes. The survey data clearly shows that good practices only find their true effectiveness in the context of worship that engages people in genuine encounter with the living God.

6

Church growth through change

Forgetting what lies behind and straining forward to what lies ahead,
I press on toward the goal for the prize. (Philippians 3.13,14 NRSV)

Change or decay

The Revd Henry Lyte, lying on his deathbed in 1847, penned an immortal
poem of honest faith when he wrote the emotionally charged words of 'Abide
with me'. However, I do worry about the impact of one of his lines on the
Anglican psyche, the one that puts the dread into newness: 'Change and
decay in all around I see; O thou who changest not abide with me!'[1] I think
Henry Lyte was talking about his own dying body, but the body of Christ
has to keep on being renewed in order not to die. The truth uncovered by
survey after survey is that churches that do not change decay, and churches
that do change grow. It is truly change *or* decay. Most churches need to
make a choice between having a comfortable death or an uncomfortable
life. Some may choose the former but, if sufficient numbers of individual
churches decide to choose life, then the national Church will start to grow
again.

The table below shows average attendance trends, from various diocesan
surveys in recent years, in churches making and not making changes.
Churches were responding to the question: 'What have been the main
changes to your church services and church life over the last (three) years?'
Churches that had not made major changes were invited to say 'none'.

Table 6.1 Average attendance trends in churches making and not making changes

	Churches making changes	Churches not making changes
Monmouth	+10%	−3%
St Asaph	+14%	−3%
Willesden	+8%	+2%
Kensington	+19%	0%
Lichfield	+3%	−22%

The Lichfield survey relates to electoral rolls 1996–2002, the others to attendance 2002–4.

There is one exception to the general rule that changes to church life and services are associated with attendance growth. In most of the surveys a number of churches reported that they had changed the liturgy or prayer book to a more modern version. This was particularly so in Wales, where churches have been moving from the green prayer book to the modern language gold one. Churches that have made such a change show just the same attendance trend as churches making no changes. It may be that changing the colour of the prayer book has about as much impact on non-churchgoers as offering brown eggs instead of white impresses a group of vegans. Something more radical, for example PowerPoint not prayer book, or something more relevant, for example better ways of befriending newcomers, may be needed for a real impact to be made.

There are eight types or categories of significant change that *are* associated with congregational growth in the survey forms, and these are listed below.

Eight changes that lead to church growth

- Planting new congregations;
- Worship less formal, more relaxed; better music;
- Better provision for children and young people (family services, better groups, paid staff);
- Improving welcome and integration – front door;
- Better small groups and pastoral care – back door;
- Regular use of evangelism courses as part of an evangelism and incorporation strategy;
- More lay involvement in leadership;
- Improvements to buildings.

This list is not in order of importance except that the top five are the most commonly cited and the ones with the biggest average attendance trend response. So these five appear to be the most important or effective good practices.

1 Planting new congregations

The evidence for the growth dynamic of newly planted Anglican churches is laid out in *Hope for the Church*.[2] The same growth dynamic is present in newly started congregations kept within the umbrella of the planting church, usually in the same building. As examples, eight churches in Kensington reporting planting a new congregation since 2002 saw their attendance rise by 26 per cent to mid 2004. Seven churches in Willesden that started new congregations in 2002–3 grew their attendance by 12 per cent, double the average rate. A group of six churches in Lichfield that planted a new congregation in 2002–3 saw their collective attendance rise by 14 per cent by November 2003. Around the country the most common planting move relayed to me has been replacing one main Sunday morning service with two. Sometimes this is because the building has got full, and the style of the two new services is similar. More usually, there is a deliberate intent to create two services of distinctive style (usually 'traditional' and 'informal') out of the original 'compromise' event. In almost every case reported to me the total numbers have risen. This may be partly because people tend to come more frequently when they know the service is to their preferred style every week, but new people are added as well. This is not just because of the new 'no need to compromise' style but also because the two smaller congregations are hungrier to attract new people to their empty spaces, and some people feel more able to join something new than break in to an established community.

Apart from this, there appears to be huge variety in the congregation-planting scene. Local conditions, the resources at the church's disposal, and the type of people the event is aimed at are probably the main determinants. As an example of such variety, below is a summary list of the new congregations started by half of a group of 20 large churches in the Diocese of Lichfield between 2002 and 2003. From compline and supper to youth worship, to café church, to a language-group service, to a traditional daily office, the variety is total. These churches had been in overall numerical decline but, stimulated by a process of teaching, conferences and consultation, they were trying new things in order to attract new people to Christ through the church and so grow again.

Newly planted congregations or worship events

- Sunday morning service divided into two;
- Monthly plant on estate;
- Sunday evening café style prayer and praise fortnightly;
- Weekly Sunday evening youth congregation;
- Sunday evening supper and night prayer;
- Urdu speaking congregation 4.30 p.m.;
- Daily services;
- 14s–19s MAD group;
- Parent and child monthly midweek.

A diocesan survey in Llandaff revealed the following new services or congregations with a similar wide variety of styles:

New services

- Seasonal and occasional, e.g. Celtic evening liturgy;
- Toddler church;
- Quarterly prayer and praise Sunday afternoons;
- All-age service Sunday mornings;
- Completely new church;
- 9.30 a.m. traditional and 11 a.m. charismatic services replace 10 a.m.;
- Non-liturgical band and multi-media Sunday morning;
- Monthly weekday for elderly – car transport team;
- Monthly young people's Eucharist;
- Monthly evensong;
- Informal evening worship;
- Monthly all-age on Sunday mornings;
- Café church;
- Party church 9 p.m.–2 a.m. Sunday–Monday.

Most congregations seem to have their own natural size ceiling, some of them surprisingly low. It is also surprisingly difficult and destructive to get some congregations to make major, or even minor, changes. The main way by which the Church as a whole changes, therefore, may also be through the starting of new congregations.

2 Making worship less formal, more relaxed, and with better music

This is not quite the same as 'more modern'. It is possible to take the tension out of a worship event while keeping it traditional in character. The litmus test is what happens when something goes wrong: is the atmosphere awkward and charged, as though something shameful has happened, the event spoiled, or is the atmosphere relaxed enough for a joke, a smile and a picking up of the threads without embarrassment?

We do now live in a more informal age. The generations who sat in straight rows at school, had to keep quiet, and learnt through 'chalk and talk' teaching methods may find a formal service at least to be familiar even if they do not like it. For the generations for whom school was a more relaxed affair, however, where learning was individually packaged and happened by exploration more than by passive listening, a formal church service in an alien style of building can be a complete impossibility. So churches able to make their worship accessible through lighter liturgy, greater participation, friendly, relaxed leadership, allowances for individualism, welcome of noisy children, songs that ordinary people understand and can join in with, sermons that engage not lecture, and buildings that relax not intimidate have a better chance of attracting and holding new people.

In St Asaph, 7 churches reported that their main change between 2002 and 2004 had been to make their worship more informal, relaxed or creative. Their combined attendance rose from 585 to 640, by 9 per cent. In Kensington, 15 churches reported making their worship more informal, user friendly or modern in the same period. Their combined attendance rose by 32 per cent. In Lichfield, 8 of the group of 20 churches reported changes to their service styles as follows:

Changed service styles

- More informality;
- Various adjustments to time and mix;
- Monthly family praise replacing HC;
- New structure for the family service;
- More lay and teenage involvement;
- Healing ministry offered;
- More varied pattern;
- New evening pattern targeting distinct groups.

Many churches today are installing data projectors and screens for use in church services for hymns, liturgy, church notices, sermon illustrations, video clips, and so on. Apart from the power of a new communications tool, the projectors also have the advantage of providing a ministry opportunity to teenagers and other technically minded people who enjoy the new technology. They obviate the need for hymn and prayer books, and enable people to sing with their heads up and nothing in their hands. All this can produce a surprisingly large change in the worshipping atmosphere. The new equipment provides opportunities for worship and teaching to be visual as well as verbal; can make worship feel more corporate, less individual; makes church seem more credibly wired up to the modern world; relieves newcomers and the dyspraxic from the embarrassment of fumbling through hymn books and losing the place in the prayer book; and generally makes the experience seem more interesting, flexible, varied, stimulating, accessible and relevant.

In a worldwide survey of factors associated with growing churches, the only universal feature of all growing churches was discovered to be 'joy and laughter'. Joyless churches shrivel but 'a cheerful heart is a good medicine'.[3] Congregations too uptight or disapproving to laugh at the vicar's jokes are unlikely to exude the welcoming warmth of the convivial Saviour met in the Gospels. I was once about to announce the opening hymn when the wardens interrupted with a surprise fire drill. When all had trooped out to the gathering points, been checked over and at last reassembled in church, hugging myself with inner delight, I was finally able to make the announcement. 'The first hymn is "Light up the fire, let the flame burn".' The congregation convulsed in laughter for several minutes before being able to proceed. Some strange therapy was deep at work as a Christian community was cemented together in simple joy and innocent laughter.

I am, sad to say, a tone-deaf dunce in a family of musicians. When I start playing the piano, the others start leaving the house on suddenly urgent errands. Yet even I recognize the vital role of music in the life and future of the Christian Church. Music is the congregation's bonding experience, it carves out and gives expression to the range of human emotions, it defines the culture of a worshipping community, it is the joyful expression of human creativity carried up to the edge of heaven itself, it expresses and often teaches the theology of the people of God. It is fun as well as worship. Good, relevant music attracts. Poor, irrelevant music repels. Many people will only allow themselves to be associated with the sort of music that fits the image they want to have of themselves. If we want teenagers to sing in worship we have to have the sort of music that enables them to look cool while doing so. Like designer labels, an image conscious person's music is a public statement of who and what they are: it is their identity, their affiliation, their football team. All this is even more important in the age of the consumer who will buy into high quality church and reject the irrelevant than it was in the age when people came out of habit and duty whatever fare was offered.

In every one of the surveys, a significant number of churches had been busy improving their music provision. In St Asaph, 9 churches reported that their music had become more contemporary or varied. Their attendance rose 2002–4 by 15 per cent. In Llandaff, 5 churches reported livelier, more contemporary worship, and in Cashel, 7 reported improvements to music provision, with similar growth results. In Kensington, 6 churches reported that their music provision had become more modern and varied. Attendance at these churches rose 27 per cent.

Cathedrals have always known the truth that investment in music pays off. They pour vast resources into choir schools, professional singers, great organs and the best professional organists. Some parish churches still ride high on their traditional church music and robed choirs. It is a highly traditional thing for a church to invest heavily in its music. What is new in many growing churches is the more contemporary and popular music style. In the early days of modern church music the usual story was the replacement of choir and organist (paid) by a band of modern musicians from the congregation (unpaid). Increasingly today part of some churches' investment in high quality modern music has been to reprofessionalize the leading of church music, usually by paying a music director. When planting a new young adult or youth congregation, it is probably essential first to organize high quality music provision before daring to initiate a worship event. The appointment of the music director is just as key as the appointment of the minister.

Yet it is striking that churches that will spend £50,000 on the organ or £150,000 on the roof without pausing for much thought are quite unlikely to spend £1,000 on musical instruments for the youth band, or £5,000 on a better sound system, or £10,000 a year on a part-time director of music who will train and lead the next generation of church musicians. Perhaps the criteria we use to decide what to spend money on need to be adjusted. What spending will help grow the community of the people of God? What spending will help grow the next generations of Christians? What spending will help grow the worshipping heart of this church?

3 Better provision for children and families

Churches shrink older and grow younger. Although the overall number of children in church has been going down faster than the number of adults, where churches have found ways to improve their provision for children and families on Sunday mornings they have usually started to grow again. In the St Asaph survey, for example, 7 churches reported improving their child provision (one or two reopening long closed Sunday schools). Their total attendance rose from 485 to 577, 19 per cent. In Kensington, 17 churches reported improving their child provision, or starting or developing family or all age services. Their attendance rose 13 per cent. In Cashel and Ossory, 7 churches reported that they had developed family services or improved their child provision on a Sunday morning. Their collective attendance rose from 522 to 580 between 2002 and 2004, a growth of 11 per cent in a diocese in overall decline.

Evangelical churches have been developing family or all-age services for many years. Some models involve the children leaving part way through, or arriving at the Peace. Others include the children through the whole service. Others have the children entirely separate from the adult congregation, perhaps in different buildings. But high-church Anglicans have been slower to go down this route, perhaps influenced by the 'Parish Communion Movement' with its slogan 'The Lord's people round the Lord's table on the Lord's day'. If all worship must be formal and eucharistic, it limits the scope for child-friendly, easily accessible worship events. However, it is clear that, around the country, catholic churches with growing congregations today are usually achieving this with family, all age or child-friendly services, often non-eucharistic. Normally these are not instead of the main weekly mass, but in addition to it. For some churches the family service will be monthly, and will often attract the largest congregation. But the ideal is to offer weekly worship in the more accessible style as well as the deeper, traditional one.

The priest inherited a church decimated by divisions and defections to Rome. He networked around the local community, started a toddler group in the church hall, and radically changed the style of worship – less mystery and heavy formality, more informal, accessible, welcoming and child-friendly. A Sunday school was begun. Young families began to come on Sundays and a new community to develop. Numbers on Sunday mornings rose within four years from fifteen to over a hundred.

---

4 *Opening the front door – closing the back door*

The church member was chatting over coffee at the end of the service to a lady who had come for the first time. 'It's a very friendly church,' said the old hand, encouragingly. 'I don't want a friendly church,' retorted the visitor, 'I want a church where I can make friends.'

Once upon a time many people aspired to little more than 'attending a service'. They tended to leave immediately it ended, only to reappear as the first hymn was announced the following Sunday. A much higher proportion of churchgoers today aspire to rather more than this – their aspiration is to 'belong to a community'. It is much easier to break into a small community than a large one, to be noticed as a newcomer and to be welcomed into the friendship life of the Christian community. Similarly, it is much easier to drift away from a large community unnoticed than it is from a small one. Small churches that are spiritually and relationship healthy do not need to organize their welcome and integration because it will happen naturally. When a new couple turn up on the edge of the village church community, they will be instantly noticed and someone will be inviting them round to tea because it is the natural thing to do. The congregation of 20 will have grown by 10 per cent!

Of course, things are not always that healthy.

The bishop and his wife had been on holiday and were driving home from the airport on a Sunday morning in holiday clothes. As 10.30 approached and they entered his diocese they decided on impulse to pull into a local church and join the service. They were given a hymnbook and sat on the next to the back pew. As they were saying their prayers at 10.29, heads bowed, the warden came up to them and said, 'I'm sorry you can't sit there, that's Mrs Jones's pew'. The bishop looked up startled and the warden said, 'Oh my God, it's the Bishop'. After the service, the bishop had a little chat with the warden, who ended up repeating, 'We've got to change haven't we, we've got to change!'

The warden, of course, was right. There is no more certain way to ensure that newcomers do not return than ordering them off Mrs Jones's pew. To be fair to the warden, she did it only because she was afraid of Mrs Jones, but the result was the same. Some churches may have to face down their 'Mrs Jones's' in order to become friendly and welcoming to newcomers.

But what happens naturally in the healthy small community where Mrs Jones does not rule must be organized, taught and modelled by the clergy and leaders of a large one. My wife and I left parish ministry for an itinerant 'Springboard' one. We started going to a nearby church where a friend was the vicar. After five months I said to my friend, 'Okay I've had a rest now, I'll take a service for you if you like'. Soon I was leading a communion service. At the door at the end of the service many in the congregation thanked me 'for visiting us today'. We had sat in a pew and worshipped with this congregation of a hundred people for five months and had not been noticed. I only became visible when I preached. They were good Christian people yet the group dynamics defeated them. It was easy to attend a service at that church, but almost impossible to join the community. Little wonder that most of the people who tried attending did not stick. They were offered no relational glue. Eventually even we left, and joined a church that was actually larger but had a high quality integration policy. As we arrived we were invited to join a cell. Immediately we could meet with a small group who offered the welcome, community and friendship we had lacked before.

I was spending a day with a church that had shrunk in Sunday numbers from 180 to 100 in a handful of years. Part of the reason why was obvious – the people only really became energized when they argued about the church's baptism policy. But then one person spoke up and said 'For the first two years only the clergy ever spoke to us'. I marvelled at why he and his wife had stayed, unwelcomed, for two whole years, until it transpired he was a retired vicar himself. 'Yes', he said, 'until one day I took a service and at the door on the way out the people said, "You're vaguely familiar, have we met before?".'

Churches that grow tend to be those that have a welcoming front door that is wide enough to walk through. The job of welcome entails finding each new-comer several friends within the first few weeks. This is a centrepiece of any contemporary evangelism strategy, for these days people tend to belong before they believe. Many need to experience the reality of Christian com-munity before they can accept the reality of Christ's presence within it. The love of God is discovered in the love of his people. Normally this welcoming into the community needs to be done by a team of lay people. It cannot be the vicar's job because, increasingly, the paid clergy are covering a multiplicity of churches and services, and leaving it to the vicar restricts the absorptive capacity of the church. The welcome team may need training and support from the vicar but theirs is the front line role. Part of the training will be in the basics like *not* asking the question over coffee at the end of a service 'Are you new?' and getting the dusty response 'I've been coming to this church for 32 years', but rather 'I'm sorry, I don't know you, my name's Fred, what's yours?' But it will also be about the subtleties of reading the body language and attitudes of the newcomers. Many are anxious to be befriended, but some want to be left alone. There is still a small proportion of churchgoers, some of whom gravitate to cathedrals, who are too bruised or private to even want to be talked to, let alone befriended.

But churches have a back door as well as a front one. People leave as well as arrive. Churches with weak relationship glue are leaving the back door wide open because people are able to walk through it unhindered by the trauma of leaving friends and community. Contemporary churchgoers tend not to come every week. It is hard enough for a warden or vicar to notice who is *not* in the service today, but trying to sort out those who are not here because they are away visiting relatives from those not here because they are lying in bed ill thinking 'those people from that church don't care about me' is nearly impossible. Especially in larger churches people tend to drift away gradually, coming less and less often, finding that no one seems to mind or notice, and eventually, perhaps after a really long gap, being too embarrassed to come back again. They have left without wanting to or meaning to – it just happened.

Sometimes, of course, it will be the clergy who notice, care and visit. Usually, however, the back door will have to be guarded by ordinary church members and to be kept as tightly shut as possible by the way in which the church organizes itself. Larger churches close their back doors by acting small as well as large, either by encouraging all church members to join a small group of some sort, or by multiplying their congregations so that each one is of a manageable, human relationship scale where most people know most people. A pastoral care team of some sort or another is organized to offer friendship and ministry to those in any sort of trouble or drifting towards the edge of the community. One church with 30 pews, where everyone sat in the same place every week, appointed 10 pew-monitors to keep an eye on 3 pews each. Their job was to notice who was missing and to find out why, and to notice who was new and to start befriending them. In another church the wardens started quietly taking a register so that they could keep track of people and follow them up with pastoral visits if they had been absent for three weeks.

Seven of the 20 churches in Lichfield made improvements to their 'front door–back door' arrangements as follows:

Front door–back door

- Better welcome and nurture of newcomers;
- Welcome team created;
- Youth cells set up;
- Launch of lay-led pastoral care network;
- Attendance register/lay follow up of non attenders/systematic visiting of members;
- Lay people trained for visiting/sick/assistant eucharistic ministries;
- More involvement of lay people.

Churches in Kensington that had improved their front door welcome, their small group pastoral care or their back door ministry during 2002–2004 found their attendance grew by 25 per cent in just two years. Paying attention to the front and back doors can make the difference between a dying church and a growing one.

The large, famous church in the university town could have 20 or 30 newcomers' slips filled in each Sunday. Yet it was shrinking. How can a church with 20 people asking to join it every week still be in decline? The reason was that the church was slow to respond to the slips and, in truth, was not really sure how to respond. Someone would come the first week, not be spoken to in the big crowd, fill in the slip, fail to get a response, not be spoken to the second week, still not get a response to the slip, and then leave. They would not give the church a third chance. They could not find their way from the front door into the life of the church, so they walked straight out of the wide-open and adjacent back door.

Recognizing this problem the church first of all began asking people at the start of services to stand, turn round and chat to the people in front of or behind them. That way all the newcomers were spoken to straightaway, ideally by regulars who might start to befriend them. Second, the church's administration was improved to ensure that each person received a phone call or visit from the church within seven days of filling in a newcomers' slip. The contact would include an invitation to a newcomers' meal where they would meet other people in their situation, some church leaders, and some cell group leaders who were anxious to find new members. As part of this strategy, the church had set up a cell structure in order, in part, to offer every member a small-group home. Once into a cell, then the new member would begin to belong to the community and be unable to drift out unnoticed through the back door. Needless to add, this church is now growing in numbers.

---

5 Evangelism courses as part of a strategy

The evidence uncovered about evangelism courses such as Alpha and Emmaus is that they have a significant role in the growth of the church, but only if they are part of an overall strategy. One church 'tried' Alpha a couple of times and it was okay, but most of the people on the courses were going to church anyway and they could not find enough takers for the third course, so they stopped. Another church set up a number of 'touching points' with the local community – a gardening scheme for pensioners, 'dads and lads' events usually based around sport, a parent and toddler group, and so on. Three times a year those who were newly in contact with the church through a touching point were invited by their new friends to a join an Alpha course. At the end of the course, home and cell group leaders were on hand to invite Alpha graduates to join their small groups. The course was part of an ongoing strategy, which ensured both that the supply of takers did not dry up and that Alpha graduates had somewhere good to move on to at the end of the course.

Advertising is a useful background to the job of inviting people to join evangelism courses, but most only come in response to a personal invitation from someone they already know. Part of the strategy should be to encourage church members not to be so fully occupied with church that they no longer know anyone who is not already a Christian. Another part should be to encourage people who have been on a course and benefited from it to bring a friend to the next one.

It is no use assuming that once someone has made a decisive step of faith or met the risen Jesus for the first time during a course they will 'become like us' and want to come to the 10.30 service on a Sunday morning. The cultural leap may be just too great. If process evangelism courses are to work at building the church then the range of worship events on offer needs to include those where Alpha graduates might feel reasonably at home. Something new may need to be started, perhaps small scale and centrally aimed at people who have completed a course. There may need to be something on offer to attract their children away from Sunday morning football. Many will have a need to keep going with a Christian small group or they will drift away quickly through the back door once the Emmaus course is over. In other words, the best strategy will weave all the eight changes that lead to church growth together in a clear-minded way that recognizes how they interrelate and depend on each other.

6 More lay involvement in leadership

Traditional Anglicanism has run for centuries on a shepherd and flock, a minister and ministered-to, model of church. The clergy have 'taken' the service and the congregation has received it. On the way out, people thank the vicar in the same way that they thank the hairdresser or the dentist for services received. The great revolution in our ecclesiology, through which we are still living, is the change to a whole people of God, a ministry of all believers, model of church. Apart from being better biblical theology, and better practical politics in an age with fewer professional clergy, such a model is also better for church growth. Around the world, churches without professional leadership have better growth trends than churches with it. Those who take an active part in church leadership and ministry tend to grow in commitment, confidence and stature as a result. The Church of England is a slowly stirring but still snoozing giant. Its impact on the world grows from midget to mammoth as the Christian ministry and testimony of the vast bulk of its hitherto passive and silent members is unlocked, enabled and deployed. This is the central task of the apostles, prophets, evangelists and teachers whom Paul exhorts, in Ephesians, 'to equip the saints for the work of ministry'.[4] It is probably the central task of most clergy today – to get the prayers, the ministry, the service, the gifts and the testimony of the people of God out into the world in which they live.

So it is no surprise that churches that have been changing in the direction of increasing the involvement of lay people in their running and leadership have also tended to grow numerically. In relation to church services, this may have begun with rotas for sidespersons, flower arrangers, children's group leaders, lesson readers, intercessors, chalice holders, refreshment teams or music groups, and continued with banner groups, family service teams, welcome teams, lay pastoral care teams, drama groups, testimony interviewers, administrators, worship leaders, prayer and healing ministry groups, congregation-planting teams, data projector operators, sound technicians and even vergers!

Thus church worship moves from being something done by the professional for the people to something done by the people together, individuals using their gifts and abilities for the good of all. Eight churches in St Asaph, for example, reported increasing lay involvement in church worship and leadership. Attendance at these churches rose 10 per cent in the two-year period. Among six churches in Kensington reporting more lay involvement (and training for it) there was attendance growth of 9 per cent. The larger churches in Lichfield that have taken steps to start growing again have largely taken steps that have to be implemented and run by their lay members (see, for example, the front door–back door strategies). Not only that, the whole process involved calling together for day conferences not just the clergy but also at least half of each PCC – the lay leaders were seeing the issues and making the decisions together with their clergy.

7 Improvements to buildings

Sometimes churches grow numerically and spiritually despite their buildings. There is a church building in an Urban Priority Area of East London where the heating has not worked for 15 years. Yet under a new priest the congregation has grown many fold in the last few years. People come well wrapped up and light a lot of candles. However, quite often it seems that improvements to buildings can enable numerical growth to happen. One huge medieval church had no separate rooms where children could meet, and nowhere to use for refreshments after services. Given the presence of pews filling every part of the space, only traditional, formal-style worship was practical. Rooms were made in the transepts for children's groups, a kitchen and refreshment area made in the narthex, and side pews were removed to create an informal worship space to one side. All this enabled a new, informal service that included children and families to be started alongside the traditional service. Numbers attending nearly doubled immediately the reordered building was reopened.

From the surveys, several of the rural churches in Cashel and Ossory reported basic improvements like having electricity for the first time or fitting a toilet to the church building. Four churches in Kensington reported improvements to their church buildings, and their attendance rose over two years by 18 per cent.

There is, of course, an issue of motive and purpose for spending money on buildings. It should not be done lightly, for large sums of money are usually involved. Is the real motive to make the existing congregation more comfortable or is the motive missional – to make the church more effective in attracting newcomers and drawing all into the arms of God?

Tools for change through spiritual renewal

There are many ways in which churches change and so find new life and growth, but there are two particular approaches widely used today that are proving of value across all settings, sizes and traditions of churches. One approach (church life audits) focuses on the inner life of the church, while the other (mission action plans) majors on the church's engagement in mission with the world around it. Neither approach is a quick fix. All salespersons for quick fixes should be politely shown the door, but both can help churches take a fresh look at changes they need to make if they are to fulfil their calling to engage in God's mission with fresh focus and energy.

Church life audits

Two examples in particular are widely in use across the Church in England today. The first is the work of Christian Schwarz as recorded in his 'Natural Church Development' materials.[5] Schwarz picks up the biological pictures of the Church found in the New Testament, such as in Jesus' words: 'Consider the lilies of the field, how they grow.'[6] Living organisms grow naturally, their growth potential built into their genes. A church is a living organism. If it is healthy it will be growing. As Cardinal Newman once put it, 'Growth is the only evidence of life.'[7] If a church is shrinking, then it is withering away and dying because it is unhealthy.

Through survey work covering 1,000 churches in 32 countries, Schwarz identified 8 quality characteristics that are more developed in growing churches than in those that are not growing. A large number of members of each church are asked to score each quality characteristic for their own church as they see it, and the scores are then compared with the growth trend of the church. The eight qualities that emerged as significant in all this were:

- empowering leadership
- gift-orientated ministry
- passionate spirituality
- functional structures
- inspiring worship services
- holistic small groups
- need-orientated evangelism
- loving relationships.

Growing churches possess these characteristics to a significantly greater extent than do shrinking ones. These descriptions of growing churches, these keys to growth, were found by a different process from my own work and are organized in a different way. However, they have an uncanny similarity. They are all covered and named as significant in the chapters of this present book. Maybe we are on to something!

Schwarz also found that it was little use a church having most of the quality characteristics but falling down on one. Among larger churches, for example, the characteristic that most frequently emerged from the surveys as the weakest was 'loving relationships'. No matter how good the other seven characteristics, churches like this were being severely hampered in their growth and development. From this developed the concept of the 'minimum factor' – this being the weakest of the eight qualities. It is this quality that limits the size and development of the whole church. Schwarz's picture of this is the open beer barrel made up of staves of differing lengths. The church is the beer barrel and the people are the beer. The amount of beer in the barrel is determined by the length of the shortest stave. A church grows and develops to the next stage by first identifying what that shortest stave is and then by concentrating on improving the quality of that aspect of its life. Once the limiting quality aspect is put right then the now healthier church will grow naturally without the need for further growth policies until that point where the level is up to the length of the next shortest stave.

A healthy churches exercise is, therefore, a diagnostic tool. It identifies what is wrong in the spiritual heart of a church that is stopping it from going to the next stage of its growth and development. Once the church community has identified its strengths and weaknesses in this way, it is able to pay attention to its limiting factors and so to grow naturally again.[8] The theory behind all this can be found in *Natural Church Development Handbook* and how to conduct an exercise in your own church in *Natural Church Development Implementation Manual*.[9]

Another approach to Church Life Audits has been developed by Canon Robert Warren in the UK context, and is designed to enable churches to conduct their own exercises. It is easier to use than *Natural Church Development*, and is set out in his book *The Healthy Churches' Handbook*.[10]

Robert Warren tested and refined his material with large numbers of churches in various English dioceses and finally came up with seven quality characteristics – the seven marks of a healthy church. A healthy church:

- is energized by faith;
- has an outward-looking focus;

- seeks to find out what God wants;
- faces the cost of change and growth;
- operates as a community;
- makes room for all;
- does a few things and does them well.

A healthy churches exercise involves members of a church each scoring the different marks according to their own experience of the church and the scores being added together. The mark with the lowest score is the limiting factor that needs attention. This diagnostic tool is only useful, of course, if the church then actually does something to strengthen the weaknesses its members have identified. One church found that its members gave easily the lowest score to 'has an outward-looking focus'. The parish was a deprived urban area, with problems that the church community was hardly touching. After much thought, prayer and debate they raised some money through selling a property and applying for grants, redeveloped an unused part of their building underneath the church itself, appointed a manager and opened an arts centre for the local community. The church now has a more balanced life and ministry, and development has occurred. Whether as a natural spin-off from this the church itself will grow numerically, only time will tell.

It is possible to conduct a healthy churches exercise in a mechanical or business way, putting right weaknesses on the surface but not addressing the fundamentals. One key to making an exercise effective at a deeper spiritual level is to look into the inner heart as well as the exterior actions of the church. To leap straight from identifying a weakness to a plan for strengthening it may fail to change underlying attitudes. The tool for this job is repentance. If a church is faced with the truth that it is inward looking, a secret club in a needy world, it may, for example, want to come together in a service of corporate repentance before it frames the acts of repentance that constitute living in a different way in the future. Sackcloth is a more solid foundation for growth than is easy triumphalism.

A few dioceses have asked every church to conduct a healthy churches exercise, and many individual churches elsewhere have chosen to do so. Much of the value of such an exercise may lie with the process rather than the outcome. It is a way in for churches to consider and discuss their spiritual health and what can be done about it. In some churches this will be the first time in living memory that such a debate has taken place. Putting the spiritual health of the church at the top of the agenda may in itself be crucial and God may honour whatever honest attempt at growing healthier emerges.

Mission action plans

The first diocese to ask all its churches to produce mission action plans (MAPs) was the Diocese of London under Bishop David Hope in 1993. This was part of a general strategy for moving a previously declining diocese into mission and growth mode. The full story of the subsequent turnaround in London is told in Chapter 8. A typical MAP is a five-year plan for action in mission drawn up by the local church. There may have been open meetings and a process of consultation and the MAP itself will have been debated in and approved by the PCC. It has been put to me that in London at that time there were many parishes for which all three parts of a MAP were novelties – mission, action, and plan. It can be particularly effective for a church that has for years simply gone round and round the Church's year, or just simply existed, or just slowly declined and drifted, to be asked to review the past, take stock of the present and plan developments for the future. Whatever the content of the plan, the process of making it has the potential to change the culture of the church.

The diocese appointed a Parish Ministry Development Adviser (PMDA) for each episcopal area. The PMDA's job was to help parishes both to frame and implement their plans. There were thus two further major cultural changes. First, the diocese was putting resources into parish development, offering to help churches grow and develop, and expecting them to respond positively. Second, the classic option of writing a plan, posting it to the bishop and then sitting back, job done, was blocked off. The PMDA would be round next week to discuss the first steps. The diocese did not only want the parishes to make plans, it actually wanted them implemented, and had people on the ground to ensure that happened.

The Diocese of London is still operating the system and many churches are now on their third MAP. The MAPs are not the only reason for the numbers turnaround in London, but they have had an important role to play, as spelled out in Chapter 8.

When he was still Archbishop of York, David Hope led a similar process more recently in the diocese. The MAPs were part of a longer process entitled 'Living the gospel'. For the first phase of this, the archbishop invited parishes to respond to a phrase in the then new Diocesan Mission Statement, which read 'We commit ourselves . . . to attending to God in worship, prayer and the study of the Scriptures'. Tapes and booklets were produced with titles such as 'The Archbishop's School of Prayer' covering each topic and to be studied by the parishes. Starting with the basics of worship, prayer and Bible study parallels the areas of spiritual renewal for growth considered in Chapter 17. In the second phase, a year later, each church was asked to draw up a parish MAP and send it in to the Archbishop by Easter 2002. Some parishes did not respond to the challenge and many were late, but most eventually sent in a plan to the Archbishop. They were offered 'parish companions' to help them frame their plans, but on this occasion there was no money in the pot to pay a team of PMDAs. Typically a church would describe its situation, offer up its own mission statement if it had one, review its strengths, weaknesses and opportunities, and headline a list of plans and aspirations for mission-development and growth over the next five years.

In the absence of a team of full-time PMDAs, the diocesan response to the plans, and help offered towards implementation, has been limited. Whether or not this is a crucial weakness will be discovered as the five years from 2002 unfold.

Other dioceses and areas are now asking their parishes to produce mission action plans, and some individual churches have produced them of their own volition simply for their own benefit. As yet, MAPs have not been written up in one accessible volume like Robert Warren's book on healthy churches. Those interested in using MAPs to assist the renewal and development of local churches might seek information from dioceses such as London, York, Llandaff, Blackburn, and Lichfield that have already made a start.

Comparing the two approaches

It is worth noting that, while church life audits start with the life of the church, mission action plans focus on the church's engagement with the world. Yet both aspects are needed for a wholesome renewal. A church that seeks to renew its inner life but has no overflow into the world around it has a very suspect form of renewal. Equally, a church that develops a whole new level and focus of engagement with the world around it, but whose inner life is not transformed by that process, may well be avoiding issues that need to be addressed for a truly authentic engagement. So both aspects must be addressed in some way at some stage by all churches seeking to renew their lives and grow as agents of the kingdom of God.

It is clear from the increasing popularity of the two main tools or processes on offer for helping churches get into the heart of renewing their lives that much renewing change is actually taking place. Some of the fruits of this will be long term, and not all of them will be to do with evangelism or increasing the size of the community of faith. However, there is enough going on to suggest that this ancient denomination is capable of renewing change, and so of a whole new lease of future life.

7

Growing the Church through fresh expressions

Where two or three are gathered in my name, I am there among them.
(Matthew 18.20 NRSV)

The mixed economy church

In the mid 1950s, a large new Odeon cinema opened in the centre of Sheffield, and my parents occasionally took me to see *Battle of the River Plate* or *The Ten Commandments*. The show started at around 7.15 in the evening, and people organized their lives to catch the bus that got them there in time to queue for popcorn and take their seats in the vast auditorium. There was one film on offer just once or twice a day – take it or leave it. If the cinema industry had stuck with this, it would have died. As it is, cinema audiences turned round with the multiplex. Suddenly there were many films on offer, starting at all times of day and night, in an attractive environment including a smart restaurant. Today's people no longer queue obediently to see the film the cinema chooses to show at the time the cinema chooses to show it in the vast barn the cinema built long ago. They demand to see the film *they* want to see at the time *they* want to see it, in the intimate environment that suits *them*. The cinema industry has had to adjust to this new reality or die.

Yet in giant 'Odeons' and 'village flea-pits' all over the country, many churches still offer their set product at their set time on Sundays in their 1950s' environments, and wonder why fewer people come. And multi-congregation, multicultural, multiplex churches meeting in appropriately modernized environments tend to buck the trend and grow.

Having said that, there are still some Odeons around, kept going by the quality and impact of key blockbuster films, their lower cost base, and the culture of a new generation. For many younger people, film has become an exploration of ideas about the meaning and purpose of life, and cinema is more than entertainment – it is a means of acquiring shared quasi-spiritual stimulus and experience that become tomorrow's topic of conversation. It is not necessary to watch the film together in order to share the experience and discuss it in a small group afterwards. So it is that some traditional cinemas have survived because of the success of multiplex in making cinema popular again, and because there is not yet a multiplex around the corner. The cinema industry is growing again with a mixed economy of tradition *and* innovation, Odeon *and* multiplex, a good time *and* meaningful shared experience.

It may be that the future of the Church lies in a similar mixed economy. In the foreseeable future, the inherited style of church, meeting for a fairly fixed format in a large building at a fixed time on Sundays, will meet the needs and aspirations of some. Others will need a flexible church, wrapping its multiplex nature around their own requirements, before they will make their spiritual explorations as members of the visible Christian community.

Flying with two wings

In this picture of the contemporary Church it is an aeroplane struggling to stay aloft on only one wing, spiralling downwards and widely expected to crash out of control. The one wing it has is the traditional, inherited model of church – a proper liturgy in a proper building with proper clergy at the proper time on the proper day. The wing it is lacking is the 'fresh expressions' wing of new styles and concepts of church suited to the variety of people and life-styles in the postmodern world. The task today is to construct the other wing in mid flight before the plane crashes. Only then can the jet-powered Church soar and fly again.

This second wing is not a replacement for inherited church. A plane with only a starboard wing is in just as much trouble as a plane with only a port wing. The growth of the Church requires a 'both-and' approach, not an 'either-or'. However, the balance at the moment is not exactly in favour of radical fresh expressions, and so new effort and resources should be devoted to multiply-ing them, to extending the second wing needed for high flying. Moreover, the fresh expressions wing of the Church will need the traditional wing to finance its enlargement, and to provide most of the construction staff. Just as the traditional cinemas are surviving on the back of multiplex popularity, so the traditional wing will need the fresh expressions wing to popularize 'church' for new generations, to share the costs, and to provide it with future leaders.

Solid church and liquid church

All the churches in the town were solid – solid stone buildings with heavy wooden notice-boards giving firm invitations to solid citizens to attend robustly constructed liturgies at concrete times firmly set in the deep roots of the sacred Sabbath.

And hardly any teenagers ever came.

So the churches got together and appointed a youth worker to see what he could do. He made some contacts in the local secondary school, started club nights for games and Bible study, took groups to Christian music gigs, started a couple of teatime cells, focused on mentoring potential future leaders, organized short holidays with a Christian teaching and fellowship content, and even led a monthly Sunday night youth worship event in the local youth centre. Young people would call at his house just to hang out, eat, pray. A new church of some sort has been started, but it is fluid, hard to pin down, difficult to describe, lightly structured, fast evolving, tricky to control, underground and nearly invisible – the solid churches have spawned a liquid church and are perhaps unaware it is a church at all.[1]

Jesus said, 'Where two or three are gathered in my name, I am there among them'.[2] If 'church' is what goes on when at least two or three meet in Jesus' name, then this liquid church is no less a church than all the solid ones. Its core activities of evangelism, community, teaching, discipling and worship are the core activities of any Christian church. It is rather nice to have 'liquid church' in a brewing town (for the town in question is Tadcaster) but the general truth is that liquid church is able to metamorphose its shape and culture to fit liquid postmodern lives in a way that solid church finds very difficult.

Yet the liquid church is still the fragile child of the solid ones. It depends on them for money, its leaders are products of solid churches, and many of the members started out in Sunday schools in solid churches. Moreover, the Christians the liquid church has matured are starting to pour themselves back into the solid churches as they pass through their teenage years, and they may become the future leaders. Liquid and solid churches are not rivals but complements.

Who is my neighbour?

St Michael-le-Belfrey church in York, made famous by the late David Watson, has only a tiny parish of its own, and so has very few 'Christendom' duties to perform. Rather than arranging its life around pastoral care for an already 'Christian' country, its main focus is evangelism in a largely non-Christian city. Its major project at the time of writing is the planting of a congregation in a nearby health club. There are also an 'alternative worship' congregation and a new, Chinese, congregation. Ironically, its new staff office complex looks out on the statue of the Emperor Constantine, splendidly seated in arrogant recline by the side of the Minster. Constantine was proclaimed Emperor in York in AD 306, and it was his conversion to Christianity in the early fourth century that began the Christendom that has so recently been replaced by the post-Christian culture to which St Michael's is being a missionary church.

St Michael-le-Belfrey, with its fresh expressions, two wings, multiplex nature, is one of the two largest churches in the Diocese of York. The other one is at York Minster, sheltering Constantine in its embrace just twenty metres from the door of St Michael's, and as solid a traditional wing church as you could hope to meet. The two churches support and complement each other well, each recognizing the importance of the other in reaching people it itself cannot reach. However, what they have in common is that they are gathered communities, with no recognized geographical base of their own.

The Church of England has been organized for many centuries into geographical parishes, a division of the country wonderfully well suited to the world of the medieval feudal economy in which most people lived and died within a very small geographical area. There is today no move to abolish the geographical parish system, but there are moves to supplement the geographical parishes with relational ones. The world of today is mobile and many people live relational lives. It matters little to them where they happen to sleep – their meaningful relationships are with work colleagues, stage of life affiliations, interest groups or peer groups spread over a wide area of the country. The purpose of the parish system is to reach everybody, but increasingly it is failing to do that because many people no longer relate to geographical units. Therefore, if the Church of England wants to be true to its original purpose – to be the church for everyone – it needs to supplement its geographically defined parishes with some relationally defined ones, in which 'neighbours' do not live next door to each other but are part of the same people subgroup. York Minster, St Michael-le-Belfrey and the liquid youth church in Tadcaster are three examples of the relational church, but many more are probably required if Anglicans are going to reach the parts of the country that the geographic parishes cannot reach.

Growing the Church away from its parish roots

Many fresh expressions are best given birth within the context of existing churches – the new congregations at St Michael-le-Belfrey being examples. The great majority of innovations in recent years have fallen into this category. However, sometimes thinking 'outside the box' demands new missional units outside the old parish system, for example, a web-based fellowship, or a sport-based group, or a relational community for young adults. This category of initiative normally cannot arise (by definition) from parishes. The most obvious unit for initiating expressions of church outside the parish network is the diocese. This means that dioceses need not only to have policies for encouraging parishes to innovate but also to be making their own radical innovations. This is turn means that a diocese needs to budget some money for its own fresh expressions. For example, the Diocese of Lichfield not only has a 'growth fund' out of which grants are made to parishes to assist in their initiatives, but it also has a policy of spreading a network of pioneer relational churches for young adults in the different population centres. These are being financed either by the diocese itself, or through partner funders such as CMS.

Mission-shaped Church

It is this conviction that the Church of the future must become a mixed economy of inherited modes and fresh expressions, a plane flying with two wings, a mix of liquid and solid, of geographic and relational, that underlies the report *Mission-shaped Church*.[3] Part of the church growth solution to the cycle of decline is, therefore, a conscious movement towards a mixed economy through the generation of fresh expressions of church. This cannot be concocted in the test tubes of some centrally controlled master plan, for the fresh wind of the Spirit cannot be rendered uniform and safe by the hierarchy of the Church. Fresh expressions by their very nature are novel experiments, prophetic action, imaginations fired by the infinite creativity of God. There are many of them about at the moment. God is on the move, breaking the old moulds, pouring out new wine fit for the new wineskins of a mission-shaped Church. The task is to find out what God is doing and to help the process along.

So it is good to catalogue and describe the fresh expressions that are breaking out, to spread good practice and provoke new thinking for churches every-where that are trying to find God's own unique solutions to their own unique problems and situations.

Cataloguing fresh expressions

The *Mission-shaped Church* report includes a useful compilation of different types and forms of fresh expression. The following summary and comments may help clarify what exactly is meant by 'fresh expressions', provoke some ideas for new initiatives, and shed light on how fresh expressions relate to good practices for conventional churches in the total picture of a resurgent Church:

Alternative worship communities

These are sometimes founded by people who have grown disillusioned with traditional church but not with God. They may be postmodern and post-denominational in outlook. The worship, usually in an evening, has a premium on symbolism, creativity, use of the arts, and space for the individual to relate to God. They may be fragile or short term. The aforementioned St Michael-le-Belfrey has an alternative worship congregation ('Visions') meeting at 8 p.m. on Sundays. Interestingly, though there may be 20 or 30 at Visions there are 300 to 400 at the main Sunday evening service, most of them teenagers, students and young adults.

Café church

When Jesus gave his famous command to 'Do this in remembrance of me',[4] it is doubtful he had in mind a row of Anglicans kneeling at a communion rail consuming distinctly un-nourishing wafers washed down by three drops of Vino Sacro from a tightly held chalice. He and his friends were actually eating a meal.

The Church today seems to be rediscovering in various ways the almost sacramental power of eating together. The meal is a key feature of an Alpha course through which a group of enquirers and leaders becomes a group of friends. One parish church held a monthly men's breakfast on a Saturday morning. There was a good cooked breakfast, a speaker, some singing, prayer and some congenial friendship making, all around tables. Several of those invited had no idea they had been to church, but they had! They had been to a variant of café church. Others have discovered the idea of church as 'table fellowship'. A group meets regularly in a home around a large dining table, enjoying supper together interspersed with Bible Study and worship. For them that is their church, not an extra event to 'proper' church on Sunday, but real church in its own right. Numbers, of course, are small and unlikely to be recorded in the service register of a church and may never be incorporated into national statistics, much to my personal frustration. But a group of eight meeting round a table having supper is no less being church than is a group of eight turning up for evensong to sit on pews in the local gothic extravaganza. They might even have achieved a closer match to what Jesus meant at the Last Supper with the command to 'do this in remembrance of me'.

My parish church in Scarborough converted the redundant church hall stage into an 'open all day' drop-in café for locals with a large range of social needs, including lack of access to kitchens and decent food. The Rainbow Café quickly became a popular place of community, belonging and acceptance in the context of Christian love and care. Some café regulars did an Alpha course, others were confirmed. At least initially, church for them *was* the Rainbow Café. The key dynamic of church was community rather than worship, though worship was something towards which some of them graduated.

But none of these examples quite describes the classic full blown café church style to which some congregations are starting to move.

One small and declining Methodist church was given a last chance with a new minister. After a few months of discouragement, one Sunday morning he rearranged the chairs in church from the usual straight lines to circles around tables. The service was led more informally, items interspersed with food, and with much opportunity for participation by all the members. After the initial shock of the revolution to their Sunday routine, this congregation began to grow, and grow fast.

My youth church, Scarborough Rock, was getting into a rut – the same old modern songs on the same old data projector with the same old ear-splitting band, with the same old computer games, jigging on the same old dance floor. So we rearranged the furniture one day, placing the chairs around tables and putting party food and drink on the tables before the young people arrived. This definitely proved to be a nice surprise, as did the atmosphere of worship in the rather full café we had created. The bishop came one week and presided at a memorable communion service where the bread and the wine were passed around followed by the pizza delivery. Youth café church had arrived, and we liked it!

Cell church

An increasing number of churches appear to be 'moving into cell mode'. For some this may involve little more than renaming the old home groups, but for others it has marked a fundamental shift in both their self-understanding and their way of life. In a 'pure' cell church, each cell meets weekly and is the home for worship, word, community, pastoral care and mission, so the cells are being real church in their own right. The central leadership might control a teaching and prayer programme as part of the regular cell activity, so there is coordination and direction. Church growth happens through multiplication of cells. Sunday worship becomes an event to be attended by cell members if they can fit it in as well as their primary commitment to the cell meeting. It is the time when the cells get together to celebrate their common life. Part of the attraction of cell church is that it simplifies and focuses the Church's inner life. In the extreme form, all other meetings, organizations and structures are closed down so that everything except the PCC happens through cells. Many 'programme sized' churches of, say, 150 to 400 members increasingly find their traditional programmes hard work to maintain. Office holders are hard to replace; leaders burn out; communication is difficult, and administration seems to soak up time and energy. Postmoderns want to join a relational community not a bureaucratic organization, need a place in the small as well as the large. Also, cell structures need many cell leaders, each doing a manageable job of leading and pastoring a small group of people. Cells are good for growing relational leaders naturally and organically.

Cell church has become increasingly popular in recent years, and appears to be well suited to the postmodern culture. Cell church is a *bright* idea, rather like team ministries a couple of decades ago. But the lesson of team ministries (drawn out in Chapter 3) is that *bright ideas* do not necessarily turn out in the end to be *good ideas*. There are one or two spectacular examples of cell churches that appear to have expanded wonderfully, but there are also other stories from churches that have not grown through the adoption of cell principles. As with everything else, what is needed is the gathering of some systematic data with which to analyse the experience of a large number of cell churches. Until the evidence is in and analysed, the jury should still be out in the cell church case. It is certainly a bright idea and it now needs someone to show whether it is a good one for growing the Church.[5]

Churches arising out of community initiatives

If many people start to *belong* to church before they *believe* its message, this may give those with the social skills and confidence to be 'joiners' a distinct advantage. The good news is that churches in Urban Priority Areas (UPAs) that start community projects can enable people lacking well-honed interpersonal skills to belong to the community of the church. From that sense of belonging and ownership may come a new ability to embrace the love of God and the salvation of Christ. The drop-in centre that starts a Bible study or an Alpha course, the parent and toddler club that incorporates a brief worship event, the community project that is able to offer a Christian counselling service, all offer routes through belonging as clients to belonging as members and believing as Christians. However, the aim may very well not be to find individuals who can progress through the various stages until at last they end up in the 'proper' worship event that the core members attend on a Sunday morning. Rather, it is to create fresh expressions of Christian community and worship in the setting and culture natural to the group of people involved.

I know only too well from personal experience that the setting up and running of community initiatives tend to be major and demanding under-takings. They can soak up the energy and focus of an entire church and are by no means a guarantee of any net growth in regular worshippers. The main motive for community initiatives has to be love, care and compassion for the human predicament, not bolstering the attendance register figures. Yet there is some evidence from London that UPA churches with community initiatives have also done rather better for numbers. In addition, because community initiatives are normally financed by grant-making trusts, they need be no drain on the church's regular finances. One interesting side effect of the community initiative in my UPA church was that vandalism and break-ins ceased almost completely. The church was no longer an alien presence in the community – a legitimate target – it now belonged to the local community and the vandalism hassles subsided. When the church is newly perceived to be 'on our side' rather than being a group of outsiders commuting in to the building, Christ's invitation to 'come to me, all you that are weary and are carrying heavy burdens'[6] is more likely to gain a response. Relevance to the local community is one of the ways to grow the Church through fresh expressions.

Multiple and midweek congregations

Labelling a church with more than one congregation as a 'fresh expression' may come as a slight shock to those used to early communion, matins and evensong. However, the multiple-congregation church has a new inten-tionality about it in a multicultural world. A church with a Radio 3 culture decides to start a new congregation with a Radio 1 culture. A church with a grandparent culture decides to start a new family service. A church in which there is constant tension between those aspiring to tradition, dignity and reverence on the one hand, and those aspiring to informality, modernity and intimacy on the other, decides to have two morning services instead of one. The first service is properly traditional, the second properly modern, and the two main groups are able to get on with relating to God in their own culture. The same church may well then start a Sunday evening service aimed at teenagers and young adults without children. This has its own style and subculture different from both the family service and the traditional service in the mornings.

Some urban churches, especially in London, have in recent years been adding ethnic or language group congregations to their multiple-congregation, multiplex church life. St Matthew, Walsall started to attract some Asian Christians to its Sunday morning service. The church then discovered that others would find it easier to worship in Urdu and so an Urdu-speaking congregation was begun, meeting on Sunday afternoons. Soon the congregation was also using Hindi and Punjabi as new members arrived. St Michael-le-Belfrey attracted some ethnically Chinese church members, and then also took the plunge with a Sunday afternoon service conducted in Mandarin. During the General Synod Service in York Minster in 2004, as 'Fathers for Justice' conducted their protest for the media from the minster roof, down below in the square between the two churches the Chinese congregation was conducting its first baptisms, in Mandarin, using a hired-in birthing pool. Such is the rich tapestry of life in a multiplex church!

New-style midweek congregations tend to have an even wider variety of style than Sunday ones. The afterschool family service, the Friday night youth event, the parent and toddler pram service, the school service in the local parish church, the Saturday teatime all-age service, the 'lift, lunch and communion' event for pensioners, the retirement home service, the Tuesday night worship, supper and small group event for Christians with busy or working Sundays, the office-workers' lunchtime service, the daybreak prayer service for commuters, the daily office, the men's breakfast, various café-style events, post-Alpha groups . . . the list and the creativity are endless.

However, it should be remembered that the Church has always held midweek services, traditionally the Wednesday morning Prayer Book communion being perhaps the most common and best attended. Until recently, numbers attending midweek had not been counted and so it was possible to reassure ourselves that 'obviously' more people were coming midweek to compensate for the (measured) loss on Sundays. Numbers attending midweek services were counted in the Church of England for the first time in 2000, but in this year attendance at weddings and funerals was included. From 2001 onwards the forms have asked for numbers at regular worship events only. The national totals for 2001 to 2003 are as follows:

Table 7.1 October count average attendance of adults (thousands)

Year	Sunday	Weekday	% of whole
2001	868	108	11
2002	838	103	11
2003	853	104	11

These figures do not yet show any discernible overall trend. But it looks as though numbers at weekday services are fairly stable, probably because falling numbers attending traditional style services are balancing out rising numbers attending the new fresh expressions coming on stream. Many fresh expressions are small and fragile and we would not expect them to dominate the numbers trend for some time to come.

The child figures, however, do appear to show a clear switching to weekdays:

Table 7.2 October count average attendance of children (thousands)

Year	Sunday	Weekday	% of whole
2001	173	56	24
2002	167	62	27
2003	164	66	29

The first striking feature is that children form a much higher proportion of weekday congregations. The other is that the growth in weekday attendance is matching the fall in Sunday attendance, leaving overall child numbers the same. This may suggest that the child-centred weekday fresh expressions are growing fast while the traditional adult only events are shrinking. However, there may be another explanation: the census is being taken in October, the month of many school harvest festival services. When parish returns are looked at closely, it becomes apparent that most churches record few if any children attending on weekdays, and then the occasional church has figures of '253' or '125' in just one week of the four-week count. The likelihood is that this is a local school's harvest service. Nevertheless, there does seem to be a sign of hope for growth among children on weekdays.

A particular problem of fresh expressions growing up on weekdays and in a variety of settings is that some may not be recorded in church attendance registers and therefore not be picked up in the national statistics. The definitions and collection methods used are designed for the inherited mode of church, for solid church, and therefore may be misleading. By definition, we do not know *how* misleading because the very problem is that we do not know how many events we are missing. There are two main solutions to this problem, if it exists. One is for church leaders to make sure they include all such fresh expressions of Christian worship in their returns, not just the respectable ones in the church building on a Sunday. This requires a change of mindset for some, and a change of theology for others. The key change is towards acceptance that these other events are in themselves stand-alone genuine expressions of church. There may, of course, be a difficult decision to make as to which events constitute 'church worship' and which do not, and here some theology and common sense judgement have to be brought to bear.

The other solution is for the national statistics form to be modified to try to pick up as many fresh expression events as possible. Archdeacons' enquiries and other local diocesan initiatives could also try to pick up data on any so far 'invisible' congregations. However, such attempts would have to be clearly separated from parish share assessment and collection activity, otherwise churches may start hiding their fresh expressions from their income-hungry dioceses. One multi-parish benefice I visited recently had managed to hide an entire church, gothic building and all, from the diocese simply by failing to mention it on forms for many years. The church had never had a quinquennial and never been assessed for parish share. Brilliant, now why didn't I think of that when I was a vicar? If it is possible to hide traditional churches from those wanting to tax them, how easy it is to hide fresh expressions! Therefore, it is important for the future that dioceses find out about every church attender, not for taxation purposes but for mission purposes. Moreover, we do not want to develop a situation where solid church (easy to count) keeps paying for liquid church (hard to pin down) through attendance-based share mechanisms.

Network-focused churches

A large handful of Anglican network churches has been started in recent years. Each relates only to a rather large and vague area but to a specific people-group as parish – usually younger adults and their children who live their lives through work, leisure, music or stage of life affiliations. There is normally a stipendiary vicar but no church building. This reduces the cost-base of the network church and enables it to avoid becoming geographically defined. Rooms may be hired in a variety of places. Each network church is expected eventually to relate to the diocese as a proper parish, paying a full parish share, but has to be allowed to phase that in as it begins to grow. Funding for the first few years of the stipend can come in a variety of ways. The network church in Huddersfield (The Net) was financed directly by the Diocese of Wakefield. It has grown steadily over the last few years and is looking towards the time when it can divide into two. The network church in the Potteries was financed initially by the Mission Funding grants for 2002–4 distributed to dioceses by the Church Commissioners. The network church in Scarborough was financed by the deanery. There were three vacant posts in the deanery and the diocese said that only two could be continued. The deanery eventually decided to amalgamate two pairs of parishes, so requiring only one traditional post to replace the three vacated. The spare post was allocated to a network-church-planter.

Network churches, like cell churches, are clearly another *bright* idea and the experimental ones are to be welcomed and supported. However, it is still too early to be sure that they are a *good* idea or can be financially viable in the long term. If someone could spend time accumulating data on as many as possible and doing some sort of monitoring and assessment, it would be of great benefit to the fresh expressions wing of the Church.

Schools-linked congregations

Schools can make good premises for church congregations on Sundays. It is sometimes easier to encourage people to worship in a familiar location than a strange one. Part of the barrier to joining a church is fear of an unfamiliar building. Even more of a fresh expression is starting a congregation at after-school time, perhaps when the church itself is next door to the Church school. Children and their carers who collect them can come round as school ends for a drink, a biscuit and a short all-age act of worship. In other cases, Christian schools workers spend time in schools leading assemblies, taking RE lessons, looking after Christian Unions, and running lunchtime clubs. Sometimes these activities and groups can actually become church for the young people who attend them.

There are obvious problems with school-linked congregations. What happens to children and their parents when they leave the junior school with the Monday 4 p.m. service and go on to secondary school? How can the members of a 'Rock Solid' lunchtime club be introduced to the wider church world before they have moved on from it? These are issues to work through, not reasons for failing to take the opportunities available through links with schools.

Seeker churches

The key concept here is that Sunday church is primarily designed for the sake of enquirers or seekers. It is likely to be less participative, more of a presentation, and will explore everyday life themes using a variety of creative arts. It always needs to be backed up with a second worship event during the week that is designed for the worship and nurturing of Christians.

Attempts to use the Seeker format in Britain do not appear to have met with much success. This may be partly because of the large investment of time and effort involved in putting together a high quality presentation every week. It is almost certainly because it is not an easy or natural thing in British culture to invite people to come with you to church in order to try it out. However, Seeker church events once in a while can more easily fit into the programmes of real churches. In this context they are rather more than a traditional guest service, but may, because of their infrequency, not quite rate the description of a fresh expression of church.

Classic church plants

These involve starting a new congregation in a different building from the parish church that is likely to become at least semi-independent from it in time. It is likely to have its own geographic area as a daughter church, and could end up eventually as a new parish church in its own right. The worship event may be in a style not greatly different from that of the planting church, though it is likely to start off being more informal. Many hundreds of classic church plants have been set up by Anglican churches in recent years, and on the whole they have grown very successfully.[7] More recently there has been a growth in the number of transplants between churches. In the Diocese of London a typical transplant occurs when there is a vacancy in a small, struggling or possibly dying church. Instead of contemplating closure the bishop or archdeacon asks a nearby large church to send a sizeable group as a transplant team to inject new life into the moribund church. Possibly the curate from the large church will become the vicar of the other one, or else a new leader is found. These appear to be working very well in that, typically, the church that has received the infusion continues to grow after it, and the donor church recovers its strength quickly just like any other lifeblood donor.

In the Diocese of Wakefield, much smaller turnaround teams have been put together by diocesan initiative to help churches in a 'last chance' situation. Maybe six or ten lay people commit themselves to the struggling church for perhaps three years in order to provide a nucleus around which the church can start to grow again. Early signs from turnaround teams are encouraging.

New interest in traditional forms

There is in the current church scene a lively interest in retreat centres, movements and communities. Some have become tertiaries of religious orders without becoming full members. Many are influenced by the music and spirituality of Taizé or Iona. 'Holiday church' at events such as Spring Harvest, Keswick, New Wine has become an important part of the worship diet of many Christians. 'The Order of Mission' (TOM) has been set up by St Thomas's Church in Sheffield as a postmodern missional order with clear monastic features coming out of a charismatic Anglican-Baptist LEP. The Prayer Book service in an ancient building with highly traditional music and culture is likely to remain not as a ghetto for survivors from the past but as a regular ingredient in a multiplex, multi-congregation church. Minster models from the pre-parish era are being discussed as an alternative to the parish system for rural areas with few stipendiary priests. The past, as always, is likely to have a bright future in the Church of England.

Youth congregations

Churches that try to keep their teenagers in the same worship event as their adults on a Sunday morning usually fail. For one thing most teenagers spend their Sunday mornings in bed unless they have a sporting or musical activity to get up for. However, churches that are able to offer their young people a specialist worship event, probably in the evening and run by specialist youth leaders or the young people themselves, usually succeed.[8] Youth worship events take various forms:

- a monthly celebration for the local churches in the area;
- a single large church's youth fellowship getting together;
- a distinct congregation in a multiplex church;
- an independent unit.

Some youth churches are for teenagers only, others embrace the whole 13–30 age group and so are primarily young adult churches to which teenagers aspire to belong. These have the advantage that teenagers have plenty of role model young adults around them, and they are also more likely to be self-funding. Funding is a constant headache for most specialist youth churches or congregations. So is what happens when young people grow out of their teens, and a congregation with a wider age spread at the very least postpones this problem. Some people worry about whether youth-church is proper-church because church should be for the whole people of God, but we rarely worry in the same way about all the parish churches with no one left in them aged under 60. The ecclesiological perspective needs to take the full set of congregations in a church and area into account. What matters is that all age groups have an opportunity to get together with people like themselves in order to worship God.

The youth worship scene is lively and fast moving, and not very well cata-
logued. It is crying out for a systematic survey of what is going on and what is
working well. Yet it also gives a lot of hope for the future. Churches, groups
and congregations that are well led and relevantly organized tend to thrive
and so to prove that young people today will respond to the Christian gospel
when it is wrapped in appropriate packaging.

How important are fresh expressions?

It is clear from the above long list of categories of fresh expressions around in
the Church today that some are numerically more important than others. The
dominant types are multiple and midweek congregations, and classic church
plants. These are the two areas in which there is most activity and which also
yield the most solid results, at least in the short to medium term. The evidence
for this is reviewed in Chapter 5. They are also the two areas that many people
may be surprised to find described as 'fresh'. Some Anglicans have been
planting new congregations and churches all their lives. In fact, every ancient
parish church is itself a classic church plant.

A fine argument could be had about whether such developments should be
thought of as fresh expressions, but the semantics involved are probably
of only academic interest. The point is that, when it comes down to what is
going on in the real world, it is not that easy to distinguish between good
practices for the inherited church and fresh expressions. What does matter is
to find the initiatives that will grow the local church and not to worry about
the label to attach to them.

Also numerically significant today is the number of churches going into
cell mode and the increase in youth worship events. The other, more clearly
revolutionary, models of church tend to be fairly rare, fragile and small. Yet
one or two of them could become major players in the Church 20 years down
the line. We need every experiment we can get up and running and to observe
them with prophetic insight to discover in this era of rapid change what God
is doing in and saying to the churches.

Fresh expressions – fresh doctrine?

The Christian Church in general (and the Church of England in particular) are
subject to various strands of turmoil and change at the same time. Matters of
doctrine and of church order can get tangled up with each other. The agenda
set out in this book for modernizing the Church of England with fresh expressions, more effective management, updated working practices and spiritual
renewal is intended to be more or less doctrine free. It can be adopted by

Anglicans of almost any theological persuasion. Underneath it, certainly, is a relatively high doctrine of the Church – as Christ's own bride with an imperative to become strong and beautiful – but it is not part of any other agenda. It can be a natural reaction for traditionally believing Christians to view all agendas for change with suspicion as potentially undermining the historic faith. Thus it is possible to retreat into a 'no change' ghetto, mistaking this for a proper defence of the faith and protection of the believing Church. Rather, I would argue that the appropriate response for traditionally believing Christians living with a fast-moving culture outside the Church is radicalism in matters of church order and conservatism in matters of church doctrine. We can only defend the faith by renewing the Church.

Yet the way we do things sometimes changes the way we believe. The words of the songs we sing shape the bones of the faith to which we cling. The old proclamation evangelism carried with it a doctrine of crisis-conversion in which a new Christian crosses the Rubicon of eternal salvation through repentance from sin, which assumed a doctrinal understanding of Christianity. Evangelism through helping people belong to the Church before they believe its message carries with it a relational understanding of Christianity; and process evangelism courses can sometimes seem to offer life in all its fullness without bothering too much with sin and the danger of damnation. Is it actually possible to change the presentation of the faith without changing the faith itself?

When I was a child, Lucozade was sold in large cellophane-wrapped bottles in chemists. My mother bought it for me only when I was ill. As medicine for a recuperating child it worked wonders because I actually liked it! Then some marketing genius got to work. The bottles, though not the price, became smaller, and Lucozade was suddenly on sale almost everywhere except the chemist. Instead of a pick-me-up for the sick it became an energy drink for the fit and active. This was wonderful for me because for the first time I felt allowed to drink Lucozade when I wasn't ill. Now I always carry it in my tennis bag. But it tastes to me as though it is *exactly* the same stuff! The manufacturers have been radical with the bottling and the marketing but conservative with the product. Sales have rocketed. Yes, it is now seen as energy for life rather than salvation from sickness, but a sick child with a taste for the stuff reacts just the same today as I did 50 years ago. It is the way in to the product, rather than the product itself, that has changed. Fresh expressions are not a new religion, they are bringing the old religion out of the chemist shop into the marketplace of the world and offering it to those who think they are spiritually healthy as well as those who recognize they are sick.

Fresh expressions as part of a growth strategy

Dioceses and the national Church

Part of a strategy for growth by fresh expressions entails research, finding out what is working well, and what is not, around the country, and disseminating the news. Another part of the strategy is for national and diocesan leaders to give encouragement to churches and clergy to try new things. We need a culture in which churches and clergy can become more highly regarded through trying new things and failing than through being safe and conform-ist. The Archbishop of Canterbury has recently set up a new agency, called 'Fresh Expressions', with which to replace the 'Springboard' initiative in evangelism. The job of Fresh Expressions is to renew the Church's vision, gather news of what is happening, support new growth, and develop appropriate training.

Sometimes ideas for fresh expressions are beyond the resources or imagi-nations of individual churches. Deanery chapters and synods, as well as ecumenical bodies such as 'Churches Together', should from time to time take a look at the whole picture of church life in their area and consider the scope for fresh mission initiatives. The result may be a youth church, a relational young adult church, or something brand new dreamt up for the first time. Perhaps it should be part of the job description of every rural dean to encourage the churches of the deanery to take and see through fresh missionary initiatives. Rural deans should also be able to hand out application forms to the Diocesan Mission Initiatives Fund designed to make grants avail-able for fresh expression initiatives. Many deaneries these days are being asked by their dioceses to plan clergy deployment for the future in their area on the basis that the diocese can afford a given number of posts in the deanery. Deaneries that simply look at how to join up existing posts are simply managing decline, but deaneries that are able to think radically about new sorts of post and people for the fresh expressions of a newly missionary Church may succeed in reversing their decline.

National, diocesan or deanery strategy for fresh expressions is not about telling the individual churches what to do, or even about laying some uni-form process of discernment upon them, it is more about providing the right environment in which the parochial initiatives can flourish. Parishes become part of the strategy when they consider the scope that they themselves might have for fresh expressions. Some parishes might conclude this is not the route for them. For example, most of the examples given in the category listing above fit most easily into an urban setting. Small rural churches may see little in there of relevance to them. In part this is simply because there seems to have been less innovation in the countryside than the towns, or perhaps it is because rural innovations have not been collated as well as the urban ones. In part, it is also because fresh expressions that a large urban church can bring about single handed would require the resources of a group of small rural churches, and this might be harder to organize. So the call to rural parishes is not to wash their hands of fresh expressions because they do not sound relevant to their situation, but to use their imaginations to invent and pioneer the fresh expressions that will make a difference in the countryside.

Part of the local church response might also be to bring in the consultancy expertise made available by the wider Church through agencies like Anglican Church Planting Initiatives, The Sheffield Centre for Church Planting and Fresh Expressions.[9] Local churches might also try networking in order to tap into the experience of others – for example, there is an informal network of relational, non-geographic parishes. Help might come from diocesan missioners or Anglican streams such as the New Wine network.

At the heart of having a strategy in a local church is the working out of one or two priorities into which God is leading this church, and then to concentrate resources on that priority. The aim should be to do one or two things well, not a number of things badly. It takes courage to do new things. Failure and dissent are very real possibilities. The queue of people with a ministry of discouragement, ready to say 'I told you it wouldn't work', may exist in reality as well as in the anxious imagination of the vicar. Fresh expressions are best attempted as the considered, prayerful, policy of the whole church rather than the pet project of the isolated vicar. The vicar may indeed be the prophet, but vision needs to be shared and owned if it is to gather transformatory strength. Fresh expressions arising out of shared vision are more likely to pull the church together as everyone works cooperatively towards the agreed objective.

So let fresh expressions become a normal part of the routine agenda of every church, and let a thousand new flowers bloom in the garden of God that is the Christian Church. Yes, it takes the imagination and courage of the risk taker to give birth to fresh expressions of church, but without them the Church may carry on withering away. Who dares wins!

8

Growing the Church in practice – a growing diocese and a growing stream

All the saints greet you, especially those of the emperor's household. (Philippians 4.22 NIV)

Church growth today is happening not only in a wide range of individual churches but also in some groupings of churches. The two groupings examined in this chapter were chosen as examples partly because they are indeed growing but also because I have been able to conduct surveys of their member churches and so draw some conclusions and identify some principles that are more widely relevant to the wider church scene.

A diocese in the capital

It seems that in the early days of the Christian era, the Church in the capital city was especially large and vigorous. Paul says to the Christians in Rome that their 'faith is proclaimed throughout the world'.[1] Moreover, there seem to have been plenty of Christians among the government officials and the ruling elite, even when Rome was pagan; and Rome was quite a gathering place for Christians from elsewhere – people like Epenetus, 'the first convert in Asia for Christ', but now a prominent member of the Church in Rome.[2]

London and its commuter belt have long seen a higher proportion of its citizens in church on Sunday than most of the provinces. Like Rome, London is a melting pot of peoples: all road, rail and airline routes seem to lead to London. So London is a special case, but this does not mean that lessons cannot be learnt from it for elsewhere. This is particularly so because this chapter is an analysis of the turnaround in attendance and membership of the Diocese of London, which covers most of London north of the Thames. In the period under review, the same turnaround did not happen in the Diocese of Southwark (London south of the Thames) or in those parts of the Diocese of Chelmsford with a million inhabitants of London north of the Thames. This means that the turnaround in fortunes was not caused primarily by the external environment of the capital but by the internal policies, fresh expressions and spiritual renewal of the diocese itself.

The numbers

In the more rural parts of the country the electoral rolls (ERs) of churches may contain many names that have little to do with the church's life today. However, Londoners tend not to join ERs unless they actually belong to the church in question in some meaningful way. The ER is, therefore, a meaningful measure of membership. It can be seen from Figure 8.1 that membership of the diocese plummeted from around 80,000 in the late 1970s to around 45,000 in 1990. The sudden drops followed by slow recovery seen in the graph are, of course, dictated by the fact that rolls cease every six years and everyone then has to re-sign.

Figure 8.1 Electoral rolls in the Diocese of London

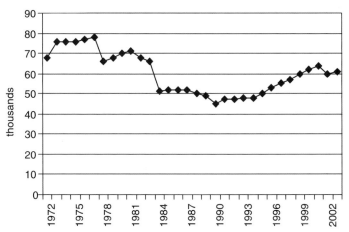

It may also be that the vigour with which churches compile their rolls is affected by their perception of whether the size of the roll will help determine parish share. The system in London did change in the early 1990s, but has now been stable for a decade. Under this system, each deanery is given a share that is spread among the parishes by local bids and agreement, without applying any formula. Some churches are still wary of pushing up their own figures in case their neighbours notice, and others simply have a postmodern lack of interest in signing up for membership of anything. The diocese has implored churches to make their ERs a realistic measure but there are still churches that do not work too hard at persuading all their people to join the roll. On balance, therefore, although the trends need to be treated with some caution, they are probably just as likely to underestimate recent growth as to overestimate it. In summary, therefore, it looks as though the drop of 40 per cent through the 1980s has been followed by a growth of 33 per cent since 1990.

For usual Sunday attendance (uSa), the published figures show a rise from 41,000 adults in 1990 to 47,000 in 1999. For various technical reasons too tedious to explain to even the most patient reader, the numbers since then have been very hard to estimate but could easily have been rising at 3 to 4 per cent per annum.

Total attendance through the week on an average Sunday in October in the Diocese of London has also been increasing significantly in every year since the count began in 2000. Growth is clearly fairly rapid and has continued for a number of years.

I also have data from the survey of the clergy of the Willesden Episcopal Area undertaken in 2003 and the Kensington Area in 2004. These surveys are unaffected by fears of massaging to protect parish shares, and the attendance figures appear from much personal follow-up to be honest and robust estimates. The collective conclusion of the Willesden clergy was that adult attendance in their area rose 6 per cent in 2003 and child attendance rose 10 per cent, giving a rise in total attendance of 7 per cent. The collective estimate of the Kensington clergy was that adult attendance rose 16 per cent from 2002 to 2004 and child attendance 24 per cent. The growth was slightly more rapid in 2004 than 2003. Between them Kensington and Willesden account for about half of the whole diocese.

The conclusion is that, although there is some uncertainty about the speed of growth in numbers, all three measures available tell the same basic story: the Diocese of London has been in significant numerical growth since the early 1990s and it is still continuing. If the clergy of Kensington are to be believed, it may even be accelerating.

This is a book about how a diocese caught in a cycle of decline can turn this round into a cycle of growth. London is a diocese that has already achieved this, thus proving to the other dioceses that new, strong numerical church growth is entirely possible for Anglicans in the UK today.

The rest of London

Figure 8.2 compares uSa in London with that in Southwark and the London part of Chelmsford dioceses.

Figure 8.2 uSa of adults in Greater London

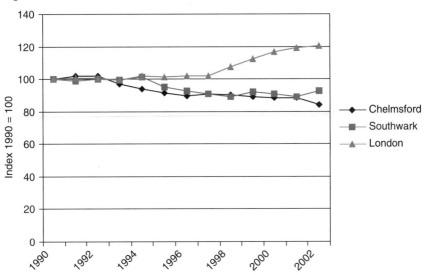

It can be seen that the trends diverge in the early 1990s, showing that the Diocese of London did not simply benefit from some change in the culture or composition of the people of the capital city. Attendance in Southwark continued to decline up to 2001, but a rather startling reversal of this occurred in 2002 when total uSa in the diocese rose according to the official statistics from 35,400 to 37,200, an increase of 5 per cent. As is normal when numbers start to turn round, the percentage increase in children was greater than for the adults. A booklet written by the then area bishop, Colin Buchanan, in 2002 shows attendance counts for the Woolwich area.[3] These were stable each year until 2001, in which year there was a sudden, startling increase of 8 per cent spread right across the churches and deaneries of the area. Attendance in the Chelmsford part of North London was 20 per cent lower in 2002 than in 1992, whereas attendance in the Diocese of London was 20 per cent higher.

So, just maybe, in the most recent years there has been a turnaround in Southwark Diocese, around ten years after it began in London. This needs to be tested and investigated for the lessons that can be learnt.

The causes of growth

During 2003, I investigated the causes of attendance and membership growth in London through a process of interviewing a number of diocesan leaders to obtain their overviews, analysing the individual churches' attendance and membership returns, and visiting a number of fast growing churches to discover their stories. A full report, entitled 'A Capital Idea', is available from the London diocesan website.[4] Since then I have gathered further data and conducted more interviews on behalf of the Willesden and Kensington areas. The following is a summary of the factors involved in the turnaround and the new growth of the diocese that have been gleaned from these different sources:

The role of diocesan leadership

The start of the turnaround is traced by diocesan leaders to the launch of 'Agenda for Action' in 1993 by Bishop David Hope. Under this, every parish was asked to submit a mission action plan (see Chapter 7). Successive initiatives ('London Bridges' 1998 and the current 'London Challenge') have maintained momentum and helped parishes to update their MAPs. The London Bridges programme was very clearly focused on growth. Every church was asked to look at its parish in a mission-oriented way under three headings:

- recruiting new believers;
- renewing the household of faith;
- rebuilding a broken world.

The London Challenge sets out strategic targets and programmes for the growth of the Church. The main numerical challenge is to grow electoral rolls to 70,000 by 2005. Once again, although financial problems and targets are laid out in the Challenge documents, the main focus is on mission. The primary focus is not on asking each parish to pay a growing amount of money each year but on asking each parish to offer a growing number of Christians to God each year. Rather than sacrificing growth to the solving of financial problems, the solving of financial problems is seen to be an incidental result of growth.

It would be wrong, however, to imagine that these top-down MAP initiatives work by themselves. The realities are far more complicated than that. In fact, those parishes I have found that have refused to join in the MAP exercise appear to have a rather better growth trend than the majority that have joined in! It is probably now time for somebody to research the impact of MAPs on parish life in a sample of churches both in London and other dioceses, such as York, that have adopted MAPs more recently.

At the same time as 'Agenda for Action', the diocese began to look for a new type of clergyperson to fill vacancies, or at least it began to write the job descriptions and profiles in a different way. No longer is the vicar expected to be a parish chaplain or a congregational pastor but rather a leader in mission and an enabler of other people's ministries. The diocese as a whole grew to accept that, in London, Christendom was dead. From now on they would be a missionary church in a non-Christian society.

Diocesan leaders have also moved from being wary of the church planting and transplanting movement to being leaders of it. Archdeacons and bishops are on the lookout for opportunities to set up new youth congregations or to arrange a transplant from a large church to a dying one. The policy in regard to churches in danger of closure is to invite a team in from another church to revive them. This has been enormously successful.

The diocese has taken steps to slim down its boards and committees, recognizing that many of them were just talking shops that would not be missed but which were soaking up valuable time and energy. For example, there is now no board for social responsibility and no diocesan pastoral committee. London never was a diocese that set up a lot of team ministries, because the dangers (see Chapter 2) were foreseen and recognized. In recent years those that were set up have been disbanded as an unsatisfactory experiment. The common fund system since 1994 has removed measures of church size from the factors determining parochial financial contributions. Growth is not necessarily taxed. In fact, when growing churches complain to the diocese or deanery about projected increases to their common fund payments, they are sometimes successful. The normal message has been 'You put me into this parish in order to grow the church, now you want to tax away all the surplus needed for the next stage of growth – back off!' Helped by the presence (and growth) of a considerable number of large churches in the Diocese of London, the payments expected of larger churches are much lower than elsewhere. For example, one London church with an attendance of 300 adults in the Diocese of Chelmsford had a parish share payment in 2003 of £142,000. If it had been a few miles to the west, over the border into London Diocese, its share would have been half this amount.

In all these ways – by MAPs and other initiatives, by clergy selection and job descriptions, by planting and closure policy, by cutting committees and team ministries that don't work well, and by growth-friendly financial management – the policy and leadership of the Diocese of London has been a necessary, though not sufficient, element in the turnaround and growth story.

The key role of the parish clergy

The clergy are not thicker on the ground in London in relation to population or church attendance. However, congregations are bigger and there has been no great move towards multi-parish benefices. In 1999, London had 553 full-time stipendiary clergy for 478 churches – 1.16 per church. The national average was 0.59. Enabled and supported by rising congregations, the number of stipendiary diocesan clergy actually rose from 541 in 1996 to 557 in 2001 at a time when, nationally, numbers fell 5 per cent. So there has been no decline cycle involving a shrinking workforce, as elsewhere.

But the quality of the clergy may be more important than the quantity. Every story of rapid church growth appears to start with the appointment of a new incumbent. The new policy of finding leaders in mission, helped by the high proportion of livings under diocesan patronage, has borne much fruit. More-over, growing churches not only grow numerically, they also grow younger. Churches with rapidly increasing numbers of young adults have a dynamism, excitement and inspiration about them that causes some of the members to think about ordination. A still developing conveyor belt of ordinands from growing, dynamic churches with a growth ethos has cranked into motion. There are now around 150 ordinands in training from the Diocese of London, most of them much younger than the national average. Almost half the recommended candidates in recent years have been aged under 30, and the average age of clergy newly ordained in London was 35. The diocese attempts to cherry-pick the ordinands it thinks will make the best leaders in mission to be its own curates, and these are likely to be offered livings in the diocese at a later date. Although some livings are hard to fill (in areas with problem schools, in some UPAs, and in some demanding suburban parishes with little developmental potential), on average there are more candidates for posts in London than elsewhere. This is not just because people like working in the capital, it is also because the diocese itself is clearly attractive to growth or mission-minded clergy.

The average age of the clergy in the Diocese of London is 46, compared with the national average of 51. This gives the London clergy a significant edge when it comes to church growth. The table below compares the electoral roll experience of churches with incumbents aged over 55 in 2002 with that of churches with incumbents aged under 45:

Table 8.1 Electoral rolls in churches with older and younger incumbents, Diocese of London

Age	Number	Number that shrank	Number that grew	1996 total	2002 total	% change	1996 average	2002 average
Over 55 in 2002	88	32	56	14,336	15,273	7	163	174
Under 45 in 2002	69	24	45	8,186	9,925	21	119	144

The older clergy still had growing electoral rolls, but those of younger clergy grew three times faster, though from a smaller base.

The role of social change

As the death of Christendom is more advanced in London than in many other places, the clergy are being asked to do fewer Christendom duties. For example, the London clergy on average take one funeral a month, in Sheffield it is one a week. The churches with very few occasional offices in London are the ones that are growing the fastest. It is probably true that leading a growing church is a full-time occupation. Far more of the London clergy are able to be full-time church-growers than is possible in other parts of the country. Clergy who spend half their week taking funerals, weddings and baptisms, or acting as chaplains to different groupings, are trying to lead churches part-time. Far from churchgoing being the tip of the Christendom iceberg (and so inevitably declining as Christendom disappears), the gathered communities seem to be growing as social change ushers in the new post-Christian society. Moreover, as nominalism has now more or less died in London, there are fewer faithless church members to weaken the spiritual life of the churches. When people on spirituality searches, or people looking for a place of community and belonging, make contact with the church, they are more likely to meet a group of committed, articulate Christians.

Church growth appears to be concentrated more in the inner London areas than the outer suburbs. This is partly associated with the size phenomenon, in that the suburbs tended to have larger congregations to start with. It may, however, also be associated with social change in the inner areas, where population growth through the 1990s was about 10 per cent – double the rate of the outer areas. And the percentage of minority ethnic churchgoers is higher in the inner areas as well. By the same token, growth has been more rapid in the Urban Priority Area (UPA) parishes than in the more affluent ones: electoral rolls went up 16 per cent in the UPAs and only 6 per cent elsewhere. Again, this is partly associated with size but perhaps also with pockets of gentrification that have begun to appear in some UPAs.

The role of immigration

The Anglicans who arrived in London in the 1950s and 60s from the West Indies did not encounter a diocese skilled at welcoming 'people not like us', or even wanting to try. This culture, however, has now been transformed. Churches welcome ethnic diversity, celebrate it and grow in numbers and spiritual dynamism and richness through it. Many of the fastest growing churches have become international in character, including anything up to 30 nationalities or language groups in one church community. Many people also move to London from other parts of the country, but population growth in London has not been much more rapid than elsewhere – there has always been rapid population turnover in many parts of the capital city. Usually this is seen as bad for church growth because the most common time for people to stop churchgoing is when they move house.

The role of large, strategic churches

Figure 8.3 shows that almost all the membership growth in the Diocese of London has been in the smaller churches. The very large have stayed about the same. Holy Trinity Brompton and other similar larger churches were already very large in 1996 and have not grown numerically since then.

Figure 8.3 Diocese of London ER change 1996–2002 by starting size group

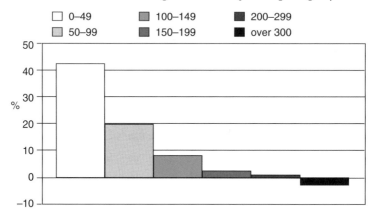

The same finding comes from the more recent Kensington Area question-naire. Churches with over 100 adults in 2002 grew by 9 per cent up to 2004, but churches with under 100 grew by an astonishing 40 per cent, with the number of children going up by over 50 per cent.

Once churches reach somewhere between 100 and 170, the growth can sud-denly stop – they have hit the glass ceiling described in *Hope for the Church.*[5] In Kensington, for example, churches under the ceiling grew 37 per cent between 2002 and 2004, churches at the ceiling grew 2 per cent and larger ones over the ceiling grew 8 per cent. So unless churches can be helped to keep growing through the glass ceiling, the overall attendance growth in the diocese might slow right down as there are fewer and fewer small ones left.

The large churches, however, have played a role in the growth of the small through transplanting. Holy Trinity Brompton has sent out a number of groups to revitalize other churches. Other large churches are now doing the same in moves either approved or inspired by the diocese. St Stephen's East Twickenham, for example, has sent out three such groups in recent years and found that the gaps left by them at St Stephen's have been filled within months by newcomers. When existing leaders move on with a planting team, new leaders have the space in which to emerge from the congregation, and newcomers find spaces in the ongoing life of the church in which to find a home. So the planting church has actually grown numerically itself as it has given away groups of its own members.

The transplanting model is applicable to other areas that do not have such large churches to do the sending. For example, Wakefield diocese is sending in small-scale 'turnaround teams' to some struggling churches, with equally gratifying results. The parish share system is a financial arrangement whereby the strong are asked to help the weak. A far more effective way for this to happen is by transfer of people.

The role of church traditions

The experience of growth has been shared by all three main traditions. The catholic and evangelical wings appear to form a highly effective alliance, sharing many of the same values and finding similar routes to growth. Table 8.2 divides the growth experience of a sample of churches by the tradition of the training college of the incumbent. This may not say much that is mean-ingful about the tradition of the church: colleges may represent a breadth of tradition, some clergy go to colleges that are not quite their own tradition, other clergy change over time, and some become incumbents of churches not in their own tradition. However, it is the best rough and ready division yielded by the available data:

Table 8.2 Attendance change by theological college tradition of incumbent

College tradition	No. of churches	No. grew	No. shrank	1996 ER total	2002 ER total	% change	1996 ave	2002 ave
Evangelical–Charismatic	88	56	32	13,846	15,374	11	157	175
Catholic	105	62	43	12,285	13,250	8	117	126
Middle/Liberal	32	21	11	3,928	4,353	11	123	136

The experience of the different traditions does not, therefore, look all that different, although it may be that some of the larger evangelical churches are the ones that bother the least about getting their members on to their electoral rolls. The evangelical churches are bigger to start with, so the average church has added 18 to its electoral roll in the six-year period, com-pared with an average of 9 to a church with an incumbent of catholic tradition. Of the overall increase in electoral rolls, 52 per cent was in the 39 per cent of the churches with an incumbent from one of the evangelical colleges.

Members of New Wine Networks

New Wine is a network of individuals most of whom are Anglicans and many of whom are Anglican clergy. The current membership list contains around 700 names. It offers summer camps and conferences, training events and support networks. The style is charismatic-evangelical and the uniting feature is a common vision and a set of common values, reproduced below:

New Wine's vision

To establish churches throughout the nation, which will reach their communities with the gospel of Jesus Christ and his Kingdom by being continuously renewed by the Holy Spirit.

Core values

Local Church life that is welcoming, relational, accessible for all generations, and builds community and family life.
Worship that is passionate, intimate, joyful, inspiring, culturally appropriate and enables encounter with God.
Leadership that is anointed, visionary, courageous, full of faith, and releases church members into their God-given ministries.
Mission that is strategic, holistic, inspired and empowered by the Spirit, concerned for the poor, and encourages new church planting initiatives.
Teaching and training that is Bible-based, interesting, thoughtful, relevant, appropriate and is applied to every area of life.
Discipleship that encourages prayerfulness, holiness, integrity, generosity and enables us to serve like Jesus.
Ministry that is inclusive, gift-orientated, life transforming and expresses God's love and power.
Theology that is orthodox in doctrine and morality, founded on the person and work of Jesus Christ and the coming of the Kingdom of God.[6]

It can be seen that many of the New Wine values embrace features identified in this book as being good for growth, for example, worship centred on encounter with God, relational community for all ages, church planting. Moreover, the context of the values and vision appears to be that of a church-in-mission in a non-Christian culture. If there is one single division between shrinking and growing churches, this may be it – those trapped in Christendom mode are shrinking, those that have gone beyond it to mission mode for a post-Christian world are growing. So, if the findings reported in this book about what makes churches grow in the British Isles today are true, we would expect churches led by New Wine members to be growing.

The numbers

A survey was conducted in 2004 that yielded information from 53 incumbents belonging to the network. It is not exactly clear whether these 53 are a random sample of members, but they do cover a wide spread in terms of geography and church size. Usual Sunday Attendance was 2.5 per cent higher in 2002 than 2001 and 6 per cent higher in 2003 than 2002. In the Church of England as a whole attendance went down at 2 per cent per annum in the same period. Moreover, the number of children attending rose by 12 per cent over the two years compared with only 7.5 per cent for adults – so the New Wine churches appear to be growing younger. The average New Wine congregation appears to have an average age of around 40, compared with 47 for the Church of England as a whole and this is clearly one major reason why numbers are growing:

Table 8.3 Age profile in New Wine Network churches 2001–2003

	Attendance 2001–2003
Under a quarter of adults are under 45 years old	−2%
A quarter to a half of adults under 45 years old	+8%
Over a half of adults under 45 years old	+10%

It is the younger congregations that are generating the growth.

The ERs of these churches grew by 14 per cent (2 per cent per annum) between 1998 and 2004 – years at the same stage of the six-year re-signing cycle. During the latest six-year period available, ERs in the whole Church of England fell about 18 per cent (−3 per cent per annum). It is clear that New Wine style churches are growing in both attendance and membership in contrast to the Church of England as a whole. Once again it seems that good practices, fresh expressions and spiritual renewal do result in numerical growth, though this is by no means universal to every church, as shown below.

Features of growing churches

Church size

The rapid growth, as in London, is restricted to the smaller churches – those with under 100 attending in 2001:

Table 8.4 Attendance growth by size of church 2001–2003, New Wine Network

Size in 2001	No. of churches	2001 uSa	2003 uSa	Change	% Change
under 100	15	995	1388	+393	+39%
200–399	27	6050	6271	+221	+4%
400 plus	6	4014	4362	+348	+9%

Area of the country

The table below shows that the growth in attendance is not shared by New Wine churches in the north, being mainly confined to churches in London and its Home Counties commuter belt:

Table 8.5 uSa changes 2001–2003 according to geographical region

Region	No. of churches	2001 uSa	2003 uSa	Change	% change	Size 2003 (ave)
North	16	2789	2732	−57	−2	172
London & Home Counties	22	5871	6890	+1019	+17	313
Other South & Midlands	13	2037	2195	+158	+8	169

Some settings would seem to be more receptive to New Wine values and growth-features than others. Or maybe it is just easier to grow a church in the South-East than the North. This conclusion is also borne out in diocesan attendance statistics, there being a tendency for northern dioceses to suffer more rapid attendance loss than southern ones.

Clergy age and length of service

In the New Wine churches, the most rapid attendance growth would seem to be in the early years of an incumbency:

Table 8.6 New Wine Network attendance growth 2001–2003 by length of incumbency

Length of incumbency	Growth 2001–2003	% growth
5 churches with incumbent over 12 years	1752–1753	0%
24 churches with incumbent 5–12 years	5156–5527	+7%
10 churches with incumbent 3–5 years	1995–2496	+25%
11 churches with vacancy in 2001, 2002 or 2003	1252–1219	−3%

The churches that had a vacancy in the period lost only 3 per cent of attendance on average, but this compares with a growth in churches that had no vacancy of 10 per cent. The difference, therefore, is 13 per cent – very much in line with the findings reported in Chapter 2.

One reason for the comparative numerical success of New Wine churches is that their incumbents are younger than the average (around 48 compared with the national average of around 52). Churches with an incumbent aged under 45 saw their attendance rise 19 per cent from 2001 to 2003, while those over 45 saw attendance rise only 4 per cent. If members of the New Wine stream, or of any other stream, are interested in the long-term growth of their churches, they have actively to recruit and nurture young ordinands.

Reasons given for attendance change

In 53 forms there were only 15 negative influences mentioned, the most important being a recent vacancy:

Table 8.7 Negative factors in church growth

Reason	No. of churches
Recent vacancy	8
People come less often	3
Sent out planting groups	2
Loss of staff	1
Members leaving area	1

On the other hand, 96 positive factors were mentioned between the 53 churches. It can be seen that most of these come under one or other of the eight general causes of attendance growth given in Chapter 5:

Table 8.8 Positive factors in church growth

Positive factor	No. of churches
Alpha	12
Congregation planting	10
Better child/youth provision	8
Worship more relevant, modern	7
Love/pastoral care	6
Quality of welcome	5
New leadership	5
Intentional evangelism	5
Improved small groups	5
Introducing cells	4
Clarity of vision (MAPs)	4
Biblical preaching	3
Prayer	3
New youth/children's worker	3
Other new staff members	2
Population growth	2
Every member ministry	2
Giving newcomers a job quickly	2
Transfer from problem churches	2
Improved buildings	2
Healings	1
Sense of fun	1
More open baptism policy	1
New 20s–30s group	1

There is no mystery or magic about the growth of New Wine churches – the same systematic set of factors is at play amongst them as in other churches –

but New Wine members are applying the good practices, fresh expressions and spiritual renewal programmes described in this book in greater numbers and to greater effect. Their vision and values are in tune with the culture (at least in the South). Most of the reasons given for growth are not specific to charismatic-evangelical culture. They can be, and are being, adopted by churches across the traditions. However, we must expect the New Wine network to continue to be a growing, renewing force within the Church of England as its churches grow in size and new members join.

Part 3

Delivering the human resources for growth

Good practices, fresh expressions, social relevance, and even spiritual renewal in the churches can come to nothing if the leadership is weak, inappropriate, or badly prepared and supported. It is widely agreed that leadership is the single most important key to the growth of the Church. Every single major church-growth story in the Diocese of London in recent years starts with the appointment of a new incumbent. If the Church of England as a whole wishes to grow and prosper in the future it has not only to encourage change for growth in the parishes, but also to deliver the resources needed to enable that change to succeed. These resources are both human and financial. Of the two, the human resources are the absolute essential – Christian leaders can be effective without money, but money without leadership is useless.

The chapters in this part of the book, therefore, are about developing the human resources needed to deliver the future growth of the Church. The first two chapters are about the stipendiary clergy – Chapter 9 covering their recruitment, selection and training, and Chapter 10 their ongoing deployment and resourcing. Chapter 11 looks at how the development, training and employment of lay people by diocese and parish should fit into the growth strategy.

9

Clergy selection and training for a missionary Church

> Let no one despise your youth, but set the believers an example.
> (1 Timothy 4.12 NRSV)

Come back when you are older'

This has been the reaction many committed young people have received over the last 30 years when enquiring about the possibility of ordination, whether or not this has been the official policy of the Church. This is extremely undermining for many young people when they are in the process of discovering what calling God has on their lives. It implies that God cannot use church leaders until they are aged around, say, 35, by which time Jesus had carried out his entire ministry, died, risen again, saved the world from sin and death, and started to reign in heaven over the whole universe. However, some Anglicans would still consider him too young to be vicar of Christ Church! The same people would certainly have looked down on Timothy.

For many potential ordinands, coming back later is not realistic. They are likely to train for a different profession, and then pursue it while getting married, taking out a mortgage, and starting a family. Some do make big sacrifices to come back at a later date, for others it is too late. Even for those who do return, their years as a young adult in ordained ministry have been lost to the Church.

For some other potential ordinands the problem is not so much being told to come back when they are older as being put off by the sheer length of the process leading up to a selection conference. Students coming up to the end of finals need decisions during their final year rather than an eighteen-month exploration of their call before even the decision about whether to send them to a selection conference.

The official policy of the Church of England has, for some years now, been to reverse the fall-off in young ordinands. The proportion of young candidates recommended for training at selection conferences is greater than the average. The continuing problem for young ordinands is mainly with the culture of the Church at a more local level – for there appears to be a consensus at the national and diocesan levels that the Church now stands in need of greater numbers of young clergy, broadly for the following three main reasons:

1 Young ordinands are needed if the Church is to grow

Chapter 3 argued that the loss of young ordinands has been a major self-inflicted wound from which the Anglican Church is suffering and that the loss of young clergy has been a major cause of both the ageing and the shrinking of congregations.

It is hard to see how the missing generations, now in their teens, twenties and thirties, can be won back to the Christian faith except through Christians from those same generations. In the Diocese of Monmouth, half the present clergy are due to retire by 2013 and the average age of the remainder will then be 57, but there are very few young adults and teenagers now left in the churches of the diocese. The average age of the adult churchgoers is 60. The average age of the serving curates is 45. Unless such a diocese can find a new way of growing young disciples and recruiting young ordinands it is hard to see who will be leading any reversal of its decline by 2013.

2 Young ordinands are needed to be the future leaders

There are 107 serving bishops listed in the 2004–5 edition of *Crockford's Clerical Directory*.[1] All but 13 of these were ordained in their twenties; 59 (55 per cent) were ordained aged 23–25. Yet the most recent data indicates there are just 4 ordained clergy currently in the Church of England aged under 25. One of these is female (my daughter as it happens), leaving just 3 who may be allowed to continue to be bishops. A further 152 clergy are aged 25–29, which is just 1.7 per cent of the total stipendiary diocesan clergy. There are far more stipendiary clergy aged 65–69 than there are aged 25–29.

The average age of those consecrated as bishops is already rising – from 47 in the late 1980s to 51 today. Yet, with an average age of ordination of around 46, there is not much time left for most clergy to gain the experience needed to be a bishop or take some other senior position. So, in the future we will either be consecrating bishops after a very short apprenticeship or the House of Bishops will get older and older, with bishops either serving for a very short time or staying on beyond 70.

The army does not recruit colonels. It recruits officer cadets who become second lieutenants, who are fully expected to be young, daft and make mistakes. They are also fully expected to learn from these mistakes, and from their seniors, and become captains within about three or four years. By their late thirties they will become majors and lieutenant colonels with great professional expertise and experience. It would be crazy, however, to commission a colonel at 40 and expect him or her to have all the necessary expertise and potential to be a general.

The Health Service does not recruit consultants. A forty-year-old solicitor wishing to change professions cannot walk into a consultant's job. He or she must start at medical school, and then become a junior doctor, in the same way as younger medical students. A forty-year-old junior doctor will not have the same experience and expertise as a forty-year-old consultant who qualified as a doctor at 24. If the National Health Service recruited only medical students who were over the age of 30, so that they had some experience of life and the patients would trust them more, it would have grave difficulty finding consultants, professors and other senior people.

If the ordained ministry is also a profession where professional skills and experience are valuable, then we should be concerned that the present generation of bishops and other senior clergy is just about the last to be both fully experienced and a long way off retirement when given seniority. We need more young ordinands for the sake of the long-term future of senior leadership.

3 Young ordinands are needed for chaplaincies

Young clergy are needed not only for the successful running of churches, but the lack of them is also being felt in chaplaincy work. Most chaplaincies deal primarily with younger people and are often well served, therefore, by younger clergy. This applies to schools, universities, prisons and armed forces. Only hospital chaplaincies tend to deal with a similar age range to that normally found in local churches. The armed forces are facing a serious problem in the recruitment of chaplains, especially when it comes to clergy in the same age bracket as the other serving officers. In today's dislocated society, a chaplain may be the main point of contact with the Christian faith and Church for very many young people and young adults. Chaplaincy work is likely to be a key component of tomorrow's missionary Church, and it needs a ready supply of young clergy to staff it.

But could we find the people?

It may be thought that, with the rapid decline in the number of young people in the churches, it is unrealistic to expect to find many more young ordinands than the few who come forward with a calling already. However, the Church of England does still have large numbers of young people, students and young adults in maybe 50 or 100 key larger churches in the cities, suburbs and university towns. Some of them will have met with discouragement when making an initial enquiry, others will never have thought of the possibility of ordination because all the clergy they have ever met have been middle-aged or elderly. There are no role models left. To a nineteen-year-old, the thought of ordination may seem about as remote as the prospect of becoming a grandparent.

Yet substantial numbers of young adults leave university and 'student' churches each year for some sort of full-time Christian work, often temporary, sometimes overseas. Some become church lay assistants, youth workers, student workers or chaplaincy assistants. These jobs are usually low paid and last about a year. The fact that graduates still take such jobs shows that many do possess some sense of calling to Christian ministry. Yet many are never encouraged to think seriously about full-time professional ministry in the Church as their chosen career. For many years now, St Aldate's Church in Oxford has taken six or eight lay assistants a year, most of whom are recent graduates, with the express purpose of giving them training and experience, and sending those with a call on to ABM and ordination. A single church in this way is providing three or four ordinands in their twenties every single year. If one church can achieve this, so can others.

If there is any doubt about the number of young people committed to their calling to professional ministry in the Church and prepared to train for three years in order to fulfil that calling, readers should visit some of the theological colleges that house branches of the Centre for Youth Ministry (CYM). These young people have not been anywhere near vocations advisers, directors of ordinands or selection conferences yet they are happily training for professional ministry in the Church, albeit with children and teenagers. The commitment and the potential supply do exist if channelled in the right way.

A culture of recruitment

It is common enough for Anglicans to lament the lack of young ordinands, less common for us to do something about it. This is partly because the culture, and perhaps the theology, is that the Church should sit back and wait for people with an inner sense of call to come to it. The job of the Church is not to recruit the suitable but to screen out the unsuitable. However, many jobs are about calling and vocation, and they are advertised in the church press every week. Simply raising awareness of the possibility of ordination in the mind of a young adult does not commit the Church to ordaining that person. Many organizations actively recruit graduates at careers fairs and milk round events but still carry out their full selection procedures once they have gained the interest of the students. Large organizations tend to have huge recruitment budgets. The number one objective of the Territorial Army, for example, is recruitment, and so this is the priority area for its budgeting and for the deployment of its most able personnel. The active recruitment of young adults who are then prepared to go through the screening process has to be the name of the game.

Although the official policy has become more friendly towards young vocations, this is of limited value if the culture of the Church has not. If the culture is only the sum of our own attitudes, it can change if we change. Ordinary church members and parish clergy are the front line encouragers of vocations – all of us need to keep our eyes open for young people with potential. For young ordinands, 'potential' rather than 'track record' has to be the key selection principle but it is still possible to arrange church life so that young people are deliberately given experience of church leadership in order to identify future leaders. The traditional way of doing this has been to recruit late teens, students and young adults as assistant leaders on summer Christian camps and house parties. This is still a good route, but in recent years some churches have been discovering an additional way of offering young people early leadership experience – as cell leaders. Youth fellowships and churches organized on cell lines should be well set up as nurseries for church leaders. One of the purposes of cells should be seen as the identification, nurture and early growth of future clergy.

Recruiting young ordinands

1 The role of parish clergy and other leaders

Some clergy and churches seem to produce a steady stream of ordinands over the years, others never produce any. This may be something to do with the relative quality of role models and church life, but it is also to do with intentionality. Some clergy and churches seek to nurture leaders and to keep a lookout for potential ordinands, others do not. The Church today needs every parish priest and every church member to be a potential active recruiter of young ordinands. However, dioceses and national institutions have a role in training and support. How to develop young leaders and spot potential young ordinands should be on every CME programme. The Church Pastoral Aid Society is starting to work with the incumbents of the key large churches around the country with significant numbers of young adults to raise awareness and share good practice in the business of discovering potential young ordinands.

2 The role of Diocesan Directors of Ordinands (DDOs)

Many DDOs are acutely aware of the lack of young ordinands and are expert at encouraging them. Their delight at a new enquiry may well be tempered when the person turns out to be yet another fifty-year-old. In other cases, the age group, culture and church tradition of the DDO is so far removed from that of the potential ordinand that barriers are in place straightaway. It would seem logical to appoint as DDOs younger clergy who will be seen as attractive role models by the primary group the Church is trying to attract.

3 The role of recruitment teams

This is a concept that Ministry Division is hoping to trial. A small group of cool-looking clergy, all aged under 30, spends a few days in a university town or city. Their first day is spent running a stall at a university careers fair, alongside other major potential employers. Their presence will have been advertised through university chaplaincies, Christian Unions, and so on. Their presence will also speak volumes about breaking down stereotypes and opening up minds to possibilities. The next evening, they run an enquirers' event at a large local church, which has been advertised widely around the diocese as well as at the careers fair. Similar sessions could be run at events such as Greenbelt, Soul Survivor, New Wine and Spring Harvest. The concept of recruitment teams is that they are available not just for first-contact work but also to mentor young potential ordinands through the minefield ahead leading to selection conferences.

What is wrong with having older ordinands?

The reality that the Church of England needs more young ordinands if it is to thrive in the long term should not be used as a stick with which to beat older ordinands. God can call people of any age into the ordained ministry. The problem is not that there are too many older ordinands, but that there are too few young ones. However, it is also important to bear in mind that the costs of training are significant. Other things being equal, it is better value for money to train someone for a forty-year career than for a ten-year one.

Can we afford more clergy?

If an active recruitment policy became successful and the supply of older ordinands did not dry up, then the costs of training would certainly rise. More importantly, so would the cost of paying the clergy. Could the Church of

England afford to pay all the clergy if their numbers stopped going down, or even rose again? The answer to this question is 'no' if numerical decline continues in the parishes. Some clergy would become unemployed as stipendiaries. But the answer is 'yes' if church membership ceased to decline and even rose again. The point is that this is only likely to happen if the supply of suitable young clergy increases. There is a risk in training much larger numbers of young priests, but there is an even bigger problem if we do not – without suitable leaders the Church of the future will continue to decline.

It would, therefore, be unfair to suggest to young ordinands that the Church of England can guarantee them a job for life. It cannot – but then neither can anyone else in today's fast-moving world. It has to be put to them that there will only be a job for life if they are successful at leading the mission and evangelism of the Church.

However, most young adults today do not look for a job for life – that is seen more as a life sentence than life security. Ordination needs to be marketed not as '40 years doing the same thing' but as the key that unlocks a whole mosaic of opportunities. These will include chaplaincy of an Oxbridge college, being a padre in the British Army, leading a church, doing pioneer missionary work planting a church, having a responsible position as chaplain to a health trust, and all sorts of new opportunities as yet not fully formed.

Getting the mix right

The Church of England will be best served by a stream of young ordinands from every tradition, but the reality today is that almost all the key churches still containing large numbers of teenagers, students and young adults are of the evangelical or charismatic traditions. Most young ordinands will inevitably come out of those traditions. This causes a problem for some Anglicans, who are unhappy to see their own tradition in decline. The appropriate response to this situation is not to make things hard for potential ordinands from those two traditions. If the Church of England's mission is to survive at all, it desperately needs all the leaders it can get who have grown up in and absorbed the values of growing churches with vision for the future.

The best response is for the Catholic and central traditions to take radical steps to reach the younger generations themselves. The Church in Wales has very few evangelicals, and hardly any key churches with significant numbers of teenagers, students and young adults. Its best response is now to think and plan towards the planting of new churches for these age groups in each of the major population centres in Wales. The logic is simple – if the key churches no longer exist, new ones have to be started that are designed to be the nurseries for the future leaders. The possibility of cultural relevance to younger generations is not confined to evangelical-charismatics – other traditions may need to learn from their relative success but then adapt the lessons to their own tradition.

However, it may be that part of the postmodern future is that the old demarcations break down. They are probably already more fluid and fuzzy than once they were. The new pick and mix society is uninterested in maintaining fine and distinctive traditions, but is interested in finding and adapting the best parts of all of them. When a new monastic-style missional order is founded by a Baptist-Charismatic-Evangelical LEP (St Thomas Crookes, Sheffield), with a high-church archbishop as figurehead, then the distinctions seem to be breaking down. The Order of Mission (TOM) may point to a future where the crossing of boundaries is perfectly normal.

New types of people for a new type of Church

If one arm of a future policy for clergy selection is to go looking for young ordinands, another needs to be to go looking for a wider variety of people types. Progress has been made in this – at least ordinands are now of both sexes, but further change is probably needed. In the Christendom model of Church, clergy are principally pastors to congregations, chaplains to local communities and theologians for a Christian society. It is those qualities that the selection procedures are traditionally designed to uncover and promote. But this world is fast being left behind. The Church of the future must be a missionary Church or a dying one. Parts of society may still have some Christendom characteristics, other parts have become post-Christian, other segments are fast changing from post-Christian to non-Christian. The pastor-chaplain-theologian may be ill equipped to lead a newly mission-focused church. Dioceses and parishes that designate the prime task of the vicar to be the 'leader in mission' rather than the 'private chaplain to the flock' are already the ones that tend to be growing. This trend is likely to accentuate. Clergy in the future may be much less likely to be church leaders and more likely to be church planters.

This is not to say that pastorally minded clergy are becoming anachronistic. The giving of personal love and care is a universal requirement of the Christian Church for all time, and the Church will always require leaders who can model and teach it, but we will require a greater range of people to give leadership in the future. We have to ordain, or employ, people to be agents of change as well as people who can pastor others. If the Church of the future is to fly with two wings, the inherited church may need leaders who are good at keeping things going, whilst the fresh expressions church may need leaders who are good at starting things up. Below is a summary list of personal qualities – on the left are those that are helpful to a traditional model of ordained ministry and on the right those that are increasingly needed in a changing world and changing Church. Sometimes our selection procedures and our culture have screened out the 'right hand' types of people in favour of those on the left. Now we need actively to recruit them:

Future shapes of ministry

Pastor to the flock	Leader in mission
Church curator	Church planter
Chaplain	Missionary
Settler	Pioneer
Conformist	Entrepreneur
Being safe	Taking risks
Maintaining existing forms	Pioneering fresh expressions
Doing the ministry	Ensuring it is done
Father Cork	Enabler of others' ministries
Multi-competent dog collar	Specialist team
Single-church leader	Oversight of churches
High-cost operation	Volunteer-led
Lone Ranger	Collaboration in the team
Middle-aged	The young
Manager of decline	Inspirer for growth
Building-centred	Relationship-centred
Rock of stability	Manager of change
Authority figure	Authenticity advert
Establishment figure	Counter-cultural leader
Independent operators	Working together

Recently a new criterion has been added to the list of personal characteristics required of ordinands – its title is 'Mission and Evangelism' and it reads:

> Candidates should demonstrate a missiological outlook that permeates thinking, prayer and action, with a commitment to the missionary calling of the church and to preaching the Gospel. They should show an awareness of the interaction between Gospel and culture. Candidates should show potential as leaders of mission and a commitment to enable others in mission and evangelism.[2]

This should help pioneer church planters and entrepreneurial mission leaders fit the selection criteria better than in the past. It should also demonstrate that these are now people for whom DDOs and selection conferences are looking as future ordained leaders of the Church.

Investing in recruitment

There is a management theory that suggests money is better spent on recruitment than on training. For many jobs, natural aptitude and gifting are more important than high quality training. It is more efficient to spend money finding the right people in the first place than to pour money into trying to train employees who will never be any good at the job in question. It is easy to argue that being the incumbent of a church is one such job where gifting and natural ability are of great importance. If this is so, then the logic is that the Church of England should spend more money on recruitment than it does on training. In practice, today it spends some money on screening out unsuitable applicants but virtually no money at all on active recruitment. Training is clearly also important, but more resources are also needed for recruitment if the twenty-first century Church is to be appropriately staffed.

Training clergy to lead the growth of the Church

This chapter has concentrated more on the subject of recruitment than on initial training partly because this is where the gap in thinking and provision seems to be. If, however, recruitment and selection of clergy need to be geared towards growing the future Church, so does the training of clergy. The future of clergy training is a large, complex and controversial subject that is beyond the scope of this particular book. However, the art of leading churches into growth needs to be learnt – not all clergy are born with all the right instincts, insights and abilities. Once ordinands have been found who are capable of growing the future Church, they should be trained for the job they have been recruited to do. This concept is not always to the fore of current training practice. It is still possible to characterize some training course or college experience as being education in theology rather than training for a job. This is almost inevitable when colleges and courses are staffed primarily by theologians rather than practitioners.

The need for help and training in growth leadership, and the hunger of so many clergy for it, is proven by the popularity of the well-known 'Leading your church into growth' and other similar courses in recent years. Whatever the future format of ordination training, it is time to match the training offered more closely to the expectations and aspirations of the future clergy who are anxious to become fully equipped leaders in mission. This inevitably involves bringing in new sorts of college staff or visiting speakers and devising new sorts of course. It also implies a greater emphasis on practical experience in placements. Theology and biblical studies cannot be abandoned, but they need to be woven into a training programme for missional leaders.

Having looked at how policies for the recruiting, selection and training of ordinands can be reshaped as part of an overall strategy to grow the Church, it is now time to move on to policies for deploying and resourcing the clergy as missional leaders once they have been ordained.

10

Deploying and equipping the clergy

> The Lord appointed seventy others and sent them on ahead of him in pairs to every town and place where he himself intended to go. He said to them, 'The harvest is plentiful, but the labourers are few' . . . The seventy returned with joy, saying, 'Lord, in your name even the demons submit to us.' (Luke 10.1,2,17 NRSV)

From secret isolation to sharing in the joy

It is interesting that, although Jesus sent out his followers two by two (a practice followed by Paul and Barnabas and other early missionaries), the Church of England sends out its foot soldiers to every town and place one by one. We have also dispensed with the second stage of Jesus' process, that of reporting back and sharing in the joy of telling each other the stories of what happened. The result is that what should be a communal mission with stories and joy flowing between its members is often turned into an isolated, lonely ministry carried out in secret from the rest of a church that shows little interest in the individual once the institution service is over.

Many recent developments in deploying, supporting and equipping the stipendiary clergy are designed to move them on from an individual model to a corporate model, from isolationism to teamwork, from secrecy to storytelling. Some clergy work in teams of one sort or another. Most clergy now have access to a system of periodic reviews of their ministry. Some, after years of being accountable to nobody, find these threatening at first, others have been thrilled that at last someone outside their own parish has shown an interest in what they are doing. The setting up of group and team ministries has been partly motivated by the desire to help isolated, and potentially idiosyncratic, clergy to live in a healthier way. Other clergy have developed their own cells or support groups with friends from college, meeting every few months to compare notes and support each other. Bishops and archdeacons may have systems of calling on newly appointed incumbents after, say, six months to talk to them about how things are going.

It is central to this chapter that simply leaving isolated individuals to get on with clergy life without support, ongoing training, accountability, and the joy of sharing the stories of what the Holy Spirit has been doing, is a good way to destroy the Church. Some stable and able clergy swim strongly when thrown in at the deep end, as do some strong-minded mavericks, but others find simply staying afloat in today's choppy waters hard enough by themselves, let alone fishing for people while doing so. One diocese traced a large proportion of its overall attendance drop to just a handful of parishes where there had been a pastoral breakdown of one sort or another. There are many able, saintly clergy without growing churches, but there are few growing churches without able, saintly clergy. The only universal feature of growing churches appears, from research conducted by Christian Schwarz,[1] to be a culture of joy and laughter. Joyless clergy cannot lead joyful churches. Joy is infectious. A joyful workforce will probably mean a growing diocese. Helping the clergy to reach their full potential as disciples whom Jesus sends out into every town and place and who report back with joy must be a central plank of any strategy for the growth of the Church.

The total number of paid clergy

If the falling number of paid clergy is one of the main reasons for falling church attendance, then we would expect attendance to be falling faster in dioceses that have lost clergy faster. In fact, this is not the case. The attendance trend in dioceses holding on to paid clergy numbers appears to be, if anything, slightly worse than the trend in dioceses shedding paid clergy rather fast, as shown below:

Table 10.1 Dioceses holding on to stipendiary clergy 1997–2002

Diocese	Clergy 1997–2002	Adult uSa 1997–2002
Bradford	122 to 120	−12%
Coventry	149 to146	−15%
Exeter	268 to 270	−12%
Leicester	170 to 168	−8%
Norwich	200 to 209	−2%
Truro	123 to 127	−16%
Wakefield	172 to 170	−10%
Winchester	247 to 249	−7%
Total	1451 to 1459	−10%

Table 10.2 Dioceses shedding stipendiary clergy 1997–2002

Diocese	Clergy 1997–2002	Adult uSa 1997–2002
Derby	200 to 174	−18%
Gloucester	168 to 149	+1%
Lincoln	229 to 205	+1%
Manchester	324 to 290	−11%
Ripon & Leeds	162 to 144	−8%
Sodor & Man	22 to 19	−12%
Southwell	198 to 167	−5%
York	290 to 250	−13%
Total	1593 to 1398 (12%)	−8%

Figure 10.1 Per cent fall in adult uSa in groups of dioceses losing stipendiary clergy at different rates 1997–2002

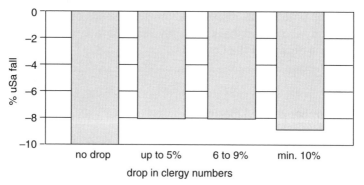

There is no correlation between changing numbers of unpaid but authorized ministries (NSMs, OLMs, Readers) and changing attendance. Dioceses shedding paid clergy at a fast rate were not compensating for this with increasing numbers of the unpaid. It would seem that there are more important factors at work determining attendance trends than the number of clergy deployed. It is likely that it is much more important to deploy clergy well and to have the right sort of clergy than simply to go for quantity. This also means that reducing the number of clergy either for financial or supply reasons need not result in loss of attendance or membership.

Making appointments – finding the best people

Making new appointments is a complicated business: PCCs, parish representatives, patrons, bishops, deaneries, DBFs, all have a voice in the matter. This means that it is very hard for any one group or individual to change, accelerate or improve the system without the others. People have to work together if they want the key matter of clergy appointments to become part of an intentional strategy for growth in a diocese.

The first requirement is clarity of purpose – the objective needs to be to find the best leader in mission. By this is meant the person most likely to lead the healthy development of the church in question so that it grows in size, ministry and kingdom impact. The motive of trying to find a suitable new post for a certain vicar who wants a move will never find the best leader in mission except by extreme good luck. Neither will a diocesan policy of making only internal appointments in order to avoid bringing someone new on to the payroll. Similarly, patrons who present the first person they stumble across are unlikely to find the best missional leaders.

The two systems that do stand a chance of finding the right leader in mission are the list and the advertisement. A large patronage society such as CPAS may have a long enough list of clergy interested in a move to be able to make suitable matches between parishes and clergy. However, the best way of opening up posts to as many people as possible is to advertise in the church press. A system of application, shortlisting and competitive interview stands the most chance of identifying the best new leader for the church. The interviewing panel will be able to compare the response of the different candidates to their questions concerning how they would lead this church into growth and development.

A study comparing the effectiveness of the various different systems of finding new clergy (bishops juggling; patrons or vacancies lists; old boy networks; just finding somebody, anybody; head hunting; advertising and competitive interview) is surely overdue. The study would compare the track records of groups of clergy appointed by different systems, and would enable the Church to choose or modify its systems on the basis of evidence rather than opinion and anecdote.

Sometimes, however, job advertisements, especially for posts in certain areas, get a very poor response. Clergy spouses are likely to be working, which greatly restricts the mobility of the ordained half. Mysteriously, God appears to be calling more clergy to the south of England than he is to the north. Active seeking of individuals may sometimes be necessary, though always bearing in mind the damage that may be done to the priest's current parish by a premature move to a new post.

For the efficient working and growth of the Church of England, the most able clergy should probably lead the largest churches. Half of Anglicans worship in just 15 per cent of the churches, and patrons and dioceses should take particular time and trouble over these key appointments. A problem is that leading a large church is usually more demanding than leading a small one, but the stipend remains the same. Should the clergy of large, strategic, churches be offered an enhanced stipend in recognition of their larger responsibilities? Many Anglicans would say 'no' because of the principle of the stipend, but then archdeacons and bishops get paid more than incumbents for their wider responsibilities, and curates get paid less for their narrower responsibilities. Some rural deans also receive an enhanced stipend for their responsibilities. Part-time hospital chaplaincies can also enhance a stipend. It would be interesting to experiment with an enhanced stipend for a few large churches to see whether that helped attract a better field of applicants. It would be surprising if it did not, because that is how able people are attracted to demanding jobs in every other sphere of life.

But clergy whom God has called to lead the mission of the Church are also likely to be motivated by the opportunity to exercise their mission and gifting in a promising environment and supportive diocese. When Bishop Nigel McCulloch became Bishop of Wakefield and renamed it 'The Missionary Diocese of Wakefield' (a title that framed every job advertisement) he attracted to the diocese clergy who identified with the missionary aspiration. These, mainly young, clergy led a group of growing churches that helped to halt the attendance decline in the diocese as a whole.

So attention should be paid to the question 'What kinds of job advertisement and description will best attract suitable leaders in mission?' Advertisements containing long lists of virtues and tasks that would daunt St Paul are unlikely to attract well focused candidates. The first advertisement I glance at in today's church paper seeks a vicar to encourage youth work, excite with new thinking, challenge us spiritually, and bring people to Christ, while at the same time delighting in our choral tradition and accepting our existing vision for the use of the new church hall. Gentle pastors will be put off by the first four requirements and missional leaders by the last two. Advertisements to advance the growth of the Church need to describe real people, not compendiums of all gifts, virtues and inclinations compiled by committees.

Some posts do not necessarily need ordained clergy: for example, a colleague to oversee the pastoral ministry of a church might be a trained counsellor rather than a priest. One deanery decided to replace a traditional incumbent's post with a church-planting post to grow a relational church for young adults in the general area. The person appointed from the competitive interviews was a Canadian Lutheran lay person who now lives in a vicarage and draws a stipend.

Increasingly, dioceses able to show how they will support the church growth work of missional leaders will be more likely to attract them. For example, a diocese that has set up a 'Bishop's Mission and Growth Fund' for awarding grants to parish evangelism and growth initiatives should use this as a lever for attracting the sort of clergy who would take advantage of the fund once in post.

Making appointments – quickly enough

A large proportion of national attendance loss is currently happening during vacancies of over six months (see Chapter 2). A vitally important plank of any growth strategy is therefore to find ways of stopping the loss of people during vacancies. The simplest solution is to shorten the vacancies. Like everything else, such a policy should be monitored and evaluated to see if the new shorter vacancies have stemmed the flow of people out of the churches at vacancy time.

Many clergy over the years build up their own personal contacts and following, often from people they have been involved with pastorally. Some of these people will drift away when 'their' vicar has left and before a new one has a chance to substitute for that person. During a vacancy, newcomers may not be picked up on so well, and, if the vicar is normally involved centrally in the pastoral care programme of the church, it is easier for people to drift away unnoticed. It may be during a vacancy that Sunday standards slip. Churchgoers have a stronger streak of consumerism in them than they once did. Habit and loyalty will hold a congregation together for only so long in the face of a lower, less certain, quality of church life and services.

In the contemporary world, churches grow only if they change and develop. There is a culture of not making changes during vacancies, and churches that do not make changes shrink. In 'programme' style churches the vicar is often holding a lot of organizational strings. After a while, these begin to unravel, job vacancies and confusion develop, and the organizational life of the church suffers. Lay leaders begin to get tired and morale slides. Prolonged absence of the leader inevitably means a church, like any organization, has to reorganize to adapt. Many months later when a new vicar finally arrives, the church must reorganize again to adapt to having a new, and probably very different, leader again.

In some distant golden age, long before the first cautious whisper of the word 'privatization', I spent some years advising the government on its railway policy. The wisdom of the experienced railway operator was 'when you reorganize, you bleed'. Energy and focus are absorbed for months at a time first by the planning, then by the act, and then by the outcomes of the reorganization. The operating efficiency of a railway neglected by its managers starts to deteriorate. The workforce has trouble adjusting to the new arrangements. Key tasks fall by accident into the hands of the inexperienced and unprepared, while old and treasured skills are set aside. The trains break down more often. The only person who knows why is old Joe the Rivet Tapper, who was made redundant. He was the last man alive who could jiggle the tightness of the key assembly on the motor bogies so that the stresses balanced and they kept on working. But the managers never met old Joe – they just saw his age on the record sheets and shunted him off on to his final siding. And now it is such a mystery why the trains don't run so well any more.

Reorganization may be worthwhile if it is for a strong, positive, long-term purpose of modernization or improved efficiency, but reorganizations without such a purpose are always a bad idea. The granddaddy of all such reorganizations was, of course, rail privatization. Leaving a church without an incumbent for a year or so is asking it to reorganize twice for no good purpose whatsoever. Allowing a smooth handover from one incumbent to the next may be to avoid both reorganizations.

The worst affected churches for attendance loss in vacancies are those large enough to run with programmes (over 100 adults on a Sunday) but not large enough to run with a strong team of paid assistant staff (say over 250 on a Sunday). These churches are losing perhaps as much as 25 per cent of their attendance during a twelve-month vacancy.

Vacancies can be shortened by starting the process of finding a replacement incumbent as soon as the present post-holder's departure is made known. There is no need to wait until after she or he has gone to start the process rolling. In most situations where incumbents have done a reasonable job, it is entirely right for them to have an input into the process of finding a replacement. There is also the, much exaggerated, fear that incumbents can change their mind and rescind their resignation. On the rare occasion when this does happen, it will be embarrassing if the job has already been advertised, but that is a much lesser problem than leaving the parish leaderless for too long. Often the most important thing a church needs in leadership is continuity. A diocese can introduce systems that give tight deadlines for the various parties to go through the stages that lead up to advertising a job and seeking candidates. The aim should be to interview candidates within a month of the old vicar's leaving. This gives enough time to make the appointment, for the successful candidate to give three months' notice and to have a month to move before being instituted just under six months after the beginning of the vacancy.

We know that such a timetable is entirely feasible because it still quite often happens today. In fact, it is still standard policy in some dioceses to fill vacancies in under six months. It should be in all. Occasionally an appointment is even made while the old incumbent is still in post – everything is possible given goodwill on all sides. It is always possible to set a realistic first target if a sudden change in culture is impractical. One diocese, newly aware of the problem of long vacancies, calculated that its average vacancy length was nine months. It decided, as a first step, to attempt to reduce that average over the coming year to eight months.

If dioceses did all suddenly attempt to fill vacancies more quickly, they would be frustrated, because the supply of clergy is fairly fixed. They would actually be attempting to employ a greater number of clergy at any one time, and probably could not afford to do so at least in the short term. So a policy for cutting vacancies needs to involve a cut in the number of posts the diocese is trying to fill. The new policy will be to employ the same number of people as before but to do so by having fewer posts and keeping them filled. This will have the spin off value of making a number of vicarages redundant and so alleviating financial problems (see Chapter 15).

That churches shrink while they have no vicar for an extended period can be seen as an unwelcome finding by those trying to make churches less dependent upon their clergy. This is a necessary process as the number of paid clergy keeps going down. However, small churches that share an incumbent appear to shrink less during vacancies than single-vicar parishes. If you share your vicar with ten other churches you may hardly notice when the vicar leaves! In fact, the very smallest that lost their own vicar many years ago are the one size group in recent years to have shown some numerical growth. I do not have enough data on this to offer systematic evidence but the examples I have seen do suggest that pastoral reorganizations that group extra churches under one vicar do not have the same attendance impact as long vacancies provided that the surgery is done quickly and neatly. Pastoral reorganization plans need to be in place before clergy leave rather than, as is so often the case today, beginning the discussion only after the clergy have left.

So losses in long vacancies are not about overdependence on the clergy. They are about organizations being asked to run for a long period without a leader. No organization can do this successfully in the long term, and I am not aware of any other walk of life where they are asked to. Occasionally a school may run without a head for a term, but attempts are always made to find one. In the armed forces, as in many management posts, the new post-holder is in place before the old one leaves so that there is a handover period. No chain of shops would survive routine twelve-month gaps between managers. Moreover, it is useless to expect the work of becoming less clergy dependent to take place during vacancies, because there is a new priest waiting somewhere in the wings with an unknown style of ministry, who may create new dependencies. Responsibilities are shared by being given away, not by being abandoned. The work of becoming less clergy-dependent is best done while a vicar is in place, helping the people to live in a different way, handing over responsibilities, and resourcing the new, fragile, ministries of the lay members. Usually the best way to find, train and keep volunteers (for example, to do church youth work) is to have a trained professional to do the recruiting, training and resourcing.

The range of jobs available

An unusual characteristic of clergy life is the very flat career structure. Once the apprenticeship of a curacy is over, then most clergy will be incumbents of one sort or another until they retire. Even if someone becomes a chaplain for a while, it is likely to be a sideways move not a step up in any way. Some clergy are joyfully content doing the same job for decade after decade but some become dry or frustrated or bored or worn out by it. Pastorally minded clergy are more likely to be content with the yearly cycle of clergy life, but the newer breeds of entrepreneurs the Church now needs are less likely to be so. Part of the art of deploying the clergy must increasingly be to find new variety, new challenges and new seniority steps to keep them interested and motivated. A small but increasing number of posts are now pioneer church planting jobs, and this number will need to increase not only for the obvious church-growth reason but also to provide exciting and challenging options for the clergy in mid career.

One priest, after a traditional ten-year incumbency, was asked to take on a redundant church and grow a new sort of Christian community that did not involve worship services on Sundays. He took some time to think and pray about the direction of this new enterprise, and so discovered he had been given time to rest and recover from the previous ten years. New vision, excitement and energy welled up from within as the extent of the new challenge and opportunity formed in his mind.

Traditionally, being rural dean has been seen by clergy as a thankless, onerous, low grade job best avoided if possible – the bishop's messenger. However, in many dioceses the role of the rural deans is changing. Deaneries are being entrusted with real powers and responsibilities, for example over parish share distribution, over pastoral reorganization, mission planning and church planting. Some bishops meet regularly with their rural deans and treat them as the second layer of oversight and leadership. Perhaps rural deans as a group should now be recognized with a small increment on the pay scale and the realization they have progressed in their career path.

New opportunities for older clergy

Along with encouraging younger clergy, it is vital to invest in the well-being and the mission-effectiveness of older clergy. Sometimes older clergy are simply worn out by years of demanding, stressful overwork. I have previously argued that a new culture of a maximum 48-hour working week, perhaps with two days off a week like everybody else, could do a lot to restore the vigour and fervour of the clergy. An attack needs to be launched on the guilt-driven culture of workaholism. This probably needs to be led by bishops and archdeacons, who will have to model in their own ministries the sensible work-life balance they urge on their clergy. A recent survey of archdeacons revealed that they work on average a 67-hour week – over 11 hours a day, 6 days a week. Apart from the not infrequent health breakdowns due to overwork, this also means that most archdeacons are working while tired most of the time. This is not a good example to give to the rest of the clergy – effectiveness is not measured by hours of work but by the spiritual impact of the work.

As clergy are deemed to be self-employed, there are no standard conditions of service. It is difficult for some to know even basic things like how many weeks' holiday they should take each year. A minimum guide could be helpful to some, and perhaps an extra week for older clergy would be both a practical help and a sign that they are expected to slow up a little as their bodies age. Some older clergy would appreciate the chance to spend their last working years as a curate or other assistant to a younger incumbent. Dioceses might find it advantageous to arrange some prototypes to test out the pros and cons. Other older clergy would benefit from a greater variety of early retirement and part-time packages. For example, replacing 'house for duty' arrangements with small stipends to supplement the pension might not only make financial sense for the diocese (see Chapter 15) but also help the clergy. Some clergy in their 60s might have a new lease of life if they were able to take their pension and work from their own house part-time for an honorarium or small stipend.

When an incumbent has spent ten years pouring his or her heart and soul into a parish, physical and emotional tiredness is the likely result. Under present arrangements, the normal procedure is to allow three weeks for a house move, for working on the new house to make it habitable, for coping with the bereavement of leaving behind the previous church, for sorting out the institution service, thinking through the new job, and having a rest. The result is that clergy start new posts before they are fit and ready for them. A longer recovery time, perhaps coupled with attending a 'between ministries' refresher course, could pay large dividends.

The bishop-elect went for the famous 'bishop's medical' – a notoriously thorough examination and medical check designed to ensure that only relatively well people get consecrated. The doctor discovered a condition that would kill the nearly-bishop within weeks, but which was entirely treatable. The treatment was successful and the bishop was consecrated a little late but fit and well. He owed his life to the medical. If he had stayed a vicar he would have died.

It is hard to justify a life-saving system of medical care that is restricted to bishops.

To the argument that the Church cannot afford proper medical checks for all clergy the answer is that a church that wishes its clergy to lead its resurgence cannot afford not to invest in their medical well-being. This, of course, is not to mention the obvious pastoral and fairness reasons for offering medical checks to all the Church's immensely valuable clerical workforce instead of just a chosen few. It would seem entirely reasonable to begin with a scheme for the over 55s or over 60s, or for all those taking up a new appointment, and to monitor its value by compiling a list of the problems uncovered and treatments begun. If the scheme proved its worth with the first group, it could then be extended to all. The Diocese of Liverpool, and perhaps one or two others, already have such a scheme.

Continuing ministerial education

If a diocese is to have a strategy for turning itself round from a dying to a growing organism, it will need to refocus its CME programme on this core objective. Academic, dilettante and fringe subjects will have to take a back seat. Those appointed to CME posts should themselves have a capability and enthusiasm for offering help and training in the area of growing the Church. That there is a widespread demand from clergy for high quality help in this area is proved by the sell-out nature of the 'Leading your church into growth' courses that many have attended. Perhaps the originators of these courses could be asked to train a larger, younger, team to be a national resource. Dioceses could arrange a series of local courses run by the national team that they expect all their clergy to attend.

It sometimes feels to clergy that dioceses just load more and more upon them – extra responsibilities and extra parish share – while offering nothing back in return. If dioceses are to ask their clergy to lead the resurgence of the Church through the church growth route, they need to offer training and other human resource support for growing the Church. This needs to go alongside the more helpful financial environment envisaged in Part 4. One diocese has helped a group of its clergy to network regularly with each other, sharing stories of growth initiatives with each other in group meetings and by email. Another arranges two large meetings a year for clergy and other leaders of larger churches to explore how to turn around from decline to growth. As well as providing the specific help indicated by their content, such initiatives improve morale and parish-diocese relationships.

Part of the content of the new CME needs to be in the area of helping clergy to retrain for a rather different job description from the one they may have signed up for at the beginning of their ministries. This is uncomfortable for some, but should not be considered unfair provided that quality help is offered. After all, most people in this fast-changing society have to retrain for different ways of working probably several times in their working lives. For example, many clergy are moving from pastoring one church or congregation to having oversight over several. This involves a different way of working. CME needs to be offered to help clergy adjust to the change. Other clergy realize that they can no longer simply perpetuate the old ways in the annual rhythm of the Church's year. They have to become managers of change. Change management is a difficult art, much studied by secular managers. Training needs to be offered.

It may be that it is unrealistic to expect every diocese to come up with its own CME package covering all the ways in which the professional lives of the clergy need to change to keep up with a changing world. It would be more efficient if some aspects were organized nationally. Perhaps existing training agencies could help bring about a national CME scene properly focused on high quality training for leading growing churches in the twenty-first century.

Improving clergy morale

Low morale – root causes

There is a problem with clergy morale. Partly this is undermined by the media's focusing almost exclusively on negative stories and spin in relation to decline, scandals and splits. Clergy feel devalued, that they are losing their respected place in society and their role in the local community. It feels to some that they are working for a failing, or at least increasingly irrelevant, organization. Morale is also undermined by stress and workload. It feels as though clergy must work harder and smarter to maintain and grow their churches today than in the past. Other burdens are piled on them through the evolution of the role from conducting a personal ministry to heading an organization. Child protection issues, for example, have added huge new headaches and workload on to some clergy.

Clergy spouses are today likely to have their own jobs and careers, thus adding to the household stress even though the income goes up. The incidence of clergy marriage breakup has also increased as divorce becomes more common generally and the pressures on clergy marriages seem to increase. In many dioceses housing budgets are under pressure and the inertia of a large organization makes it difficult to organize vicarage repairs and maintenance. Many vicarages appear from a distance to be typical nice, large detached houses. It is only on closer inspection that the rotting window frames and peeling paint are revealed, and inside the family has been waiting three months for the shower to be fixed and three years for the ancient, wheezing central heating boiler to be replaced.

Morale is further undermined, and workloads increased, by the realities of the decline cycle. Until recently the main cause of declining clergy numbers has been the shrinking supply – there were 11,000 stipendiary clergy in 1990 and 9,000 in 2002. Now, in many areas numbers are now controlled by the diocesan budget. The diocese says that another 20 posts must go because there is no money for them. The remaining clergy must spread the workload between them. Those with small or declining congregations start to worry that their own job is no longer financially viable. Many clergy no longer have the freehold, and fear for their future. Ordinands and younger clergy are sometimes being warned not to assume that their future pension provision is wholly safe and to make extra arrangements. How they are supposed to do this on a stipend finely tuned to be just adequate without such expenditure is not clear.

It is not the intention of this book to reinforce the fallacy that 'success' in ministry is simply measured by church growth. There are many criteria of success, and simple faithfulness is one of them. However, many clergy with declining congregations feel that decline in their church is due to their own personal failure, and morale is further undermined. Some feel that their heroic efforts at stemming decline have been wasted, and have never been noticed or acknowledged by the diocesan hierarchy. Meanwhile, the diocese is demanding more and more money for the parish share, pressurizing clergy into becoming fund-raisers to keep their own jobs going. As the average age of the clergy has been rising, so a higher proportion is struggling to maintain the workload while coping with the effects of loss of health, fitness and physical resilience.

The picture painted above is not, of course, the experience of all. That there is enormous job satisfaction in following God's calling in ministry is beyond doubt. Many clergy find their roles to be stimulating and joyful. There are advantages to the lifestyle as well as problems. Hours may be long but they are flexible and there are no long commuting hassles. Other jobs today are equally stressful. Nevertheless, many clergy will recognize the realities of the above sketch. The point for the purposes of a strategy to reverse decline is that decline is a consequence of low morale as well as a cause. It is important to take steps to raise the morale of the workforce and so to raise the effectiveness of the workforce. A joyful, vibrant ministry will be far more effective than a depressed, stressed-out one.

Making the right moves

I have spent much time in recent years with groups of clergy who lead larger churches with an adult usual Sunday attendance of more than 100. The first part of a typical day is to show the clergy that it is churches in this size of group that have sustained the brunt of attendance loss in recent years and that it is common, for all sorts of well understood reasons, for larger churches to be in numerical decline. For some clergy this knowledge takes a great weight off their minds because they had thought the decline of their own church must have been simply their own fault. To realize they are victims of a trend more than perpetrators of it does wonders for their morale and prepares them for the rest of the day in which solutions to the decline problem are discussed. Clergy going back home having been reassured that the problem is not their own fault, and newly armed with strategies that have worked else-where to turn larger churches around, tend to return with renewed energy and optimism.

The clergy of a diocese knew things were bad, but didn't really know how bad. The main thing they did know was that the finance people had said a third of their posts had to disappear in the next few years if the remaining two thirds were still to be paid. At the request of the bishop, I spent a couple of weeks immersed in the diocese's database and in a set of survey forms filled in by the clergy. At a day conference attended by all the clergy, I was able to paint a clear picture of just how bad things were in terms of the decline cycle – shrinking congregations, problem finances and work-force projections. Far from this further undermining the clergy's morale, it seemed a great boost. They were hearing the truth, clearly and objectively expressed. The clear truth is usually not as bad as the vague or imagined truth and it is easier to cope with. And Jesus was absolutely right when he said, 'You will know the truth, and the truth will make you free.'[2] Only a clear facing of the truth together conveys the freedom to discover ways to change the realities. There were signs of hope and growth revealed in the data I had been given and I was able to share them. A clear facing of the problems coupled with offering realistic ways of tackling them was a great boost to morale. Also helpful to morale was the change in perceptions about the diocesan leadership: at last things were changing from drift to decision. At last the diocesan leaders were getting a grip of the problem and even seemed to know what they had to do. So the level of trust in and of support for diocesan leaders also seemed to receive a boost.

Another key area for morale is that of pastoral care for the clergy, including systems for picking up problems early before they get out of control, terms and conditions of employment, good practice in job interviews and ministry reviews, career guidance, and so on. Some of these matters are routine and others require a specialist expertise. Most employers today provide human resources managers for these issues, yet in the Church we still expect them to be handled by the bishops and archdeacons. It is not an intelligent use of senior clergy's time to expect them to keep up to date with all the latest employment legislation, be responsible for clergy disclosure forms, and myriad other things for which a theological education neither equips nor disposes them. Allowing lay people to become part of the senior management team for the clergy may require a change in culture, and an extra salary, but for how long can dioceses afford to be without professional human resources management? The salary will probably be repaid many times over in the effectiveness of better-supported clergy and, if it is a problem to start with, could sometimes be found by reducing the size of the ordained senior team.

In parish life in larger churches the clergy are no longer the front line pastoral carers for the congregation. The vicar may have responsibility for the lay leaders, but the cell group leaders have primary responsibility for the cell members. This change is, in part, due to the simple recognition that one busy person cannot be responsible for the pastoral care of several hundred others. What has been accepted at parish level also needs to be accepted at diocesan level. One busy diocesan bishop cannot make day-to-day pastoral contact with each of several hundred clergy. Just as parishioners complain about vicars who 'never visit any more' so the vicars complain about the bishops. Both complaints are usually equally unfair, and both the clergy and the bishops probably feel equally guilty about their failure to get round every-body. One way forward is the professional specialist route outlined above. Another is to find the diocesan equivalent of the cell leader. This, once again, looks like the rural dean, who may be asked by the bishop to exercise a pastoral responsibility in relation to the deanery clergy. It is, however, no use loading more and more on rural deans and expecting them to continue leading their own churches just as successfully. Some may need to be offered human or financial resources help for their own parish so that they are freed to exercise wider responsibilities as well.

It is clear to me, having visited groups of clergy in about half the dioceses of the Church of England and Church in Wales, that morale is far higher where there is growth than where there is decline. Often, where there is growth, the problems are more acute and the workloads may even be greater. The problems of church growth can be far more challenging than the problems of genteel decline but the mindsets, energy levels, morale and spiritual resources to face them are far stronger.

A diocese able to implement just some of the programme for growth outlined in this book is likely to find that the morale of its clergy will rise as a result, and so add a further twist to the new cycle of growth. For example, the provision of a 'Growth Initiatives Fund' (see Chapter 15) offers positive support to clergy trying to do their job well, and makes them feel the diocese is an ally rather than a problem to them. Where there is a coherent and credible strategy, not for managing decline but for defeating it, then clergy motivation and morale strengthen, and when the overall numbers do start to increase, this fact should be spread around a diocese in order further to rebuild morale.

11

Training and supporting the laity

Timothy, my co-worker, greets you; so do Lucius and Jason and Sosipater, my relatives . . . Erastus, the city treasurer, and our brother Quartus, greet you. (Romans 16.21,23 NRSV)

Lay v ordained?

In a certain crematorium of my acquaintance lies a row of three doors. The first says 'Ladies', the second 'Clergy' and the third 'Gents'. 'What plumbing novelties designed for the middle sex lurk behind that central door?' I wondered to myself, pushing my way in. Disappointingly, the equipment was perfectly standard. The advent of readers, non-stipendiary ministers, and locally ordained ministers on the one hand, and paid church leadership posts occupied by lay people on the other, has partly bridged the chasm there once was between the two branches of the human race found within the traditional Church of England but not immediately apparent from the way members of the Early Church related to each other. The move from the 'shepherd and flock' model of church to the 'whole people of God' model has further narrowed the distinction between ordained and lay. Many clergy are wearing less and less distinctive dress less and less often. The dog-collar manufacturing industry faces an uncertain future.

When 'Springboard' (the Archbishops' Evangelism Initiative) ran training days on how to grow larger churches, we began to invite the incumbent and at least half the PCC of each church. That way the participants had a chance to take back what they had gained from the day into the bloodstream of their church. Just one or two isolated people attending, even if one was the incumbent, might have little chance of conveying the lessons or excitement of the day to the rest of the church. Often the incumbent would arrive in ordinary clothes, with the others, and it would be unclear which of the party was the ordained professional and which not.

So perhaps the clear distinction still made between 'CME Officer' on the one hand and 'Lay Training Officer' on the other is not always helpful. In order to work together at developing the life of the local church, the people, lay and ordained, need to be trained together. Perhaps the training functions in dioceses need to be amalgamated into a single entity that best expresses the whole people of God theology on which the future of the Church is being based. In the Diocese of Liverpool this is already a reality for 'Shared Ministry Teams', which already train with their clergy. The church that trains together grows together. I realize that I have perpetuated the very division I am here questioning in my chapter headings, but that is simply in order to cover the two categories in which we currently work, not to suggest they should be perpetuated. Training support has never been so important to the future of the Church, and it is right and proper that more resources are probably being poured into it today than ever before. However, not all training efficiently serves the purpose of growing the future Church.

The fallacy of filling the gaps

Clergy play a key role in the growth of the Church. The number of stipendiary clergy is forecast to continue falling for the foreseeable future. How can we expect the Church to grow when there will be fewer and fewer professional leaders? One answer to this question is that the very churches that have lost their own vicars – small ones in the countryside – are actually growing numerically. Around the world, churches without paid leadership tend to grow faster than those with paid leadership. We have seen that dioceses keeping their paid clergy numbers steady were losing attendance at least as fast as those shedding clergy rather rapidly, but all this is not to say the Church of England does not need paid clergy. The role of the clergy in relation to the lay people of the Church is evolving, but it is by no means diminishing. Clergy are needed more and more in order to give oversight over groups of churches, to be vision and value bearers, to equip the people for works of ministry, to offer strategic and pioneering leadership as well as to be the traditional spiritual teacher and guide. It does say that a less clerically-dependent Church has every chance of being a growing one.

The main strategy for promoting new growth through the era of clergy cuts in some dioceses is to train small teams of lay people to take on some of the work and ministry of the now more thinly-spread clergy. They are to fill the gaps left by the disappearing clergy. One diocese developed a lay ministry scheme designed for adoption by every parish. It involved finding several lay people from each parish and training them for two or three years for a range of pastoral and leadership functions in the local church. One of the lay people would become a locally ordained minister. Sensibly, the diocese piloted the scheme with twelve initial parishes over a three-year period. The pilots were deemed a success because the diocese succeeded in finding, training and commissioning a team in every one of the twelve parishes. However, what the diocese did not realise at the time was that attendance at the twelve pilot scheme churches had dropped by 25 per cent over the four years the scheme was being implemented. The diocese had monitored only the *implementation* of the scheme; it had not thought to monitor the *impact* of the scheme on parish life. There were in fact some reasons for this decline other than the implementation of a ministry scheme, although other churches without a lay ministry scheme had remained pretty much the same size. Another diocese invested heavily in the training and support of similar 'mandated ministry teams'. Attendance in 98 churches with such teams fell over 18 per cent over a five year period while attendance at 353 churches without such teams fell only 16 per cent. So why are such teams around the country apparently not producing the church growth goods it was hoped that they would?

First, the group of lay people set aside for training usually contains some of the most effective and committed leaders of the church. They are taken from their existing jobs and ministries and trained to do something else. This inevitably creates gaps and weaknesses in the churches that were not there before. Second, it might actually be that some of the new team members are more gifted or called to the functions they were previously fulfilling than the ones for which they are being trained. Third, whereas a diocese thinks it is preparing churches for a declericalized life, in practice it may be simply clericalizing a few of the laity. Some may be less effective in this role than the paid clergy they are replacing. Lay ministry schemes may be more a way of avoiding real change than of bringing it about. The structures of church life can continue as before because the gaps have been filled – a group of square pegs have had some carpentry attention to make them fit into the round holes vacated by the paid clergy. Finally, teams often focus on the internal workings of the church – its liturgy and pastoral care. One church had a three-year downturn in its attendance figures following a period of growth. I asked the vicar the reason for the downturn: 'Those were the years we were training our ministry team and our focus was all inward looking. Now the team is trained we are trying to look outwards again and hoping to grow.'

One large church had some excellent evangelists among its members. These were formally commissioned and recognized as such by the church at a public ceremony. The main result was that the rest of the congregation became demotivated about evangelism – they now had their labelled experts and it was their job to do the evangelism on behalf of the whole church.

142

Living in a different way

Churches needing to adapt to life with reduced hands-on stipendiary clergy input may actually thrive, not through finding lay people to fill the gaps, but by learning to live in a different way. For example, instead of replacing one full-time 'pastor' with two or three part-timers, it may be better if everyone simply looked after each other. The training input should then be aimed at the whole church rather than the 'local ministry team'. Instead of finding others to fill the management and organizational gaps left by the clergy, it may be better to deconstruct the organizational life of the church so that there is less managing to do. This may need people to adopt a new mental model of church – less of an institution with meeting times and office holders, and more of a relational community engaging with the wider world. Or perhaps that mental model is not so new after all and is actually closer to what Jesus had in mind in the first place. One practical way of helping churches move towards lighter structures is to introduce them to a 'cell and celebration' model of church life. Once again, it is the whole church that would need to be trained and led to live in a different way.

Even when teams are being trained for 'mission', the model adopted may be purely organizational and restricted to few labelled leaders. So the mission strategy becomes the formation and running of a lunch club – a new church activity. Yet the primary expression of mission is the outworking of the faith in the daily lives of church members. Lay training might be less about helping people run the church better and more about helping them live their lives better.

One church found that many of its members were middle managers, who found business meetings a very stressful part of life. The church brought in experts on how to run meetings well and put its middle managers on all the church committees. By giving them a good experience of meetings the church enabled its middle managers to improve their business meetings. Colleagues then started asking them 'Where did you learn that?' The answer was 'At church' – and the managers suddenly had a new opportunity for sharing their faith.

So 'mission' and 'lay training' are not only about 'doing' (church activities), they are also about 'living' – helping church members to live out their faith in their daily lives – and about 'being'. By this is meant the very nature of the Church and the way it proclaims or delivers the gospel in the quality of its relationships and buildings and common life. To be effective, this training in 'doing, living and being', and this calling out of people into ministry and mission teams, needs to be of the whole congregation, not just a chosen few.

Low-cost models

The Church of England is a high-cost operation. The clergy may not be very well paid, but costs of pensions, the housing, and of training and support mean that the total costs of the clergy are about double the stipend, and there are plenty of other costs to come out of the parish share as well. Clergy costs are all halved for a church that shares its stipendiary vicar with another, and avoided altogether for a church with no stipendiary oversight. Such low-cost models of Anglicanism lose the benefits of professional leadership and ministry for the church as well as the wider ministry of the parish priest. However, there is some compensation in that more of the church's financial resources are available to finance other ways of conducting the church's ministry. Can lay people, or at least unpaid people, be trusted to run their own churches without any professional clergy oversight?

This is already happening in certain cases where a reader or retired or non-stipendiary or OLM priest is given charge of a church. Here the ministry is trained and recognized, but not paid. It is frequently highly effective.

One vicar had two churches – a large, established one and a smaller, more recent, plant in a school hall. The small church had developed its own lay leadership and was proving itself capable of living independently and growing steadily, so the vicar concentrated on his large church. He stopped going to meetings of any sort at the small one. All he did was preside at the Eucharist once a month. A group of lay leaders, aided by the lack of buildings to care for, ran the church quite easily and efficiently. As soon as a locally ordained priest was found for that church, his plan was to leave it alone completely. With no building and no paid staff of its own the total running costs of this church were about £7,000 a year.

Part of the training function should be to assist groups of lay people to set up and operate experimental low-cost models of Anglicanism that might be part of the future mosaic of provision.

Telling my story

If the purpose of lay training is to preserve the institution then training people to fill the gaps may be the best approach. If, however, the purpose is to share the faith and so grow the Church, then gap-filling is doomed to failure. Rather, the principal focus of lay training as part of a strategy for growing the Church must include helping people to tell their own Christian stories. This is how the faith will best be communicated in the future to postmodern people whose question is not whether Christianity is true but whether it can work for them. This question is answered by ordinary Christians saying, 'Well it works for me, this is my story'. A diocesan-wide lay training programme to help people tell their stories, that is, to witness to the reality of their faith, is likely be the most direct and effective way in which trainers can help grow the church of the future.

Energizing lay people

Finding square pegs to fit into our predetermined round holes in order to keep the show on the road is not a good way to unlock the energy and enthusiasm of the square pegs. The older generations may be used to looking around the world and working out how they can fit into a predetermined pattern of life, but younger generations have been trained as sovereign consumers. Rather than adapting to the world around them, they tend to assume that the world around must fit them. Energy and enthusiasm are best generated by shaping the life of the Church around the gifting, calling and inclinations of the members of the church. Lay people should be helped to take stock of their gifting, calling and inclinations and then to work out how that should shape the life and ministry of their church. It is the church that should be reshaped around the people, not the people who should be reshaped around the church. In this way the people of the church are energized and motivated to share the life of the church with others.

It is, of course, possible to take this too far. The Christian life is about sacrifice and service as well as about fulfilling potential – churches will probably always need treasurers – but the principle still holds, that the future lies in developing people-shaped churches rather than church-shaped people.

Paying the laity

There is nothing wrong with the theology of the ministry of all believers and the Church as the whole people of God. This is more than just a fig leaf for withdrawing paid, priestly, ministry. It is always a better ecclesiology than the pastor and flock perception it is replacing, whether or not there is any human or financial resource problem that makes it more convenient, but maybe sometimes we have in our minds an outdated and increasingly unrealistic version of this timeless, biblical concept.

It is all too easy to imagine that the ministry of the whole people of God boils down to volunteers taking on all the jobs the paid person used to do. This may have been practical for a time in the 1970s and 1980s when there was more leisure around than there is today, but who are all these volunteers with spare time and energy who are going to joyfully lead and run the churches of the future? Most people today, both men and women, have their own paid work and many are struggling with long hours and stressful situations. Once upon a time, for example, schoolteachers were key leaders of church Sunday schools and youth groups. These days very few teachers have any spare time and energy to work with young people in the churches. What is more, post-modern people leading busy, mobile, varied lives are much less likely to agree to tie themselves down with major weekly church responsibilities. There may, on the other hand, be many active retired people with time on their hands, and their contribution to church life is often invaluable. If all the lay leaders are elderly, because they are the only ones with any time, then the church will develop in their image and also become elderly.

In a time-rich, money-poor society there may be little need to train lay people for paid work in the churches, but in our increasingly time-poor and money-rich society there may be both need and opportunity. So it is that the paid workforce of the Church has actually grown as the number of stipendiary clergy has decreased. Administrators, youth workers, secretaries, worship leaders, pastoral carers, evangelists, and many others have multiplied in response to the changing times. It may be that training provision for some of these ministries is better arranged at a national level than a diocesan or local one. The Church of England is now involved in the professional training of youth ministers in a number of its theological colleges. There is a need for further training streams for administrators, worship leaders and evangelists. Perhaps in the future the Church should be training some people to *run* the churches as administrators alongside other people to *lead* the churches as ordained clergy. The visionary leader and the organizational manager need different gifts and abilities that do not often come together in one person, yet both are needed. A new breed of worship leaders, trained in the full range of church music, skilled in getting the best out of amateur musicians, and gifted in leading congregations into heartfelt worship, are forming an essential specialist corps growing new-style young adult congregations. More are needed.

Thus paying, and training, a wide range of people for a wide range of professional ministries must be part of any strategy for providing the human resources needed to grow the Church of the future. Most of these posts will be set up and paid for by the local churches, though some may be set up by deaneries and dioceses. Where posts are paid for by parishes, dioceses have a responsibility to see that the income generated to pay for the posts is not taken by parish share demands. The whole point of a strategy is that all the various policy areas, instead of hampering each other, are coordinated together towards the common goal.

Helping people to network

It was the third time that teams from larger churches in the diocese had come together for day conferences on how to turn church decline around to growth. Each team summarized its church's growth initiatives over the past year on a large piece of paper and stuck it up on the wall. Most of the team then went on a walkabout to see what the other churches were up to, while two members stayed behind with their sheet of paper to answer the questions from other church teams doing the walkabout. The walkabout was a remarkably fruitful hour, everybody learning from everyone else's story and perspective.

The realities of how to grow churches are not invented by experts, they are discovered by the churches themselves. In this book I have attempted to compile and systematize things I have learnt from numerous churches up and down the country. It may be that churches are best energized to try new growth initiatives themselves not by the sage teaching of the expert, or even by the expert summary of the specialist, but by the encouraging stories from a range of similar churches. In this case, the job of helping churches to learn how to grow is not so much a training exercise as a networking one. The job of the trainer is to arrange ways in which church leaders can network with each other under the watchful eye of someone who can measure an individual story against a wider experience. Such networking can take place as a walkabout in a large venue one Saturday afternoon, it can be done through an Intranet chat room, or a newsletter, or a regular meeting listening to a new story or two each time. It could even be done at deanery chapters or synods opened up to other leaders. This sharing of ideas and stories is one of the main functions of the New Wine Network, and probably one of the main reasons why churches whose clergy belong to the network tend to grow. Isolated churches may have only their own experience and tradition to go on. Churches exposed to the wealth of life and growth in the contemporary Church are stimulated, enriched, energized. They are far more likely to pick up good practices they can apply to themselves. The answers to the growth of the Church are already out there – in order to turn the whole national Church around it may be enough simply to expose the churches to each other in networks of mutual learning and sharing.

We have now come to the end of Part 3, in which indications have been offered for harnessing the human resources of the Church for the growth of the Church. Part 4 concerns the harnessing of financial resources for the growth of the Church.

Part 4

Where finance fits in

The classic cycle of church decline and the cycle of growth with which we aim to replace it have three main components: the size and shape of the local church, the human resources to serve it, and the financial resources needed to sustain and grow it. Here in Part 4 we are considering the financial resources. The issue is clear and sharp. At the moment, financial restrictions appear to be contributing to the decline of the Church. Can we so turn things round that finance becomes an engine of growth? This will be achieved only by finding the finance both to maintain the inherited church and to give birth to the emerging styles of church that are likely to take us forward through the twenty-first century. It is a tall order. However, the contention of these chapters is that it is entirely possible to achieve these two things: to make abundant finance a means of empowering the growth of the Church, provided that we have the imagination and courage to make it happen.

Money and spiritual health

First, we look at why the way we handle our finances matters so deeply. There are far more verses in the Bible about money than there are about things like faith or prayer. It was the thing that Jesus spoke about most. He wanted us to know that the way we handle our money has an important effect on our relationship with God. If we treat our money in God's way, then we will enjoy a closer relationship with him. The Sermon on the Mount teaches that money and possessions are likely to be Jesus' major competitor for our time, attention and loyalty: 'You cannot serve both God and money' (Matthew 6.24).

What is true for Christians individually is surely also true for Christians as a group, for the Christian Church. The way we handle our money will help determine our spiritual health and impact. Most PCC members will attest that Jesus' main competitor for the Church's attention is the Church's own money. Around the country, PCC members wend their weary way back home late at night after an evening of treasurer's report, the gift day, the autumn fayre, debate about the fairness of the new parish share formula, worries about being able to pay the share, decisions about spending money on the buildings, missionary support, next year's budget, an argument about whether we should spend money on outreach to young people when the organ may need an overhaul, and so on. Prayer may have taken five minutes, the word 'Jesus' may hardly have been uttered all evening, but the PCC has spent three hours on money. In many churches, as with many Christian individuals, we may wonder where the sense of security comes from – is it from trusting in God for the future or from the investments secreted away for a rainy day?

Much of the material concerning the money side of the members-money-ministry cycle of decline and growth this book is discussing may appear to be dry and practical – to have no spiritual dimension to it. Nothing could be further from the truth. The Church of England's money – the way it comes in, the way it is managed, and the way it goes out – is at the heart of its spiritual life and future. For example, Chapter 13 argues that parish share formulae are a bad idea and should be scrapped. There are many practical reasons for this, but at rock bottom the problem is that Christian giving should not appear to be organized on the lines of a government tax and subsidy system. An appeal to give nurtures Christian generosity and kingdom values.

A quick guide to this section

Chapters 12, 13 and 14 take a look at our arrangements for sharing the costs of running dioceses between the churches. They suggest how parish share systems can be replaced with a financial regime that both generates extra revenue in a spiritually healthier way and provides a more level playing field for rational choices to be made between spending on inherited and fresh expressions.

Chapter 15 covers the problem of finding the right balance between parish funding and diocesan overheads and support – to what extent can we be more efficient or minimize spending on heritage, administration, support functions and non-core activities in order to maximize support for the turnaround and growth of the local church and the establishment of fresh expressions? Chapter 16 shows how dioceses can generate a substantial 'growth fund' to give financial empowerment to the new initiatives needed to grow the mission-shaped Church. Chapter 17 covers the role of the Church Commissioners in providing central funding for development as well as maintenance.

This will then complete the circle of the growth cycle – growing numbers in the churches enabling healthier finances and a bigger, more appropriate workforce, and a bigger, more appropriate workforce and healthier finances enabling growing numbers in the parishes.

Readers who would like more background information about church finances may find the Church Commissioners' section of the Church of England's web site a good place to start
(www.cofe.anglican.org/about/churchcommissioners/).

12

A time of transition

Where your treasure is, there your heart will be also. (Matthew 6.21 NRSV)

Some background

Adam Smith, the founding father of economics, in his seminal book *The Wealth of Nations*,[1] wrote at length on the role of the Church in the life of the nation. In it he made a distinction between two types of church. In one church the stipend or wages of the minister are paid for by the State or by some other central body or charity. The minister is not dependent on the size or generosity of his congregation for his living. In such a church, Adam Smith argues, the clergy will tend to develop other interests – they may be engaged in laudable social work, or become the country's leading expert on butterflies, or just hunt with the hounds, but they will spend little time and effort building up the size or spirituality of their congregations. In the other type of church, however, the minister *is* dependent on the size and generosity of his congregation for his income. This will, therefore, motivate him to grow and tend his flock in order to keep him in work. Smith, of course, then goes on to say that the Church of England is an example of the first type of church and the nonconformists of the second. He then contrasts the idleness of the eighteenth-century gentleman-vicar with the industry of the nonconformist minister. The centrally funded Church will wither, the locally funded Church will flourish.

Adam Smith was not, of course, wholly correct in his analysis. He reckoned without the Evangelical Revival and the Oxford Movement that were about to turn the tide of the Church of England and propel it to its high-water mark at the turn of the nineteenth and twentieth century. Economists have always had trouble grasping that people can be motivated in their work by things other than economic considerations. Smith was confounded by generations of clergy anxious to grow their churches not to secure their income but for the kingdom of heaven, the salvation of others and the glory of God.

The point is that in our own day the Church of England is undergoing a historically momentous transition from Adam Smith's first type – centrally-funded Church – to his second type – locally-funded Church.

The other problem with Adam Smith's preference for local funding of clergy is the loss of protection against the vagaries of their own congregations. Queen Anne's Bounty (which provided much of the Church Commissioners' historic assets) was created in 1704 because clergy:

> wholly depending for their necessary maintenance upon the good-will and liking of their hearers, have been and are thereby under temptation of too much complying and suiting their doctrines and teachings to the humours rather than the good of their hearers: which hath been a great occasion of faction and schism, and of contempt of the ministry . . .[2]

Many Anglican clergy have had cause to be grateful for this view down the years, though it must be a mystery to them why so many Baptist ministers, for instance, paid by their own congregations, still manage to live securely, preach the historic gospel and grow their churches. Nonetheless, what is proposed in this chapter still retains the diocese as a buffer between clergy and congregation when it comes to the payslip. There is still some way to go on the journey from the centrally to the locally funded denomination. First, though, we must take a look at one of the key contributory factors in the current move towards funding coming closer to home: the Church of England's pensions' bill.

Pensions, parishes and playing fields

There are a number of reasons why the Church of England's pensions bill has grown, the main ones being a compulsory maximum retirement age and a trend towards more clergy retiring at or before the normal age of 65. The provision of the improved retirement benefits itself has removed most of the financial incentive to go on working later. These were deliberate and laudable policy changes, but they have absorbed far more of the Commissioners' assets than expected and now also require current funding from the living Church. The reason for this is that, at the time, neither the Commissioners nor the Pensions Board undertook any proper financial planning when undertaking the liabilities. Also, clergy have been ordained later in life and so the number of pensioners has been increasing at the same time as the number of working clergy and church members has been going down. Moreover, the clergy have been living three to four years longer than the average for people of their age and so three to four years longer than the actuaries thought they would. This is further evidence to add to earlier research findings that regular churchgoers live longer than others. This first came to light in a survey of Seventh Day Adventists in California, Norway and the Netherlands, reported in the Adventist magazine 'Ministry' in September 1989, in which Adventists were shown to live an average five years longer than non-churchgoers.[3] Much of this is down to healthier lifestyles (clergy and churchgoers tend to smoke, drink and take drugs to a lesser extent than others). So being part of the community of the Christian Church and conforming to its norms of living is an excellent longevity indicator. While this is good news for Christians in general, is wonderful ammunition for evangelists seeking to prove that Christianity works, and is absolutely tremendous news for older clergy such as myself, it is definitely bad news for central subsidy to the working Church.

So it is that dioceses have turned to the parishes as the main source of their income out of which to pay for the parish clergy and their other costs. All parishes are asked to pay a significant proportion of their own costs, and some are also asked to subsidize those that cannot or will not pay their full share. Funding is becoming more local. However, it is not yet entirely local in Adam Smith's terms. In fact dioceses can go to considerable lengths to separate out the paying of parish share from the receiving of the clergy stipend. In part they are constrained by law – clergy with the freehold are entitled to remain in post and be paid whether or not there are any members left in their churches. In part it is still deemed right to protect the clergy from facing too close a correlation between their own flock and their own income. So it is that the money that parishes pay immediately gets lost in a general diocesan pot and cannot be traced through to their own vicar's stipend.

It could be argued that this is a brave attempt to combine the *disadvantages* of Adam Smith's two types of church. On the one hand the automatic stipend of type 1 may still keep at least a few clergy from the awkward necessity to earn their own living as well as just receive it. It can also protect church members from facing their own responsibilities, still relying on outsiders to pay their costs for them. On the other hand the uncertain cash delivery of type 2 has convulsed parishes and dioceses with job losses, pastoral reorganizations, fragile morale and shattered confidence. Moreover, the fact that central subsidy has been withdrawn from some expenditure heads (clergy stipends) but not others (support for bishops and cathedrals) means that spending patterns are newly distorted. For example, dioceses may review how many bishops and archdeacons they would like to have. However, the diocese gets its bishops 'free' from the Church Commissioners but has to pay for its own archdeacons. Which diocese will wish to reduce its number of bishops when it can save money by doing without an archdeacon, or a parish priest? Between 1993 and 2005, the Commissioners' spending on parish mission and ministry more than halved from £57m to £26m, while their spending on bishops rose from £11m to £20m. Efficient allocation of resources requires a level playing field on which the decision making, funding and accountability are the same for every type of expenditure.

The necessity of change

It is likely that the present transitional situation is unsustainable for reasons outlined throughout this chapter, but also because the larger churches are the ones afflicted with the greatest attendance losses (see Chapter 5). There are increasingly fewer and fewer funds available from them to subsidize weaker churches. There are fewer subsidy funds too from national and diocesan bodies. The move from a denomination of centrally funded, subsidized, churches to one of locally funded, self-supporting, churches is probably inevitable even if it has a long way to go yet.

Such a move is undoubtedly disruptive and painful, and can only be accomplished successfully through much personal financial sacrifice by all Anglicans, but for the mission of the Church it is more of an opportunity than a problem. Being forced to assume financial responsibility for their own church helps transform Anglicans from 'attenders' to 'members'. Involvement and commitment are likely to be stimulated through the taking of responsibility. Efficiency and clear priorities are promoted through the financial discipline of those making the decisions also being responsible for funding them. As Adam Smith pointed out, accountability makes for more effective employees. Clergy and laity alike have their attention drawn to their core tasks of evangelism, making disciples and growing the church, for otherwise first the vicar and then perhaps the church itself will cease to exist.

However, there is still a long and rocky road ahead of the Church of England before it can arrive at that happy place where its local costs are all met locally and its growing ministry is never under threat from financial cutbacks. At the heart of this transition is the system by which the diocese currently raises and redistributes its funds – the quota system, the parish share system, the common purse or common fund, or whatever other name it is known by in each diocese.

There are huge problems with most of the systems currently in use. I am taking the whole of the next chapter to outline these in detail.

13

The parish share

I thank my God . . . because of your sharing in the gospel . . . in the matter of giving and receiving . . . the gifts you sent . . . [are] a fragrant offering, a sacrifice acceptable and pleasing to God. (Philippians 1.4,5; 4.15,18 NRSV)

It is the contention of this chapter that most of the systems currently in use for dividing up the financial share between the churches are actually accelerating the spiral of decline and need to be abolished. Instead, a new way of doing business needs to be found, based on the principles of giving and receiving freely and joyfully entered into out of personal relationship and gospel commitment modelled by St Paul and the Philippians and summarized at the chapter heading.

Problems with existing allocation systems

1 Problems of perception

A parish share system is a subsidy arrangement. For most churches the share represents the amount of their costs that is not being subsidized by outsiders. Subsidies are cut, when they need to be, through increasing the share. For a minority of larger churches, it is true, their share is greater than the amount they cost their diocese, in which case the net outflow is indeed a church tax. Most churches, however, have come to believe that what is actually a benign subsidy system *to* them is in reality a wicked taxation system *upon* them. The way in which it is presented and managed, the 'subsidy' being hidden and unspoken, the 'clawback' of subsidy being out in the open and an endless topic of conversation, has been a fatal flaw in the whole arrangement. It drives a damaging wedge between parish and diocese. The diocese, the operator of the subsidy system, gets bitten by the mouths it is feeding because the owners of the mouths believe, wrongly, that the diocese is taking their food from them. 'Bringing in the share' has become the major point of contact between many parishes and their dioceses. Often, when a church hears from its diocese, it is in connection with a demand for money. Diocesan leaders often appear to assess local clergy and churches not on the basis of their effectiveness for the kingdom of heaven but on whether or not they are paying their parish share. Good clergy with part of their share unpaid get marked down and criticized; in return they become rebellious and disenchanted. Others, dismayed by parish share rises that seem out of control, look hard at the diocese's own central costs and demand reforms and economies. Their assessment of the scope for economies in diocesan support functions may well be accurate, but often the only way that appears to be open to them to force the issue is through conflict, which may happen in synods, boards and committees, or through personal contacts and relationships. It sours the whole life of the diocese.

2 Parish v parish

Many dioceses try to make a distinction between parishes that 'can't pay' and parishes that 'won't pay' the parish share. The idea is that 'can't pay' parishes should be treated with compassion, but 'won't pay' parishes should be named, shamed and otherwise leant on to pay up. Sometimes churches with assistant staff, who could be sacked in order to pay this year's share, are lumped into the same category as the shamelessly obstinate refusniks. Lists of non-payers may circulate around deaneries and dioceses without any background explanations. Parishes complaining about large increases in budgeted shares are told that the increase is only necessary because some parishes are letting the side down. 'Don't blame the diocese, blame those parishes that won't pay up.' Thus is born another set of potential resentments and conflicts – between parish and parish. Some resentments may be well merited, but they are nonetheless damaging to the unity of the Church.

Misunderstanding and conflict can also arise between the small and the large. Small churches may believe that a 'fair' system of share allocation is to equalize the bill per church member – a sort of poll tax system. They find themselves struggling to pay their share even though average giving per head is greater in small churches than big ones. They resent the fact that members of larger churches have it easy because they have to contribute much less per head than they have to. Some large churches, however, maintain that, in order to stay large, they have to employ assistant staff and so they have less left over for parish share. In fact, they themselves are paying their own way as a parish and do not see why they should be forced to feather-bed members of smaller, sleepier churches when they have their own missionaries and other much better causes to support. So it is that battle lines over quota reform can get drawn up along interest-group lines, each grouping supporting the mechanism that will minimize its own bills. Such attitudes and conflict are not, of course, universal; many churches rise to these challenges in a spirit of generosity, but tensions continue in other situations.

In some dioceses, another sort of parish has accumulated a vast mountain of notional debt over the years from repeated underpayment of the share allocated to them. There is no way these parishes can ever repay this debt and so the people stop trying. What point is there in aiming at a target so distant that it is clearly impossible? They might as well just allow the debt to keep increasing. They have become demoralized and demotivated. One diocese, seeking to apply the teachings of Scripture, offered such parishes a 'Jubilee' forgiveness of debts. Some saw this as statesmanlike commonsense, others were cross that the 'won't pay' brigade had got away with it. Further conflict ensued. The rather amusing final compromise was that the biblical Jubilee would go ahead this time 'but it will never, ever happen again'.

3 Self-protection

Some churches feel themselves to be driven to devise ways of protecting themselves from what they see as the 'ruinous taxation' their diocese is attempting to impose on them. Some set up their own independent trusts and other funds, separate from the PCC accounts, into which their people may give money 'tax free'. In other churches, the people will give generously to one-off gift days that are exempt from share calculations while keeping their regular giving to a minimum. Some churches deliberately understate their attendance figures on the annual form to the diocese. Others do not encourage people to join the electoral roll. So it is that systems that rely on attendance, membership or income figures supplied by the churches themselves can lead to churches effectively telling lies to their diocese, or at least to sharp practice and to accusations of cheating. It also means that churches that do not adopt the clever dodges of others are penalized financially for being so straightforward.

One church with a large student work in a diocese that relied on the October count to decide parish share was faced with a dilemma. Should it count during term time and then face an impossible diocesan bill it could pay only by sacking the assistant staff who attracted the students in the first place? Or should it be less than honest and count the congregation in September before the students arrived? It would be better not to put such a church in such a difficult ethical and practical dilemma.

---

4 Allocation mechanisms – some strange consequences

I was once vicar of a church in a diocese that increased parish quota in steps according to income groupings. As Christmas approached, the treasurer and I realized that the usual December giving would just tip us into the next 'quota category'. Every pound given over Christmas would result in the diocese's demanding an extra three pounds from us. We could not afford to have people give us money and had to beg them not to at each of the Christmas services. I have never had such funny looks from congregations during the church notices. Later on, I was vicar of a church that closed down its Sunday evening service and reopened much more successfully on a Tuesday evening. Attendance and membership went up, but the parish share went down because the diocesan formula counted only Sunday attendance. Church growth and a quota-dodge – smart move or what?!

These examples serve to illustrate the point that allocation formulae can have arbitrary and unintended consequences that serve to undermine and discredit them.

5 The Holy Grail of fairness

There are many different ways of allocating 'fair shares' between parishes. Most involve some sort of mathematical formula that includes elements of adult attendance or membership, recurring income, clergy posts, parish prosperity or 'potential' for giving based on congregational surveys or parochial census data. Some systems are based only on one variable, usually either adult attendance (a 'poll tax') or PCC income (an 'income tax'). Others are based on several factors through a more complex formula. Some are so complex that virtually no one understands them. In some dioceses the formula allocates share direct to parishes, in others it allocates to deaneries and the deaneries are invited to invent their own system of dividing up the deanery share between the various churches. Sometimes this is done by consensus, through a system of offers until the whole bill is covered, sometimes through the deanery's own formula, which may be on a quite different basis from that of the diocese. In yet other dioceses, the allocation is made on the basis of historical precedent and attempts at agreements.

It is, therefore, very hard to find two dioceses that use the same system. There is no general national advice or consultation process to indicate which system is to be preferred or which should be deemed to be the fairest according to agreed criteria. Put the same church in each of the 44 dioceses and it will have 44 very different parish shares to pay. Put it in any one of the many hundreds of deaneries that have their own systems and it will have many hundreds of very different parish shares to pay, and the differences between different systems are huge. Two churches looked out at each other across the big river that formed the diocesan boundary. The rather smaller congregation on one side of the river paid £160,000 in parish share and the rather bigger one the other side just £90,000, simply because it happened to be in a different diocese.

Yet most dioceses, if asked, explain that their main criterion for selecting their system is 'fairness'. They not only want to *be* fair in the way they spread the load, they also want their system to *be seen to be* fair so that it gains general acceptability, brings in the money from willing givers, and gives some respite to hard-pressed diocesan authorities. It is difficult, however, to see how every one of 44 different allocation systems can be the fairest possible. 'Fairness' is a universal criterion: it does not vary greatly across diocesan boundaries. If the system in Diocese A is indeed fair, then, presumably, the very different systems in Dioceses B and C are less fair, or unfair.

Moreover, ideas of what constitutes 'fairness' vary. For some it is fair to levy the same amount of money on each individual concerned. Thus a church with 200 people pays 10 times as much as a church with 20. Mrs Thatcher thought a poll tax was fair, but not many people agreed with her. For some, it is fair to take the same proportion of a church's income, no matter how generously the people are giving – so generous givers in Church A have to pay twice as much as stingy givers in Church B. For others, fairness involves making considerable allowance for variable prosperity. It is fair that well-off people in suburban Church A pay a lot more than the unemployed in inner-city Church B. Complicated formulae are devised to measure deprivation and prosperity using 'Oxlip Scores' from the census data. In some dioceses allowance is given only to UPA parishes, which means that those just above UPA status are left doubting the system's fairness to them. In others there is a sliding scale or a range of prosperity bands, but this may bear little relation-ship to the prosperity of the people who actually attend the church as opposed to those who live in the parish. Systems that rely on the honesty of church members answering questions about their own personal incomes may be fairer but everyone is then at the mercy of a complicated survey that needs to be repeated regularly. For others, 'fairness' suggests that each parish should pay its own way and not be coerced into subsidizing others with whom it may have little in common.

So the search for the Holy Grail of 'fairness' appears doomed. We cannot even agree on the criteria for 'fairness', and the consequence of the multiplicity of systems is that the actual amounts asked of parishes are nothing more than a postcode lottery.

6 Allocation methods – temporary at best

In most dioceses, every few years the level of dissatisfaction with the existing allocation mechanism from those who feel themselves to be its victims grows to such an extent that a review is undertaken. In truth, much of the dissatisfaction is likely to be misplaced anger or misdirected anxiety. The real problem may be the overall total rather than the way it is divided up. The total required is simply beyond the combined powers of all the parishes to produce without damage being done to parish life. However, the search is on for a new system that will lessen the pain.

Such a review can take months or years to conduct and it consumes a large amount of time, energy, heartache, and diocesan money. It becomes the most divisive issue, and perhaps the dominant issue, on the agenda of the Bishop's Council or the Diocesan Synod. The *Titanic* may be sinking but the people are too preoccupied about the fairness of their ticket prices to notice. The DBF demands a system that brings in the money, the fairness of the whole thing being a near irrelevance as far as it is concerned, so a new dimension of conflict threatens. Eventually, a new system is introduced. If the review has done its work, it will by definition make considerable differences to the actual amounts of money asked of individual parishes. Otherwise it was largely a waste of time. The result is that some parishes are quietly relieved whilst there are howls of indignation from others. Parishes facing large increases under the new 'fairer' system protest at the injustice and claim they cannot possibly pay.

So there is a whole new set of winners and losers from the new system. The shock of moving from one category to the other brings its own costs, however, as the new losers have to make adjustments to their other expenditure items and refocus their parish life on raising money. PCCs are convulsed, their agendas hijacked by the latest shock from the diocese, and the seeds of the next review of quota fairness have been sown.

The search for the Holy Grail of fairness and universal acceptance has failed again.

7 The cost of share systems

The periodic upheaval of reviews comes on top of the continuous running and policing of parish share systems. These activities normally absorb a great deal of time and energy. To run and monitor the collection of share is now a major task of diocesan financial officers. Highly qualified and competent people are required, who do not come cheap. One diocese was facing a £500,000 budget deficit and tasked its finance department to find some answers. The salary and office costs of the finance department? About £500,000 a year!

Senior clergy such as bishops, archdeacons and area deans can also spend a large part of their time trying to bring the quota in. One diocese, with declining numbers of clergy and people, wondered whether it needed to replace one of its archdeacons when he retired. The DBF, however, insisted a replacement be appointed because the archdeacons were the people who brought home the parish share – the DBF's enforcement officers. Some archdeacons appear to have graduated from drains inspectors to tax inspectors.

So central to the life of some dioceses has become the fight for their own financial survival that they are in danger of forgetting the real reason for their existence. When the longest and most important item on agendas is the balancing of the books and the bringing in of the parish share, it could be argued that a diocese has lost the plot. Parishes under intense pressure from archdeacons and others to pay up their share can start to do the same. Kingdom goals take a back seat to income targets. Parishes begin to behave as though their central task is to pay the share rather than share the gospel.

The problem of appropriate division of financial responsibility between parishes is, in principle, the same throughout the Church of England. It would be difficult and debilitating enough to have one process for the whole country, but to have 44 groups of people, all running in parallel, going their own way with little reference to the others, repeating each other's mistakes and spending huge amounts of their own energy enforcing and changing their systems, must look to an outsider like something approaching madness.

8 Large churches and small churches

In recent years there has arisen through the parish share system a new cross-subsidy from a minority of large churches to the majority of smaller ones. This works through larger churches receiving share bills in excess of the amount they cost the diocese plus a proportion of shared costs.

In general terms cross-subsidy systems can be defended on the grounds of fairness or for giving short-term transitional support to units that may become self-sufficient. Universally, however, in the long term, cross-subsidy systems always lead to inefficiency.

Consider the case of a chain of shops. Some branches have a brisk trade and make a profit. Others have slack trade and make a loss. The company decides to keep all the branches open and to use the profits from the better stores to pay the salaries of the staff in the weaker stores. This takes away the surplus the profitable stores need to invest in the future. Their expansion plans, and their new lines, are put on hold. They cannot employ their own extra staff and so queues lengthen and customers become dissatisfied. Success is undermined and profits fall as competitors forge ahead. The loss-making branches, on the other hand, are being feather-bedded – protected from the consequences of their own situation. They learn to be complacent, and have little incentive to be entrepreneurial and increase sales. They begin to treat their situation as inevitable, and the cross-subsidy from the profitable branches as their human right.
Such a chain of shops is not long for this world.

The Church, of course, is not a chain of shops and there is more to church finances than market economics (the widow's mite is a precious commodity in spiritual terms). Yet the problem of sending larger churches into decline and so losing them as subsidy providers for the small still remains if large churches are faced with parish shares bills that take away all the surplus they have for parish development. Assistant staff, paid for by the parish itself, can no longer be afforded and have to be dispensed with. Outreach that costs money is put on hold. Church members giving sacrificially see their own church impoverished and going backwards, and lose heart. On the other hand, small, sleepy, declining churches may be protected from the full consequences of their situation. Under most share formulae, when a church loses attendance or income, its share goes down to compensate. The church simply becomes a greater financial burden on the already overstretched larger churches.

It is no coincidence that in recent years in the Church of England the larger churches have been shrinking quite fast, while medium-sized churches have held their own and tiny ones have actually grown on average. This is not only because the financial surplus is being removed from the large churches and given to the small ones, but it is partly because of it. The result is inevitable – the cross-subsidy system is unsustainable because it erodes the size and capacity of the larger churches – it is helping to kill the geese that lay the golden eggs.

9 Moves towards independence

One response to this situation, increasingly adopted by the more assertive and less diocesan-minded large churches, is for them to cap their own contributions. Instead of waiting to hear from the diocese how much they are going to pay next year, they make their own decision and inform the diocese of it; some have capped their contributions to match their own costs; others include a more modest element of cross-subsidy to smaller churches; one or two have withdrawn from the system completely and are paying their own staff. If a financial grievance is compounding a theological difference with a diocese, then some parishes may be tempted into even further distancing.

So it is that parish share systems that are progressive, in the sense that the bigger the church or the more generous the people the more is asked, also have the potential to encourage some key churches into independence. One day, this might happen not only in individual cases, but a whole stream or grouping could pull out of the system. Apart from the other consequences of such moves, they might also cause the whole financial structure of dioceses to come tumbling down.

Very large churches that do remain within the system and are major net contributors to the diocesan budget are likely to discover that they have some newfound influence. When the budget stands on a knife-edge, then a threat to withdraw subsidy by two or three large churches has to be taken seriously. Diocesan leaders can begin to believe they have some over-mighty subjects who have an effective veto on major policy changes. From the perspective of the large donor church, it is simple good stewardship to be concerned about how its money is spent. From the perspective of the bishop, the same concern looks like interference or blackmail.

10 Taxing church growth

There is a further inefficiency problem with parish share formulae that is every bit as serious as the 'cross-subsidy, large church decline and rebellion' problem outlined above. An attendance, membership or income-based system taxes growth. An attendance system asks as much of the newcomer who has not yet learnt sacrificial Christian giving as it does of the experienced church member. A church attracts new people and doubles in size. Its income goes up by 30 per cent but its parish share by 100 per cent. The life and ministry of the church will be badly dented and it may be unable to pay its full share. Many diocesan leaders do not look at parish attendance returns, only at the parish share arrears. So the vicar of the growing church may well get branded as disloyal and unsuitable for preferment. Not only, therefore, does the parish share system lead an effective attack by the diocese on the growth of the local church, it also makes it hard for effective and entrepreneurial leaders in mission to attain senior positions.

Similar problems are encountered by churches that increase their giving. The church decides to spend its surplus on a worthwhile 'expansion' project such as employing a youth minister. The trouble is that next year the diocese increases the share demand by so much in response to the increased giving that the parish can no longer afford its youth minister. If another great effort is made to increase the giving to cover both the youth minister *and* the share, then the reward will be an even greater share in the following year.

The primary role of the diocese in relation to the growth of its churches should be to provide them with an environment in which they can grow and flourish. All too often, however, dioceses provide an environment that, in the name of fairness, attacks growth and subsidizes sloth.

11 Fresh expressions not catered for

Share formulae are designed to cover the inherited mode of church. They assume that people come to clearly defined worship events in designated church buildings on Sundays and pay money into PCC accounts. Newer expressions of church, where the people meet in small groups or on days other than Sundays, do not produce the statistic called 'usual Sunday attendance' that many dioceses use as the basis of their share calculation. Others do not have a geographical parish and so there is no 'parish population', 'potential' or 'prosperity band' measure for them. Others may have such non-standard financial arrangements that it is not possible to find an appropriate 'income' figure for them.

As the new expressions of church life gain momentum, they will move from being occasional anomalies that the system cannot cope with, to being whole categories of churches the system cannot cope with. Unless they are to be exempt from paying share, the traditional churches continuing to pay for them, the wide range of fresh expressions has to be brought into the system, but it is hard to see any sort of mathematical assessment formula catering for every situation. Something more radical will be needed to encompass and facilitate the evolving church scene.

12 Failing to balance the books

It is possible to argue that neither considerations of fairness nor of efficiency should be uppermost when judging the performance of a parish share system. What matters most urgently is to get the common fund payments in. The wages and bills have to be paid month by month. A diocese in which the system produces a very high proportion of what is asked can therefore feel that it is being successful. It may be that the collateral damage caused to larger churches, and the financial penalties to growing churches are too high a price to pay for this. Yet, in many dioceses, the system is not bringing in all the money required anyway. It is true that the increase in parish share payments over recent years has been very substantial, which is a cause for rejoicing, but many dioceses are still facing deficit budgets and having to make staffing cuts. One diocese currently has a plan to reduce its stipendiary parochial clergy by 20 per cent over the next few years, another by 33 per cent for purely financial reasons. Another has had to shed 30 posts as quickly as possible through not filling vacancies in order to balance the books because share demands were not being met.

It is not only that parish share systems are failing to pay for the existing cost base and parochial ministry of many dioceses, it is even more that they are not providing the Church with the surplus it needs to invest in fresh expressions, church planting, new sorts of posts, and all the other responses needed to create a mission-shaped Church fit for the twenty-first century. In most dioceses, the parish share system is not even getting close to providing the crucial finance for growing the new alongside sustaining the old.

A new way of doing business

In conclusion, the whole chaos of quota, parish share, or common fund systems is simply not serving the Church well.

1. It is inconceivable that every diocese, with its own unique system changing every few years, has currently found the best possible one, or even a good one.
2. Systems risk provoking conflict and dishonesty. They can lead to more serious division.
3. They do not provide a secure and stable framework in which churches can do long-term planning.
4. They fail to provide the fairness their architects desire.
5. They absorb the best energy, time and expertise of diocesan leaders and officials. They divert people at every level from concentrating on the real ministry and mission of Christian churches.
6. They asset-strip the large churches and tax away the growth of growing churches. They encourage the declining and sleepy in their ways.
7. They encourage false judgements to be made of clergy and endanger the future provision of dynamic senior leadership.
8. They cannot cater for fresh expressions of church.
9. They fail even to maintain the current levels of parochial staffing, let alone to produce the resources for growing the new sorts of expression without which the Church may wither away.

It is time for new financial arrangements that will encourage rather than prevent the growth of the Church. In short, it is time to do away with quotas, share mechanisms, common fund contributions and the rest of the sorry mess. There has to be – and there is – a better way.

14

A better way

Strive first for the kingdom of God and his righteousness, and all these things will be given to you as well. (Matthew 6.33 NRSV)

1 Foundational principles

It is frequently argued in defence of parish share systems that it is of the essence of being Anglican that we maintain a presence and ministry in every area. The alternative to a system of fair shares is characterized as simply letting each church pay for itself if it can, and allowing the others to go to the wall. Other denominations have abandoned the inner cities and the countryside, but the Church of England has stayed and must continue to stay. There has to be a system of giving and receiving by which this presence is financed. Coupled with this is the fear of 'going congregationalist'. Churches should be kept to their responsibilities to each other, to the wider denomination and to the nation. This inevitably involves a system whereby funds are channelled into areas of deprivation that can never produce self-financing church communities.

There are three vital principles being advocated here that should not be abandoned:

1. The strong should help the weak
2. The Church of England should keep a presence in every community
3. Denominational bonds should be maintained and strengthened.

It should not be imagined, however, that parish share arrangements are securing these three principles today. We are withdrawing paid ministry rather fast from many rural and inner urban areas. This process is set to continue as the scope for cross-subsidy reduces, central funds continue to dry up and stipendiary clergy numbers diminish. We actually need a better way of keeping our principles.

It is also important to be clear about the basis of the current systems whereby the strong and wealthy help the weak and poor. The basis is not a Christian or biblical system of giving freely entered into but rather a socialist model of enforced income redistribution. In such a system the 'government' (in this case the diocese) fixes a system with rates of subsidy and taxation designed on ability to pay or other fairness criteria. Money collected in, after deducting the central authority's own rather substantial costs, is then redistributed according to need. Such a process is one with which many Christians are comfortable, and it is easy to argue that it is itself based on Christian principles. Paul speaks in 2 Corinthians 8.12-15 about generosity leading to financial equality. Even here, though, Paul speaks of giving rather than coercion. Also, many of the criticisms levelled at parish share systems above are parallel to those levelled at public sector tax and spend systems of inequality reduction. There are good reasons why governments have become more wary of utopian systems in this area of public life and why they rely more on markets to produce the growth cycle of rising production, incomes, taxation and social welfare provision.

There is a third way available, however, that is neither socialist nor free market. The church has an option not normally available to governments. This is to devise arrangements to facilitate Christian giving and receiving freely entered into out of personal relationships. The New Testament churches did not have a quota system, levying demands on each local church on the basis of some formula. They gave to each other out of generosity as need arose. Members of the first church gave so that the widows could be cared for. Paul organized a collection for the poverty-stricken Jerusalem Church. The Church at Philippi collected money and sent it to Paul for his church planting work. Churches today have gift days for good causes, support mission agencies, and develop their own networks of giving and receiving.

One lesson learnt by many churches is that a gift day for a specific development or missionary project will raise perhaps two to three times as much money as one directed at general giving to a mission agency. A giving project that captures people's imagination and involvement is likely to succeed. This is both because people are motivated when they see the specific results of their own giving ('we paid for the incubators at the mission hospital') and because they give more generously when they have some control over the end use of their giving ('we gave to the mission agency but we don't know what they did with our money').

The same truth applies to the local church's giving to the rest of the diocese. Churches with a parish share greater than their own costs respond badly to their lack of knowledge of where their extra share has gone. To some it has 'disappeared down the black hole of the diocese'. People who would give generously to support the work of a specific local church down the road become grudging givers to a diocese that demands much of them but offers no accountability in return.

Moreover, there is a universal human truth when it comes to money that 'he who pays the piper *will* call the tune'. If the large churches in a diocese are now paying the piper then they will increasingly ask to call some of the tune as the price of their support. It is far better to go with the grain of this than to fight a rearguard action against it. Similarly, as the main sources of subsidy funding for parish ministry are drying up, it is important to face all churches with their true costs as part of the business of helping more of them to pay their own way.

We have now established some more principles on which to base financial arrangements. These arrangements should:

4. rely on Christian generosity out of freedom and personal relationship;
5. provoke generosity through providing specific objectives that capture the imagination of the original givers;
6. provoke generosity through granting the original givers a greater say in the destination of their giving;
7. provoke responsibility by facing every church with the task of meeting its own costs;
8. enable the strong to help the weak directly out of Christian responsibility and love rather than indirectly through 'quota coercion'.

2 Models from outside the Church of England

Before I move on to propose a new system for financing the work of the Church, here to pave the way are two examples from other parts of the Anglican Communion that show that even the concept of central funding itself is not a universal nor an inevitable feature of Anglicanism.

The Diocese of Bendigo in New South Wales has only one employee, who is half-time diocesan bishop and half-time diocesan secretary. Around 50 parishes employ a vicar each. This is a low-cost operation and the bishop has no support staff. By the same token, he has no financial responsibilities, no boards and committees, and surprisingly little administration. He actually has quite a lot of time to relate to individual parishes and to give leadership to his diocese.

The Diocese of Down and Dromore in Northern Ireland includes part of Belfast and a large surrounding area. There is no central funding for parishes in relation to their day-to-day running and each is required to be self-sufficient financially. Each parish owns its parsonage house and pays its own clergy directly. The diocese has a small central staff and the bishop has few financial responsibilities, which leaves him free to concentrate on the core tasks of being a bishop without a lot of administrative and financial diversions. The only contribution the parishes make is a modest assessment, which is divided between the administration and the development of the diocese. There is also a central church assessment for the episcopacy and for the Church of Ireland Priorities Fund, to which each cure contributes. This means that there is no need for a large diocesan finance team or DBF. The diocesan finances are dealt with by a subcommittee of the diocesan council, and by an accounts office with an accountant and small staff, shared with the adjoining Diocese of Connor, which operates a similar model. A glebes committee ensures that parsonages are adequate and well maintained by the local parish, and it would not be an exaggeration to say that most are in excellent condition. There is no need, therefore, for an archdeacon to have the role of bringing in the parish share or looking after the houses, and the diocese, with 79 benefices, functions with two part-time archdeacons, both of whom are rectors of large parishes. The diocese itself is, therefore, in Anglican terms, a low-cost operation.

Even though a number of the parishes are in deprived areas in and around east Belfast, each one is essentially expected to fund its own ministry. Where this is not possible, the diocese will review the viability of the parish and in some cases creates a 'bishop's curacy' where there had been an incumbency. On occasion some diocesan help may be given to a struggling parish where this has happened, to help it to get back on its feet again, but always for a limited time and on a reducing basis. People in the parishes of Down and Dromore know that their giving is needed to support directly the work and ministry of their local church. Spending is largely controlled within the parish, both for the needs of the local church and also for overseas mission and local charitable needs, where the giving is actually very generous. There is no major decline in church attendance, and growth is indicated in many parts of the diocese. Where needed parishes are able to help each other out financially. The numbers of clergy have been sustained and, indeed, the parishes of the diocese can pay for more than are available. There appears to be no great concern that the diocese has gone 'congregationalist'. The Bishop is involved with and has a veto over all appointments, and clergy enjoy the same security of tenure as in England. There are some central ministry posts, largely paid from the development

fund of the diocese, where these are required for support and development; and the commitment to ministry in deprived situations has been
sustained.

Such systems where the diocese is a modest affair and the parishes have
greater freedom and responsibility therefore do appear to work well enough
even in Anglican churches within the United Kingdom. The system is the
church equivalent of a low-tax 'small' government allowing local enterprise
to keep its own resources for local mission and ministry. The result is greater
efficiency and growth, though there may still be dangers to the weak and
vulnerable.

It is hard to see how an English diocese could deconstruct itself successfully
in order to change to such a system. Legal and political problems would
doubtless make the transition lengthy, messy and problematic even if a
majority in a diocese were in favour of the change. However, if there were
a will a way would be found, and there may be lessons to learn from Down
and Dromore that could be applied in England without deconstructing
dioceses. In any case, most parishes in most dioceses will have to be more or
less self-sufficient financially in the future because potential subsidy and
cross-subsidy sources are drying up.

So, is it possible to find an arrangement that reflects this reality, follows both
sets of principles outlined in part 1 of this chapter, efficiently harnesses the
advantages of local responsibility and freedom, and yet is sufficiently close to
present arrangements to enable a realistic transition to take place?

What follows is a description of such a system, the equivalent to a 'mixed
economy' in which all are responsible for their own expenditure needs, but
targeted state help is available to those who need their income boosting in
order to pay the bills.

3 Self-funding supported by Christian giving

Self-funding

1 Churches pay costs of their own ministers

Under a self-funding system, the diocese bills every church or group of
churches that share a stipendiary minister for the whole cost of the minister:
stipend, pension, national insurance and housing. This is technically known
as the 'marginal cost' of the parish to the diocese – the amount of spending
the diocese would save if the stipendiary post were abolished.

173

2 Fee income stays with the local church

At present most parishes make a return payment to the diocese of the minister's fee income. This adds an unnecessary complication and transaction cost. The diocese chases and receives this money, so reducing parish incomes, which it then needs to subsidize with the fees collected. Clergy who spend a lot of time doing weddings and funerals have less time to spend on leading their churches. It is right that the local church, rather than the diocese, receives the fee income to help them employ others to compensate. It also enables churches to move a little closer to the goal of self-sufficiency. Alternatively, if parishes still remit fees to the diocese, then the fee income should be netted off the self-funding bill.

3 Diocesan costs are shared by local churches

The diocese also has a range of other costs not attached to the parish clergy: the diocesan office, clergy training, legal fees, contributions to national costs, and so on. Probably a diocese would want to include under this heading part or all of the cost of curates in their first three or four years while they are still training. Under the system these costs are added together and divided by the number of parochial clergy. The resultant amount is then added to the marginal costs to produce an average cost for each parish.

4 The total bill

This average cost, including both the direct costs of the clergy and a share of diocesan and national support costs, is the bill presented to the parish each year. If desired, this bill could be modified by a 'prosperity weighting' that increases the bill for parishes in wealthier areas and reduces it for those in poorer areas. When every parish is able to fund itself plus a share of joint costs, then local self-funding has truly arrived. However, it is likely that every parish will *not* be able to pay its own costs out of its own internally generated income, and neither would we wish it to do so, because of our desire to see mutual support from the strong to the weak.

5 What to do with surplus funds

But, if each parish *were* to become self-funding, then the diocese will have a surplus of income over expenditure, for it has certain other income sources as well as the parishes. These include property and investment income and any funds it receives from the Church Commissioners. If a part or the whole of these funds are not required to make up for parish shortfalls, then they can be invested by the diocese in an opportunity budget for missionary activity – fresh expressions, planting, evangelism and other strategies for the future growth of the mission-shaped twenty-first century Church. The opportunity money could be offered in grants to parishes or spent directly by the diocese on its own projects.

6 Show the costs and the giving in the church accounts

The total costs – divided up between parish costs and central diocesan overheads – should appear on each church's accounts, together with the corresponding payments. Where churches pay the diocese or other churches over and above their own costs, by whatever route, the extra amount should be recorded in the accounts as part of their 'Christian giving'.

7 Balancing the books in the long term

Parishes that fail to fund their whole costs would be offered consultancy help to enable them to improve their performance. Those that failed to cover even their marginal costs, however, would be warned that their unpaid bills will be settled when the minister leaves and the parsonage house is available for sale. The minister will not be replaced and the parish will be subject to pastoral reorganization as soon as possible. The selling of parsonage houses to pay back unpaid bills should ensure that, in the long run, the diocese does indeed receive its full marginal costs from the parishes. Those that covered their marginal costs but made only a partial contribution to shared costs would be allowed a replacement minister and offered further assistance to bridge the gap. The diocese would no longer try to balance its books with centrally planned cuts in posts or with extended vacancies. The system itself should ensure balanced books.

8 The deanery option

The diocese need not bill each church independently for its costs but could simply bill each deanery for the cost of its posts and allow the deanery to divide this up by a system of bids and offers, including direct gifts between parishes. Such a system would encourage Christian giving locally within any deanery that had churches able to contribute more than their assessed costs.

9 Sources of help

As most parishes today do not pay enough parish share to cover their marginal costs, let alone their average costs, it is reasonable to suppose that, left to their own devices, most parishes will still be unable to pay under the new system without outside help. However, it is likely that the simple fact of making parishes responsible for meeting all their own costs will encourage a more forthcoming attitude. Further encouragement will come from the fee income. On top of this, outside help *will* be forthcoming, from three main sources that are outlined below under 'Christian giving'

Christian giving

Source 1: The diocesan fund

The diocesan authorities would place their 'other' income into a separate account given over to a grant-making group. The members would come from the diocesan board of finance, diocesan leaders and officials. Every parish would be entitled to apply for funding to help them pay their costs. Successful applicants would receive a cheque into their PCC account and have to show that the money is subsequently and rapidly sent to the diocese's main account out of which the diocese's own bills are paid. The best arrangement may be a pair of monthly direct debits. In this way each parish knows it is in receipt of subsidy income and is bearing the full responsibility for its own costs. The criteria on which judgements would be made would include the need to sustain parishes in areas of social deprivation. It is also likely they would look to support churches not well enough connected with others to make it easy to find support through routes two and three. It would also be possible to set criteria such as money being available only to parishes that enclose a credible mission action plan with their application form. In such ways money would be channelled into churches that have the best chance of using it positively. A voucher system could be used instead of real money.

Source 2: The donations fund

The diocese would set up a second grant-making trust, but one that this time invites donation-income from the parishes, and even individuals. This will come in the form of Christian giving freely decided upon out of prayerful generosity by parishes with surplus income. This is likely to include many of the large churches that, under the new system, have had their bills reduced by the diocese down to the level of their own costs. The trustees of this fund will be representatives of the donor parishes themselves. They too will issue an application form to any parishes requesting help and decide their own criteria for the making of grants. In this way the original givers of the money will have some responsibility for and power over the way in which it is spent. Parishes would be entitled to apply to both funds at the same time so there would need to be coordination to ensure some churches did not receive too much subsidy overall.

If it is felt that such a body would not be stable enough because the identity of donor churches would vary from year to year, then the fund could be merged with the diocesan one and donor parish representatives appointed to it. However, diocesan leaders may not wish their large donor churches to have automatic representation on a body distributing general diocesan money.

Source 3: Parish to parish

Individual parishes would be encouraged to make their own links with each other for the giving and receiving of money. The most important would probably be within the deanery. This in effect happens in some dioceses already where the parish share is simply allocated to deaneries and the churches in a deanery make offers towards the deanery share until it is all taken up. In others it happens in team churches where parish share is billed to the team as a whole. Some links, however, would be within the various streams and groupings of the Church of England. Like-minded parishes would be invited to help one another out. Other links would come from the personal contacts and friendships of the clergy or lay leaders. None of these links needs to be restricted to within the diocese in question. These could open up new routes for the funding of ministry in poorer dioceses by the giving of church members in richer dioceses. In this way mutual support can be extended across diocesan boundaries. This is a common practice today in the Baptist Union, where a thriving church in one area may be helping support the minister of a small inner city church in another. One large Anglican church in London is currently donating over £100,000 to another Anglican church in Liverpool through a link grown out of personal contact. If the request for money had instead come from the Diocese of Liverpool for its central pot to spread between parishes in a way that was not transparent it is unlikely that any money at all would have found its way up the M6.

It has not been possible so far to find a direct system of increasing 'mutual support' from richer to less well resourced dioceses. A 'self-funding by Christian giving' system is tailor made for allowing and encouraging such direct transfers to take place either from dioceses or individual parishes. The existing 'taxation' models have no point of entry for gifts from outside the diocese in question – a system of giving and grants puts that right.

If a church cannot find support from the diocese, or from other churches either individually or through the grant-making body, or from outside the diocese, then it may not be able to meet its costs. However, there may well be a reason why others have not felt it a worthwhile cause to support. The market will have done its job of identifying those stipendiary posts the future of which should be called into question.

Here are some further applications of this approach.

A system for a mixed economy Church

Under the parish share system in most dioceses, struggling to fund existing posts and maybe looking at cutting posts, all the dioceses' money is spent on keeping going for as long as possible as much as possible of the inherited church. Little money is being spent on developing new ways of being church or on funding new mission posts for the new post-Christendom world. Under the new system, it would be best if the two grant-making bodies were able by their terms of reference and criteria to make grants for both inherited and emerging church. In this way a level playing field is formed and rational decisions can be taken locally on the right balance of spending between the two. However, a good real-world alternative, at least in the short term, might be to ring-fence some money for fresh expressions, because the lobby for new things is always vulnerable to the lobby for keeping something pre-existing going whether or not it has had its day.

It might be thought that a system that empowers parishes with some control or influence over the direction of their giving would reduce the power and discretion of diocesan leaders. In fact, the opposite is the case. Under this new system, diocesan leaders have a lot of new power through their control of the diocesan fund. They have power to choose the balance between inherited church and fresh expressions, a new stick and carrot to wake up and lead forward the sleepy parishes, and the power that comes from the release of extra money into the system as the generosity of parishioners responds to the healthier giving environment.

Responding to core principles

This system of self-funding and Christian giving abides by all the principles identified above. The strong are enabled to help the weak in a much more direct and visible way than under parish share systems. The primary duty of the trustees of the diocesan fund, though, would be to ensure the Church kept a presence in every area. As the new system is likely to encourage greater generosity from parishes than the existing system, it will be more possible to stay in every place. Denominational bonds are maintained and strengthened through new networks of direct financial assistance as well as through the central hub of the diocese as at present. The system relies on the generosity of Christian giving. It provokes confidence by being easy to understand and explain, unlike the more complicated of the existing systems. It provokes generosity through giving people specific objectives, personal relationships and the ability to measure what their own giving has achieved. It also provokes generosity by allowing the givers a say in how their money is spent – it goes with the grain of allowing those who pay the piper a modest role in calling the tune. It provokes responsibility by facing every church with the task of meeting all its own costs. It also provides a framework in which the strong can help the weak not through an imposed 'tax and subsidy' system but out of Christian love.

Testing the waters

Finally, it is still true, of course, that moving to this new system of relying on the generosity of Christian giving freely entered into through personal relationships carries with it a clear risk. What happens if the PCCs of the large donor churches take the opportunity to spend their money on themselves or on other good causes? It would therefore be prudent to first test the theory of the new system that extra Christian generosity is presently dormant and waiting to be unlocked. This can be done in several ways. For example, PCCs of some large churches can be asked to debate their new giving policy if the new system were to be brought in. They would then give some indication to the diocesan leaders of how they would play things under the new regime. Slightly further down the line, the donations fund could be set up while the existing parish share system continues. Churches would be allowed to switch parish share paid over and above their own average costs into the new fund provided that the total was at least, say, 5 per cent greater than the reduction in parish share paid. The greater the switch and increase the more confident the diocese would be that the new system would yield more money.

If such a system were proven to work well in one or a few dioceses, then it would be beneficial if every diocese switched to it. Gone would be the days of every diocese going through the same heartaches and convulsions in parallel, each reinventing the same sets of wheels and then seeing them start to fall off. It would become a national system fit for the stable long term. A financial environment would have been put in place that forwarded the transition from national to local funding, found new routes for mutual support, protected the development of church life from taxation, maximized the stipendiary labour force, and empowered the Church to adapt and grow.

A self-funding system in practice

A few of the newer parish share systems being adopted by dioceses now incorporate many of the principles advocated in this chapter. One such is that being adopted by the Diocese of Chester from 2006. Each parish is billed for its costs calculated in relation to its stipendiary posts as outlined above. However, a relative prosperity factor is applied to the wealthiest and poorest 25 per cent of parishes, using employment category data from the 2001 census. This increases the bill to the wealthier parishes by an average of 15 per cent and reduces it to the poorer ones by the same percentage. Churches unable to meet their bill are first of all asked to find help from within their own deanery. If the deanery is unable fully to fund the shortfall, then the parish can apply to the Diocesan Development Fund. Income to this fund comes from 'other' diocesan income (fees, investments, etc.) plus voluntary donations from wealthier churches and individuals. Parishes will receive grants from the fund only if they can show they have a credible mission plan of their own.

The diocese will, therefore, no longer have to seek information from parishes for some formula; shares do not go up when income or attendance rises; parishes can self-assess their capacity to pay and then seek funding for the shortfall (so that the percentage of share actually paid should rise); it is a subsidy system rather than a pseudo-taxation one; fresh expressions are incorporated as soon as there is any stipendiary involvement in them; there is scope for specific Christian giving and generosity; and the diocese acquires a lever of influence to help sleepier parishes develop mission plans of their own. In short, it is a system fit for growing churches in the twenty-first century.

15

Controlling the costs

What did you go out into the wilderness to look at? Someone dressed in soft robes? Look, those who wear soft robes are in royal palaces. What then did you go out to see? A prophet? Yes, I tell you, and more than a prophet. (Matthew 11.7-9 NRSV)

The dioceses' own costs – where do they fit in?

Many dioceses have made strenuous efforts to control or reduce their 'other' costs in recent years, recognizing that these ought at least to go down in line with parochial spending. Money spent on central and support costs is money that cannot be spent on parish ministry or fresh expressions of church. So in this chapter we are considering whether controlling or trimming other costs can be a significant factor in an overall growth strategy, both to help retain as many parochial posts as possible and to provide a surplus for investing in new forms of church.

This issue is not only to do with money, it is also to do with the nature of the Church in the future. In principle, an institutional Church embedded into the fabric of national life is likely to be more expensive to maintain than a 'missionary movement' church working from the edge inwards. Are cumbersome, expensive structures that developed in an institutional Church with a lot of central wealth a handicap to the infant mission-shaped Church now emerging? Do we now need to release the money tied up in the splendour of the old Church and some of its buildings in order to deploy it for the missionary work of the new one? Conversely, it is sometimes argued that, as the parish clergy are easily the biggest cost item on the diocesan budget, it is a foolish diversion to spend a lot of time and effort on the minor expenditure items, which probably cannot be cut much anyway. What is more, diocesan officers such as missioners or trainers are important aids to parish mission and growth. They are important to the mission-initiatives drive, not expensive diversions from it. Where lies the truth?

'Other' costs

Just how big are they? One diocese recently conducted an exercise to answer that question. The aim was to show each church what level of parish share it needed to pay in order to be both paying its own costs and making an average contribution to shared costs. The answers discovered in one diocese will not necessarily translate accurately to another because, as will be shown below, dioceses vary considerably in their cost structures as they do in everything else. However, here is the cost structure in 2003 of one diocese expressed in terms of the average cost of a vicar to an average parish:

Table 15.1 Diocese A costs per incumbent

The direct or marginal cost of the vicar:	£
Stipend	17,450
Pension	4837
NI, Council tax, CME	2880
Housing costs	5625
Total	30,792
Proportionate share of diocesan costs:	
Curate & ordination training	3112
Chaplaincies	737
Church schools	413
Diocesan advisory staff	1069
Administration	5384
Other property maintenance	1602
Registrar & legal	328
Other	417
Proportionate share of national costs:	
Administration	1859
Ordination training	1450
Total 'other' costs	16,371
Average cost per vicar – direct cost plus other costs:	47,163

It can be seen from this table that the direct cost of the vicar is around 65 per cent of total costs. Put another way, the extra costs, or overheads, add an extra 53 per cent to the cost of the parish clergy. Some of this (especially the cost of curates) is money that is actually spent in the parishes. Another diocese divided up its costs for 2005 between posts as follows:

Table 15.2 Diocese B costs per incumbent

	£
Ministry in parishes (employment, housing, expenses of parish clergy including curates, archdeacons & chaplains)	38,300
Support for ministry in parishes (specialist & advisory ministry, specialist departments)	4,200
Training of ordinands	1,500
Contribution to national church	1,600
Administration & statutory costs	2,200
Total cost	**47,800**

Under these definitions, the extra diocesan and national costs add 25 per cent to the cost of ministry in parishes.

These tables do not include the costs of bishops, cathedral staff, and pre-1998 service pension expenditure, which are funded nationally. It is clear from this that, in this diocese at least, the 'other' costs are indeed very substantial and make a very great difference to the level of parish share required of each parish before it is paying its full share. Costs are not necessarily too high just because they are large, but this does make it easier to find money for growth from savings in them. To put it another way, when such a diocese is facing cuts in its overall expenditure budget, it can realistically look to cut its 'other' spending as a way of protecting parochial posts and possibly avoiding another twist to the decline cycle.

This is in no way to caricature 'other' spending as 'bad' and spending on parochial clergy as 'good'. For a diocese to be effective, all its employees and voluntary workers must work together as part of a team. This is the whole message of a book such as this, outlining a comprehensive strategy for the growth of a diocese. What the finance director 'sows' in some backroom when spotting how to wring a little extra money out of the investments, a local vicar may 'reap' when the diocesan growth fund is able to fund an Alpha group coordinator for the parish. Working together in the same team involves looking at the bigger picture and being objective about priorities, even if they are personally uncomfortable, rather than individuals simply fighting their own corner.

Cutting other spending

It is wrong to assume that other spending never contributes to the growth of the church. The training of ordinands and curates, or the salary of a diocesan missioner, may be vital to future church growth. So where would a diocese anxious to preserve parochial ministry or find funds for growth in the teeth of budget tightness turn to for savings? This would vary between dioceses, but here are some examples of places where a diocese might look:

1 Chaplains

It is possible to argue that chaplains to institutions should be paid for by the institutions themselves. This is, after all, the discipline that the diocese seeks to impose on the parishes and their clergy, and the parishes may be asked to pay not only for their own vicar but also for chaplains to local industry or education. The core business of the diocese, and the source of its funding, is the ministry of the parishes. When retrenchment has to happen, then any sensible organization protects its core business where its revenue is raised and looks to cut its marginal, non-contributing operations. This need not imply making chaplains redundant, rather talking to their institutions and asking them to phase in a move to fund them themselves. If a chaplain is so little appreciated by the organization being served that it does not wish to fund the post, then perhaps the post-holder would be more effective, and appreciated, elsewhere. New 'mission-shaped' posts resulting from new initiatives may equally yield no revenue in the short term. However, it should normally be a condition of their setting up that they become gradually self-funding over time. A church-planter, for example, should eventually have her or his costs paid for by the members of the churches planted.

2 Advisers

Parish advisory and support staff have both a direct cost and a direct use to the parishes they are there to serve. The question is whether their usefulness outweighs their cost. The cost can be measured but how can the usefulness? One way round this problem when assessing the future for such posts is to ask the parishes themselves. One diocese recently conducted an evaluation exercise in which clergy and wardens were asked their views on the value for money offered by the advisory and support staff. Posts coming out with high scores would be retained or developed, posts with low scores would be dropped. One problem with this approach is that it is hard to disentangle the value of the post from the effectiveness of the current post-holder. So decisions will need to allow for this subjective element.

Value for money evaluation exercises on diocesan operations, however, are a valuable tool for defining the optimal size and shape of the diocesan operation and so keeping costs under control.

3 Buildings

Diocesan property such as office accommodation can be both a major expenditure item and a significant component of diocesan wealth. Some diocesan offices are sitting on very valuable sites yielding scope for relocation and profit taking. As property prices have risen in recent years, it has become more sensible for a diocese to pay a housing allowance to a diocesan office holder than to pay a stipend plus a house. Average spending on church houses is £6,000 per annum, and a house valued at, say, £350,000 is costing around £20,000 per annum in lost interest on capital. So selling the house would yield a financial benefit of at least £26,000 per annum to set alongside the housing allowance. Allowances would need to be realistic, taking into account local property values, and so would need to vary between dioceses. Typically they may be of the order of £10–12,000 per annum. Unless house values are exceptionally low, dioceses should, therefore, take every opportunity to switch out of 'stipend plus house' arrangements for ordained employees into 'salary including housing allowance'. There are greater problems with doing this for the parish clergy, but where practical such a move would yield similar savings.

4 Diocesan office

Some dioceses have made considerable efficiency savings in office salary costs, helped by the use of modern office technology. For example, computer-literate senior staff may no longer need their own secretary. Further streamlining is possible. For example, annual membership and finance forms are returned to the diocesan office by every parish. Much time is spent in the office chasing up non-returns and inputting the information to the diocesan database. Asking each parish to enter its data online would accelerate response rates and eliminate the need to input data. This change is important for purely mission and church growth reasons, but it would also help cut diocesan administration costs. The mission imperative is to inform policy by reference to facts and trends. Diocesan leaders need to know where the diocese is gaining ground, and where it is losing it, and why. Under the present cumbersome system, the latest known figures are two years out of date. An online system yields up to date information as well as being cheaper – a double win. Much administrative time is also spent devising and operating parish share systems (see Chapter 14 for a suggested new system).

5 Committees

Diocesan costs are associated not only with paid employees but also with their boards, committees and synods. Travelling and other expenses can become significant items, as also can be the time of paid staff in attendance to service the committee or synod. In some dioceses, the size of committees is too large for efficient decision-making, let alone for efficient use of money (or time). One diocese has recently reduced the size of its DBF from 87 members to about a third that number. Frequent or large gatherings also soak up the volunteer time and energy of some of the Church's most committed members. One growing diocese has recently abolished many of its boards and committees on the grounds they were talking-shops contributing too little to the real life of the diocese. It is hard to tell whether their presence has been missed, or even their demise noticed.

Having outlined some areas where a diocese might cut its expenditure, here are some 'big picture' approaches for dioceses to adopt in their cost-saving strategies.

Benchmarking

One way of working out what scope there might or might not be for savings in 'other' costs is for dioceses to benchmark against each other. If some dioceses seem to operate with lower costs and fewer posts than others then the 'high cost' dioceses may be enabled to discover ways of making savings. Alternatively, the 'low cost' dioceses might realize what they are missing by living without certain key staff.

Such benchmarking exercises do indeed reveal significant differences between dioceses. For example, in an exercise comparing all the large dioceses with area systems, one diocese was found to have 26 administrative and support staff whereas another diocese of the same size was found to have 60. Among large dioceses with area systems, the size of the property team varied between 4 and 10, the size of the finance team between 6 and 14. One diocese had a schools team of 19, another of 3. One diocese employed 8 educational chaplains on its own payroll, another none. One diocese had 23 'bishops, archdeacons and their support staff', another had 14. In a study of 12 dioceses of varying size, adult attendance per support post varied between 500 and 1200.

A national benchmarking exercise could clearly yield some very helpful information for dioceses trying to shape their staffing to suit changing times and secure the growth of the Church. Subscribing to such an exercise could be part of the growth strategy of all. Such an exercise could be set up by the diocesan secretaries, be done in-house and cost very little.

A further revealing comparison is shown below. Church attendance in the Church in Wales is currently at almost exactly the same level as in the Diocese of Oxford – around 50,000. The revenue-base of the two organizations should, in the long run, therefore, be about the same. But the cost-base is very different, as the table below illustrates:

Table 15.3 Posts in the Diocese of Oxford and the Church in Wales

Posts	Oxford	Wales
Archbishop	0	1
Diocesan bishops	1	5
Suffragan bishops	3	1
Archdeacons	3	16
Deans & cathedrals	1	6
Diocesan secretaries & offices	1	6
Provincial secretary & office	0	1
Total	9	36

Issues of geography may make a rather higher cost-base in Wales inevitable (although Oxford itself is a large diocese with many rural communities). Also, many of the archdeacons in Wales have a parish to look after. However, there still remains a stark contrast between the two organizations. It is entirely possible that there are those in the Diocese of Oxford who complain about the costs of overheads and hierarchy. If so they should be very thankful they do not live in Wales.

The same contrast extends to boards, committees and synods. The Diocese of Oxford sends 19 people to the General Synod of the Church of England, every diocese in Wales sends 62 to the Governing Body. So, out of the same size of membership Oxford finds 19 people to represent it nationally and the Church in Wales finds 372.

The contrast also extends, though in a less extreme way, to the numbers of parish clergy. At the last count there were 402 parish clergy in the Diocese of Oxford and 713 in the Church in Wales.

The Church in Wales has kept going financially despite its high cost-base per member through use of historic resources. However, these are now drying up through being diverted into clergy pensions. This is a Church that will be forced to slim down significantly in the next few years. As part of this, it needs to make choices between retaining parish clergy on the one hand and its support, oversight, and administration costs on the other.

We conclude that paying attention to diocesan costs is indeed an important part of a diocesan growth strategy. In the short term, dioceses are wise to ensure that support operations share fully in any cost-cutting exercises so that the whole loss is not felt among the parish clergy. In the longer term, rational decision-making is helped by internal value for money exercises and by benchmarking operations across the dioceses.

Dioceses united

Costs can further be cut through dioceses combining functions. Some pairings already exist, for example, two dioceses sharing a finance director. In other places, dioceses are starting to talk to each other about combining their diocesan offices into one joint office. A certain amount of caution is needed here because benchmarking exercises have shown that there are currently no economies of scale being reaped by large dioceses, which are costing just as much to run per church attender or member as are small ones. However, especially as the number of clergy being supported continues to fall, there ought in principle to be considerable savings available from such amalgamations. Dioceses can also reap potential savings from adopting common solutions to IT issues, from learning to operate as members of the same organization instead of completely separate ones.

It may be there are areas of diocesan life that could more efficiently be covered once at national level instead of 44 in parallel. IT provision might be one such area. Another (see Chapter 14) might be the fixing of a replacement for parish share systems. Some training programmes could be organized nationally (see Chapters 10 and 11). There may be scope for a small working group to consider the savings and advantages of going national in the provision of a range of services.

Working together is not the same thing as everyone going the same way, local initiative stultified by national systems. Just as parishes need flexibility to respond to local situations so do dioceses. However, these actually become clearer through working together rather than in isolation, and local practices can be tested against the backcloth of other ways of doing things.

The diocese deconstructed

Perhaps the greatest potential for savings at diocesan level would come from devolving to parishes much of the professional work now undertaken at diocesan level. The key move here would be to transfer responsibility for paying and housing the clergy to their parishes, together with gifting the parsonages to the local churches. Removing the finance and housing functions from a diocese would slash its cost-base and enable more parish clergy and growth projects to be financed (see the example of Down and Dromore in Chapter 14). The advantage of this in terms of cost cutting is clear. The diocese quoted above would see the break-even parish share payments fall from the current £47,000 per annum a long way towards the simple cost of clergy of £31,000. The dioceses' own investment income averaging £9,225 per vicar could be used to make grants to parishes finding it hard to meet even their own costs, or to invest in new initiatives. Potentially, though, parish costs, and the professional skills needed, might have to rise significantly as they take on the job of physically caring for their houses and of organizing pay and rations for their clergy. Parishes might have to work independently through problems currently solved only once at diocesan level. However, pay and rations for local church staff can usually be arranged through the local Councils for Voluntary Service, givers are usually more generous if their money is going into 'their' vicar's house than into the giant housing pot at the diocese, and there is nothing to stop dioceses issuing helpful guidelines to parishes.

Most Anglicans, though, are reluctant to deconstruct their dioceses, valuing mutual dependence and support. The flip side of the cost savings is that many people would be made redundant. Such deconstruction is worth touching upon to show what could be done in terms of reducing the cost-base to a more normal level for Christian churches in the UK, but such a move may not be practical politics in the Church of England today. However, calls for such deconstruction will only grow unless dioceses can show themselves capable of reining in their costs while retaining their core functions.

Beating the heritage constraints

The decline in church attendance in recent decades has not been accompanied by a significant fall in the number of Church of England churches open. We have smaller congregations, not fewer churches. Partly, this is because the loss of people has occurred mainly from the larger congregations. Small churches in the villages and towns have actually seen some numerical growth on average. The overall decline means, except in so far as general appeals bring in money from outsiders, that the buildings and heritage costs and responsibilities are being shared among fewer and fewer people. If this trend continues, then local churches will be in ever-greater danger of being dominated by their heritage costs and responsibilities. This is especially so as standards expected seem to rise as the heritage lobby strengthens.

I was fortunate for nine years to be vicar of a large medieval Grade 1 listed church building with an atmosphere of prayer and peace that acted as a magnet for spiritually minded people. A lot of money was spent on the building, but most of it was from legacies left for the building. It was, and is, a major net asset to the ministry and growth of its congregation, but not all vicars are so lucky. For some congregations their overlarge, gloomy and expensive building is a millstone round their neck. Replacing it with a new one is out of the question both financially and because the heritage lobby and faculty system would not allow it.

One congregation had a church building with structural problems. Its architect inspected it one day and declared it unsafe. The congregation was not allowed in even to collect the umbrellas left behind there last Sunday. Members were relieved more than shocked, and decamped to a local hall the following Sunday, which they have rented ever since. The day they left the church and started renting the hall the congregation began to grow. The cost of remedial work on the church building is enormous and the congregation has no intention of trying to raise it. The church members have been cut free from the millstone that was dragging them down, and happily thriving as a consequence.

This congregation is not unique. Most stories of churches being closed temporarily for repairs, rebuilding or reordering include the information that 'the congregation actually grew in the six months we rented the school hall – some of us didn't want to go back'.

There are at least three keys to the business of ensuring the Church's buildings' legacy supports its growth rather than drags it down:

1 Attitudes

We need the courage to treat our buildings with greater objectivity and, if necessary, ruthlessness. Those that are an asset to the ministry of the church need to be cherished and improved, but those that are a hindrance should be disposed of or radically altered. Church buildings were built as mission vehicles and to serve Christian communities, not the other way around. It is true (as argued in Chapters 5-7) that the generation of church growth requires more church communities, not fewer, but each community does not require its own specialist building. Anglican churches meeting in hired premises or in church halls or dual-purpose buildings or homes are at least as likely to thrive as those in traditional church buildings. Some congregations may in the future decide, for mission reasons, to walk away from their church buildings, and let them be mothballed or declared redundant. They can then use their personal energy and financial resources for mission and ministry among people rather than on heritage work on 'millstone' buildings. They might even want to take on some different premises to use as their own base. Is the Church of England a heritage organization or a missionary organization? If Anglicans agree that they are a missionary organization, then that is where their time and money should be directed. Buildings should be kept on only if they are useful to the mission purpose. Diocesan structures in a mission-shaped Church should be sympathetic to such moves in the parishes, not obstructive.

2 Legalities

The legal framework, currently under review, for the declaring and disposal of redundant church buildings is complex, cumbersome and opaque. Even if it is not practical to simplify the system, it should be possible for the national Church or diocese to circulate parishes to explain clearly to them what they have to do if they want to leave their building. This option needs to be routinely on the agenda when churches are looking to the future, conducting vision exercises, or producing parish MAPs.

3 Faculty procedures and Diocesan Advisory Committees (DACs)

The Church's own planning permission procedure, without which changing the interior or exterior of a church building is illegal, has toughened up in recent years in response to the heritage lobby. How it works in practice, however, varies widely between dioceses. In some dioceses, churches wishing to reorder their churches to make them suitable for the mission of the Church in the twenty-first century are met with sympathy and understanding from DACs. The expertise available becomes a help to the parish, not a threat. However, in other dioceses, when I have asked clergy to name the obstacles to church growth in their area, the DAC has been on their list.

The vicar had some DAC members round to the church to consult them on a reordering for mission purposes. The members did not listen to the reordering proposals, all they were concerned about were the Victorian pillars that had been painted over in the 1960s. 'Get rid of the 1960s' paint' was their only cry.

These DACs may have become dominated by individuals with an architectural or heritage perspective. The needs of the living Church appear secondary to them. So when the bishop encourages the parishes to modernize, and the architect comes along to plan a reordering to make the narthex a comfortable meeting point at the end of the service, the DAC turns round and says, 'You can't do that – its far too domestic. We don't allow kitchens and carpets in church buildings.' If the bishop is serious about having a diocesan strategy for the growth of the churches, he may need, therefore, to pay attention to the membership and attitude of the DAC as well as simply to exhort the parishes to modernize. Perhaps in the future the alternative to modernizing a building will increasingly become abandoning it. This in itself should be enough to create a more amenable climate in heritage-minded DACs.

On the other hand, many churches, instead of viewing their buildings as a millstone round their neck, are learning to use them for a multiplicity of purposes during the week.

Passing through a picture postcard village, I pulled up at the church to have a look inside and perhaps say a quiet prayer. On pushing open the door I was greeted by a huge crowd of toddlers and their carers, with the vicar and his wife at the centre. It was the church playgroup, meeting in the medieval church itself, an integral part of the village community and a ready source of church attendance growth.

Multi-purpose buildings adapted for a range of community uses are often a good way forward both for the contribution of the church to the locality and for the reaching of new people by the church. 'Mission-shaped' church facilities are less about finding tenants to help pay the bills and more about making contacts with different groups in the community. Churches with such facilities and groups should make sure that different members link up with each of the different groups, know the people leading them, share their joys and problems, and pray for them.

In summary

There is considerable scope and need for controlling the administrative, over-sight, overheads, heritage and other cost burdens. The scope and value of actions will vary across the dioceses, but such policies should be an integral part of any comprehensive growth strategy. At the very least, a diocese that is asking its deaneries and parishes to produce cost cutting plans should have a parallel plan for trimming its central costs as well. Moreover, any diocese wishing to find new financial resources for mission initiatives, for fresh expressions, or for growing the twenty-first century Church, should be looking not just to its income sources but also to the trimming of its own cost-base in order to release the necessary funds. Parishes should view their physical assets with mission eyes as well as heritage ones, and be objective and imaginative in deciding upon future patterns of use.

16

Delivering the financial resources for growth

> If you have not been faithful with the dishonest wealth, who will entrust to you the true riches? (Jesus, in Luke 16.11 NRSV)

A fresh agenda for funding

We are today living through a fundamental shift in the source and origin of the Church of England's financial resources for the funding of its life and ministry. The main source used to be accumulated historic resources, built up through the centuries of Christendom, representing its power and wealth at the heart of the Establishment. These resources still exist, but now they are largely absorbed by the massive pensions costs of the retired clergy. As far as the working Church is concerned, the inherited, central, wealth has been drying up.

There are, however, two new, or rather newly enhanced, sources of wealth for the Church today. One is the new property wealth following the great house price boom of the last few years. So dioceses are actually wealthier than they have ever been, though they find it hard to feel wealthy or to translate their new wealth into income. The second and more important growing source of income and wealth is the new prosperity and increasing generosity of the people of God as the country as a whole gets richer. Total giving to the Church has increased in real terms for many years now at 3–4 per cent per annum despite smaller congregations. The most important new wealth, therefore, is in the local church. Today's God-given resources appear to be local rather than central. Increasingly, they are in the hands of people who are learning to be 'leaders in mission' rather than 'keepers of tradition'. It is not true to say that God is allowing the Church of England to become poor. Dioceses and congregations have never been richer. Perhaps if we read the signs of the financial times aright then our spending priorities should be changing – less on symbols of Christendom prestige for the institutional Church and more on grassroots service for the missionary Church.

For the foreseeable future, most of the finance available will continue to maintain traditional parish ministry. However, it was clear from Chapter 7 that many 'fresh expressions' also require significant funding, perhaps because they work best with new sorts of paid leadership, and that some are best instigated by dioceses rather than wealthy or go-ahead parishes. Can parish, deanery and diocese together rise to the challenge of financing enough fresh expressions to kick-start the new growth of the Church while at the same time maintaining sufficient traditional ministry to stop its inherited wing from withering away?

In this chapter I aim to show how a diocese can itself indeed generate the needed extra funding for growth initiatives and fresh expressions. This is of necessity quite a 'technical' chapter but the intent is to re-envision and inspire. I hope that, along with those who lead dioceses, readers with more localized responsibilities will get a fresh understanding of how the dioceses might enable new initiatives.

Diocesan culture and organization

Diocesan boards of finance, parsonage committees, glebe committees and their officials have a key role to play in the growth strategy of a diocese but, in order to play this role, they may need to adjust their culture and self-understanding. The traditional culture has been one of maintenance, in the case of the houses literally so! The purpose of the DBF has been to provide the resources to maintain the ministry of the Church. Budgets have been built up by first calculating how much it will cost to keep the same size of work-force and shape of operation as last year, then how much 'other' income will be available, and then how much parish share must be collected to cover the difference between the two. Finally, the bill for this is distributed between the parishes according to a given formula. Although this procedure may still be balancing the books in some dioceses, in others it has broken down because the increases needed in the parish share bills have been unrealistic. DBFs have been increasingly forced to shape their budgets from the other (and more normal) end – working from the sort of increase parishes might actually provide and then calculating how many posts can be sustained and how many have to be lost in order to balance the books.

In both these procedures, however, it is hard for categories of new spending on investment for the future even to find their way into the budget headings. The fixation is on keeping going for as long as possible as many as possible of the old ways of doing things. New spending categories can therefore be seen not as an opportunity but as a threat – further eroding the capacity to maintain the old.

So DBFs, parsonages and glebe committees need to be re-tasked, given a new culture and self-understanding in exactly the same way as the rest of the Church is changing its outlook. This is not quite to move from maintenance to mission because the existing clergy being financed are already at the heart of the mission of the Church. Their task should change from 'providing the resources to maintain the ministry' to 'providing the resources to grow the Church'. In this task, the parsonages and glebe committees are every bit as vital as the DBF, as will become clear below.

The other major need is to join up the financial and church growth thinking. Traditionally, the financial decisions have been taken with little reference to their mission impact. There has been no joined-up thinking, no overall strategy. For example, in the setting of parish share bills there has rarely been any consideration of the impact of rises on the life and ministry of parishes. A diocesan parish development officer or evangelism adviser may be working with a deanery on promising plans for expansion through starting new con-gregations. Without reference to these, or even knowledge of them, the DBF increases share bills to such an extent that the deanery can no longer afford its expansion plans. Or the DBF forces cuts in clergy posts so that the deanery is driven into retrenchment mode and no longer has the management time for its expansion plans.

The problem of long vacancies (see Chapter 3) is perhaps the most important current example of the damage that can be done through policy-making by the wearers of financial blinkers. In order to square this year's accounts and next year's budgets a diocese deliberately elongates its vacancies while thoughtlessly assuming this will have no impact on its attendance and revenue. In fact, on average, a long vacancy will drive away 20 per cent of the congregation and be the major cause of the decline cycle the DBF thought it was simply managing, not creating.

So DBFs, parsonages boards and glebe committees need both to know and to accept their role in the overall turnaround and growth strategy of the diocese and to focus on 'providing the financial resources for growth' as their core task. Assuming they are so focused, how can they pull off the apparently impossible trick of giving a financial kick-start to new growth while not taking money away from established patterns?

The growth fund

There are two ways of solving this conundrum. One is to change the structure of funding arrangements so that new individual decisions need to be taken between the different spending options out of the same pot of money. Let the different ways of spending money compete with each other on a level financial playing field. It is argued in Chapter 14 that a new system of financial apportionment will generate extra total income compared with the parish share system and so leave room for some new spending on fresh expressions.

However, it is often very hard for new expenditure claims to compete successfully with established items, and posts, so the second solution may be more practical. This is to acknowledge that the existing DBF budget is effectively ring-fenced for the inherited Church and to set up a new and separate ring-fenced fund or income flow for the fresh expressions and growth initiatives of a mission-shaped Church. We will call this the 'diocesan growth fund' (DGF). This should still be administered by the Synod and DBF and appear in the accounts, but it is raised and spent separately from its other income and expenditure.

The concept of a DGF explored here is to build up a financial asset over the long term. The funds would be managed in the usual way in order to produce as big a yield as possible without undue risk. The income earned in a given year would form the spending budget for the fund in that year. At the time of writing most commentators and practitioners (including the Church Commissioners) would say that 7 per cent plus per annum is a prudent expectation of an average rate of return including both income and capital growth. Spending the 'interest, profits and dividends' yield on mission initiatives and church growth projects is not the same thing as selling the family silver. It is true that the value of the capital asset might erode gently in real terms, but the amount by which inflation erodes its purchasing power is effectively the amount invested in the future numerical, and therefore income, growth of the Church. It is the contention, or faith, of this chapter that such investment is likely to be so productive that it will more than compensate for the falling purchasing power of the initial capital sum.

Each year it is likely that new money would add further funds to the DGF, and the resultant church growth would add extra income to the diocese from the giving of the people. So the fund should keep growing in overall size for the foreseeable future.

The growth fund would be administered by a group with two major competencies. DBF members would be responsible for maximizing the income from the trust fund and so for placing funds in the most advantageous places. Grant-making trustees would have an expertise and experience in parish ministry and development, in church planting and pioneering fresh expressions. They would be responsible for spending the money and be appointed by the Bishop's Council. The chairperson of the DGF should probably be the diocesan missioner or parish development adviser, or a mission-minded suffragan bishop or archdeacon.

Building up the growth fund

It is now necessary to pull a rabbit out of a hat. Where can we possibly find the money to create a sizeable DGF?

It may sometimes be possible to start up a growth fund by rearranging some existing funds and capital assets.

The Diocese of Lichfield managed to find around £500,000 from such sources in order to kick-start its fund. Invested in equities, this should produce an income flow of around £35,000 a year. It also found it had an unexpected increase in its stipends allocation from the Church Commissioners, and this enabled it to put £450,000 of other income into its growth fund as capital. In addition, it found it was in receipt of over £200,000 per annum of 'Mission Initiatives' funding from the Church Commissioners (Chapter 17), giving it an initial capacity to make grants for church growth of around £280,000 per annum.

Dioceses quite often end up with an unexpected financial surplus in a given financial year, usually because on average fewer posts were filled than were budgeted for. A diocese in that situation could choose to put the surplus into the DGF.

Many dioceses do not run with substantial reserves, but there are exceptions. The Diocese of Cashel and Ossory in the Church of Ireland actually collects the parish share to pay for expenditure in Year 2 during Year 1. It could, therefore, choose to put several months' total income into its DGF and simply operate with fewer months' general reserves.

The main source of capital for a DGF, however, is likely to be the housing stock and glebe assets (historic assets of land and property). Dioceses have never been richer. Their newfound wealth has come through a windfall gain; it has come about through luck rather than judgement, but it is still massive. It has come through the enormous increases in the market values of parsonage houses and other buildings and land holdings in recent years. At the time of writing, house values have stabilized, but most commentators are not expecting them to fall back significantly.

The most obvious reason why this large increase in net wealth has not registered its importance in many dioceses is that no attempt is made to estimate the market values of the housing stock. It would appear to be a serious omission for an organization to make no attempt to measure the market value of its principal assets. Insurance valuations may be known, but they bear little or no relation to the market value of the houses, which is the thing that matters. So the first step for a parsonages board newly tasked to see how to manage its assets to help finance the growth of the Church would be to have the houses valued. The usual objection is that valuations cost money. The reply to this is twofold: first of all we cannot afford not to know how much our assets are worth and, second, agents may be persuaded to do valuations cheaply if they sniff the possibility of future sales. A cheaper alternative is to use an automated valuation service provided by a property database company that is based on postcodes.

The second reason for so easily dismissing the growing wealth of the diocese is the argument that the bricks and mortar cannot be turned into cash because we need the houses as clergy homes. Their valuation is, in fact, not relevant to us because we cannot sell them. This is clearly untrue, as parsonages are being sold all the time, especially because the number of stipendiary clergy is set to fall in the foreseeable future by around 1 per cent per annum. Even 1 per cent of the value of a diocesan housing stock is a formidable sum of money. If a diocese has 300 houses and their average market value is £333,000 then it will be selling houses worth £1 million a year just to keep pace with the falling number of stipendiary clergy. With a rate of return of 7 per cent, this would yield £70,000 for the DGF to spend or reinvest in the first year and rising by at least £70,000 a year thereafter.

Normally the proceeds of a house sale are placed into a benefice building fund until the legal conclusion of any pastoral reorganization. Only then, if the funds are not needed for a new house, can the diocese release the money for discretionary spending. Some of this may go on upgrading existing houses, or be incorporated into the diocese's portfolio of financial investments.

So it is clearly possible to build up a DGF from the proceeds of house and glebe sales. In many cases, all that is needed is to direct the proceeds from already planned house sales into the DGF. This will make it comparatively easy to build up a sizeable DGF.

Some dioceses, however, are reluctant to part with their houses even when they are not needed as clergy homes. One diocese had 40 empty houses, while at the same time it was laying off further clergy because it could not afford to pay for them. Another maintains and lets out a stock of 100 surplus houses no longer needed for clergy in order to reap future capital gain and in case pastoral reorganization makes it convenient to use some of them for clergy again in the future. Such a diocese has all the wealth it needs to create a massive diocesan growth fund and transform the mission ministry it is able to offer. It prefers instead to sit on a large stock of old vicarages 'for a rainy day' and to keep parish share bills in check. Such a diocese needs to transform from seeing itself as the custodian of historic assets for the maintenance of historic posts into the custodian of mission resources to be deployed for the future growth and ministry of the Christian Church.

The redeployment of existing funds, yields on existing reserves, already planned house or glebe sales, unexpected income or financial surpluses, plus reduced support costs (Chapter 15) can easily create a financial asset to use as a growth fund.

Yet even a diocese that has *none* of these possibilities can build up a significant financial asset through more efficient use of the assets it does have. Even a diocese that is already banking on the receipts from planned future sales to balance its ordinary books can find fresh capital-value to release for its growth fund. The remainder of this chapter shows how the housing stock can be better utilized in order to produce new income even when these other options are not available.

Effective use of housing

1 Shorter vacancies

Chapter 3 showed that the trend to longer vacancies, in part a deliberate expedient for short-term financial savings, is resulting in large permanent losses of church attendance. Even as a purely financial expedient, the policy is counterproductive. But there is also another cost of longer vacancies – empty vicarages.

A management consultant was brought in by the printing firm. Its problem was that it was asset-rich but cash-flow poor. Rather like a typical Anglican diocese. Its money was tied up in two giant printing presses, each of which ran flat out for one shift a day and then stood idle for sixteen hours until the next morning. The consultant's answer was to sell one of the machines and run the other for two shifts a day. The company could solve its cash shortage, invest in expansion elsewhere and maintain production at its current rate. The company objected that it needed backup in case a machine broke down. The consultant retorted that this sort of machine hardly ever broke down but that, if it did, a maintenance contract would ensure it was mended quickly. The company could have sold the machine and lived happily ever after, but in the end it was too timid to do so.

A diocese strapped for cash but owning a lot of vicarages is also asset-rich but cash-flow poor. It also owns assets (houses) that hardly ever 'break down'.

When its vacancies are lengthy, then it also has a lot of expensive assets – parsonage houses – standing idle. A diocese with 300 houses, an average length of stay in post of seven years and an average vacancy length of one year has, at any one time, 37.5 (1 in 8) houses not occupied. Some dioceses in this situation do try to let out empty vicarages, but there are many costs associated with this and the net profit is less than the return from investing the sale proceeds if the houses were sold. If the average market value of a vicarage in the diocese is £333,000, then the value of idle assets is £12.5 million.

Now suppose that the diocese takes steps to speed up new appointments but keeps the same size of workforce. Vacancies will now last six months instead of one year. It does this by reducing the number of posts on its posts list but keeping them filled for more of the time. This will, of course, involve yet a further round of pastoral reorganization, not in order to cut the number of clergy but in order to have only the number of posts it can afford to keep filled. The diocese had been paying an average payroll of 262.5 (300–37.5). It can now reduce the number of its posts from 300 to 281.25. With clergy in post for 7 years out of 7.5 (93.33 per cent of the time) there will still be 262.5 on the payroll. There will also be around 19 vicarages made redundant and available to sell. At £333,000 each, the total market value of the 19 houses is £6.3 million. By adopting a more growth-friendly vacancies regime, the diocese has started to use its assets more efficiently and has built up a cash pile of over £6 million that can be put into the growth fund. It is employing the same number of parochial clergy, just employing them more effectively. It can maintain its 'traditional' workforce *and* find the money for financing fresh expressions.

2 Longer incumbencies

Churches grow best under incumbents who have been in post for between around five and twelve years.[1] Yet the average length of stay is around only seven years. Part of the problem of decline in team vicar parishes is their even shorter average length of stay, with many five-year contracts. One church growth strategy is for clergy to decide, and to be persuaded, to stay longer. Not too long – just ten or twelve years on average rather than seven.

If the clergy of a diocese were to achieve an increase in average length of stay, this would have the side effect of further efficiency gains in the use of parsonage houses. With an average length of vacancy of six months and vacancies every 7.5 years, the diocese needed 281 houses for 263 clergy. However, if the length of stay went up to 11 years, then only 275 posts and houses would be needed for 263 clergy. A further six houses are released to be sold, netting the diocese a further £2 million for the growth fund.

A further significant saving to a diocese of shorter and less frequent vacancies relates to the movement costs of the clergy – advertising, interview and appointment costs, decorating and ingoing works, removal expenses and ingoing allowances. If these costs average £8,000 per house move, then cutting the moves from 33 to 23 per annum through shorter, less frequent, vacancies saves £80,000 per annum. Even more important than this cost saving is the saving in annual costs per house – repairs and maintenance, insurance, council tax, and so on. Around the country these costs average around £7,000 per house. A diocese able to operate with 25 fewer houses is able to save a further £175,000 a year on its operating costs.

3 No more 'house for duty posts'

It is tempting to think that buying semi-retirement ministry with the offer of a free house for part-time duty makes good sense. The only costs that appear on the balance sheet are the running costs of the house – say about £7,000 a year. This seems quite reasonable in return for Sunday duties and a couple of days a week being the village's parish priest, but there is a significant opportunity cost of using a house in this way. The alternative would be to sell the house and draw income from the resultant financial asset. Suppose the house is worth £333,000 and the diocese is able to obtain 7 per cent, then the opportunity cost of the house for duty post is £23,000 for the house itself plus the £7,000 on its annual running costs, making £30,000 in total. Suddenly the house for duty idea no longer looks so sensible. Of course, in an area of really low house prices it may still be a cheap option, but in many areas of the country vicarages can easily be worth between £400,000 and £500,000, making house for duty posts cost around £40,000 per annum.

It can also be argued that offering a house for duty may not be the kindest thing to offer retired clergy, who will need to buy a house eventually when they finally retire. Better to encourage clergy to buy as soon as possible, to offer an income flow rather than use of an asset as the incentive to take part-time retirement posts. To give an example, suppose the diocese were to offer, instead of the £333,000 house, an annual income on top of pension of £10,000. Most of this income would be found from the saving of £7,000 in annual housing costs. A further £3,000 will be needed from interest on capital released by the house sale. At 7 per cent, this requires a capital sum of £43,000. So when the house is sold, £43,000 should go into the account to cover the payment to the minister and £290,000 should go into the growth fund.

As outlined above, the downside of this operation is that the diocese will no longer benefit from capital appreciation of its asset and it will gradually need slightly more than £50,000 to fund an increasing honorarium to its retired priest as inflation continues. The plan is that the church growth generated by wise spending of the growth fund will more than compensate for this. Nervous dioceses could, of course, reinvest part of the total rate of return on capital and spend less from the growth fund. I am not advocating this, however, because it is time for dioceses to trust in God, rather than the stock market, to give the growth. Increasing house price values are, in any case, entirely useless unless the housing is eventually sold.

If a diocese with 8 such 'house for duty' posts switched them all, over a period, to 'honorarium for duty', it would add £2.4 million to its growth fund.

4 Paying housing allowances instead of offering houses

The same principle as that established above in relation to house for duty posts can be applied to other paid posts. Suppose a diocese houses a parish ministry adviser or director of education in a vicarage. Both are full-time diocesan posts, with no parish duties, filled by clergy on a standard stipend. What rate of housing allowance would entice the clergy to give up their vicarage and buy their own house? Perhaps it would be £15,000 per annum. This would take them from an income of £18,000 plus a house to an income of £33,000 without a house. The extra £15,000, after tax, would pay a mortgage of around £900 to £1,000 a month.

If the post-holders were offered a choice of this arrangement or a house and chose the higher salary, then we have to assume they have gained from the new arrangement. The diocese, on the other hand, saves £7,000 on annual house costs and needs £8,000 per annum from the capital value of the house. This takes £114,000 of the sale value, leaving £219,000 to be added to the growth fund. If, over time, the diocese switches five officers over to the new system, it can add £1 million to the growth fund. Candidates for such an option would also include archdeacons and suffragan bishops. In their case, with more expensive housing, the potential gains are all the greater.

The opportunity may also exist to start offering the full salary-no house alternative to the parochial clergy. This would be more complicated and controversial but would also carry with it the possibility of huge savings. The costs of parsonage surveyors, archdeacons, parsonage committees and so on together with the ordinary annual costs of the houses would all be saved. The diocese is, in truth, a very cumbersome and expensive landlord. Its duties as a landlord absorb much of its management time. Problems over housing are the cause of much friction between diocese and parish clergy. Sometimes the diocese cannot or will not afford a repair or improvement the parish priest is anxious for; sometimes it just takes an age for a decision to be reached or permission to be given. Some clergy, knowing the house is not their own and that they will only be living in it for a few years, allow their houses and gardens to deteriorate, and so lose capital value. At the very least, a diocese might consider one or two experimental 'stipend plus housing allowance' packages to see how they work out. Some could be on an equity sharing basis, as outlined in Section 7 below.

One objection to the idea of clergy buying their own houses is that the vicar will no longer live in the strategic location just next to the church. However, one option might be to offer the vicarage for sale to the vicar. Part of the proceeds would finance the housing allowance and part would go into the growth fund. When the vicar moved on, the house could be sold or let to his or her successor. In order to obviate the possibility that the vicar would not wish to sell the house when she or he moved on, this option could be reserved for older clergy in their last post. Such solutions may only work in a small minority of situations, but having the flexibility to adopt them might be the key to unlocking enough of the Church's wealth to enable it to invest realistically in its future survival and growth.

5 Swapping high value and high cost houses

This is something that dioceses have been doing for many years. As vacancies arise, houses with exceptional value or exceptional running costs are looked at with a view to replacing them. However, quite often, local sentiment or some other factor has kept the house within the portfolio, and, in many dioceses, no systematic survey has been made and no current market valuations obtained. Given the current financial needs and the recent increases in house values, the time for such a systematic survey is surely now.

The house value survey should be accompanied by a gardens survey. In some areas there are still many large vicarage gardens that could be used for development. Could outline planning permission be obtained for building a house or houses in the grounds? Sometimes it might be possible to build a new vicarage in the grounds and sell off the existing house, sometimes simply to sell parts of gardens to developers.

From the surveys, it should be possible to draw up lists of houses that could be swapped or gardens that could be developed at a significant financial profit. Nothing can be forced upon incumbents and parishes. Traditionally, dioceses have waited until there is a vacancy before acting, but there is no necessity for this. Likely candidates could be circulated and asked if they are willing to consider a change. If the reasons offered are mission orientated (in order to generate a diocesan growth fund), and if contributing parishes are offered priority treatment in the making of grants out of the fund, then there may be many positive reactions.

Suppose the diocesan parsonages committee is tasked with making such a survey, drawing up a list, and then working with parishes and clergy in order to work through it systematically, and it identifies 30 worthwhile schemes; suppose the profit from each scheme averaged £70,000, then £2.1 million could be added to the growth fund.

As well as a systematic survey of houses and land, it may also pay to survey the past and forecast maintenance costs of all the houses. Some will be vastly more expensive to maintain in the future than others. Can these be weeded out of the housing stock before the big money has to be spent?

6 The glebe survey

A similar situation often appertains to glebe and other parcels of land owned by a diocese and managed by either a parsonages or glebe committee. I was a member of a parsonages board for a number of years. Quite often we would learn that someone else was trying to take possession of a piece of land that we 'probably' owned. How should we repel them? We had no systematic assets register and, it seemed, no clear idea of what we owned, let alone its market value. There may be surprising scope from a systematic survey of glebe-type assets and a policy of converting the under-used ones into financial assets.

7 Equity sharing

Mainly with Church Commissioners' funding, the Pensions Board provides value-linked loans to help clergy pensioners find retirement housing. The funder and borrower share the sales proceeds when the pensioner dies or moves on in the same proportion as the split of funds provided to purchase the house. The Pensions Board has a say in the maintenance of the houses.

There may be cases where a diocese could invite working clergy to take an equity stake in their parsonage houses. In many areas of the country it may be unrealistic to expect the priest to raise a large enough mortgage to buy the whole of a house to use as a vicarage. Possibly a diocese could offer an equity share in a vicarage to a priest, and pay a housing allowance to enable the priest to pay the mortgage. The cash inflow to the diocese would be divided between provision for the housing allowance and the growth fund as before.

8 Maximizing sale prices

When it comes to selling houses, some dioceses do not seem able to maximize their sale prices. Houses are often put up for sale in poor condition or empty of furniture. The garden is usually untended. They are not presented in the way that the viewers of TV house-buying programmes expect today. Sometimes they are put on the market with an inappropriate selling agent from another town simply because that is the agent with whom the diocesan office is used to dealing. When it comes to negotiations, the diocese might not be as nimble as a single private seller. Those on parsonage committees with experience are likely to suspect that, cumulatively, very large sums of money are being thrown away.

So, along with a systematic policy for taking value out of the housing stock and putting it into ministry and mission, should go a new approach to maximizing the value of sales. This might, first, involve finding more help from the local church in presenting and selling the vicarage. It might also involve a diocese in finding a professional to spend modest amounts on the superficial presentation of houses before they are put on the market. It would include being more careful about using the right agent and playing the market more professionally.

I have now listed a number of ways in which a diocese can extract value from its housing stock without losing any ministry effectiveness from it. To some we have attached a notional value in our fictional diocese, to others we have not because the assumptions needed to do so would be more heroic, but enough has been done to show how an average diocese could put together something in the order of, say, £20 million for its growth fund. This is the sort of figure that diocesan financial officials working off the back of envelopes have confirmed to me as realistic. A fund of £20 million earning 7 per cent per annum yields £1.4 million per annum. This is the sort of sum that could transform the ability of a diocese to stimulate and fund fresh initiatives to grow the Church of the twenty-first century.

The Church Commissioners' contribution

Since 2002, the Church Commissioners have been allocating 'Mission Initiatives' funding to dioceses. It is possible that such funding will become a permanent, and perhaps increasing, feature of the Commissioners' operation. It is straightforward to add this annual flow to the yield from the capital sum owned by the diocese when making up the total funds to disburse in a particular year. For wealthier dioceses, this funding is on a small scale, but for poorer dioceses it is substantial. Lichfield diocese received £215,000 for its growth fund from the Commissioners in 2005, an amount much greater than the yield from its capital set aside for the fund.

Having demonstrated how a diocese can, if it wishes, build its growth fund it is now time to look at how it can spend it.

Spending the growth fund

The DGF is a ring-fenced fund with clearly defined spending criteria. Experiments and fresh expressions of church can be risky and they require flexibility, imagination and quick thinking from their funders. It would normally be a mistake to entrust the distribution of such money to a Bishop's Council or similar body. Rather, as suggested earlier in the chapter, each diocese will need to appoint a specialist group to run and disburse the fund. The criteria within which successful grant applications should fall need to be drawn up with care.

- One criterion could be 'projects likely to draw people under the age of 40 into the Christian faith and community'. This identifies evangelism and church growth as the central field of activity and targets the younger 55 per cent of the population, those that the Church has been losing and needs to win back. If a diocese has identified loss of young people as its major decline problem, the age range could be tightened further in order to prioritize a concentrated response to its principal problem.

- Another criterion could be 'projects designed to start new congregations and churches or to develop new forms and ways of being church'. This puts the DGF firmly in the area of funding the emergence of a mission-shaped Church by fitting a finance fuel line to the engine of the fresh expressions wing of the twenty-first century Church.

Applications for funding would be invited from every level of the diocese. Diocesan bodies such as the bishop's staff meeting, the synod, the bishop's council, the mission division or the ministry division could make an application, so could a rural dean or deanery synod or chapter. And so could a vicar and PCC. In this way, top-down and bottom-up initiatives could compete with each other for scarce resources on a level playing field. Both one-off costs and annual salary costs would be eligible for grants. However, it may be wise to discourage or exclude spending on buildings – there are other sources of funding for church restoration and building projects. The DGF is primarily for investment in people-related initiatives.

Diocesan leaders, bodies and officers would primarily be looking for projects that the parish churches are unlikely to be able to initiate or sustain. For example, there is no youth worship and specialist ministry offered by the Church of England in a particular town. So the diocesan missioner or bishop draws up a proposal to appoint a youth minister to plant a youth church in the town, drawing on the cooperation of all the churches. Or the diocese realizes that, in a town with a large number of college students, there is no large Anglican church meeting their needs and drawing them in. One response to this is to look to appoint a suitable incumbent to the next vacancy somewhere. Another would be to appoint a team of, say, an incumbent, a worship leader and a student worker to a new non-geographic people-group parish covering the town and to ask them to plant a church for the under 30s. The DGF would provide some or all of the core finance for the initial period.

Deaneries would similarly look for projects that are a little beyond any individual parish. Possibilities might include:

- the set up costs of an alternative worship community for the area;
- a deanery children's minister or a deanery evangelist;
- a deanery mission;
- the salary of a part-time deanery evangelism course coordinator or deanery 20s–30s' coordinator.

Parishes would be encouraged to work together where appropriate, perhaps to put in joint applications, but many projects are best undertaken by individual churches. These might be in any of the areas of good practice for the growth of the Church considered in earlier chapters, for example:

- A UPA church might apply for financial help with the process of devising a mission action plan or going through a healthy churches' exercise. This might enable the church members to get away for a day or weekend to a decent venue, and bring in a helpful speaker, in order to work through their plans.
- A church might want help with the salary costs of a new staff member – a children's or youth minister, an evangelist for young adults, a student worker, or a church planter, or a cell group coordinator.
- The application might be for help in planting a new congregation – for set up costs such as musical instruments, or hall hire for the first year.

Whatever strategy a church develops for its own growth and future, some financial help from the diocese can be even more important for morale and confidence than it is for practical reasons. Even a grant of £1,000 towards a £20,000 project at least makes the church realize that it has the backing of the diocese, that it is not alone. It is also a help towards raising funds from others – the bishop has given us some money, why don't you?

The growth fund should probably exclude the funding of social programmes from its criteria. This is not because social action may not lead to church growth but because abundant funding is normally available from secular sources. The DGF should be kept for funding initiatives that do not qualify for such outside support.

The growth fund application form developed by the Diocese of Lichfield, together with explanatory notes and criteria, is included in Appendix 2 as a model for others to use.

It is vitally important to a successful grant-making strategy that the grants are not only made in a careful and professional manner but also that their use is properly monitored. Recipients will need to make progress reports that enable the DGF trustees to assess how successful the grant has been. This will enable them to learn from the past and to target future grants on schemes with a higher chance of success.

Trustees disbursing grants in response to applications, and then monitoring the results, can find it rather time consuming. One way of guarding against this is to have a minimum grant size as well as a maximum. In this way the administrative burden of small schemes will be reduced or eliminated. Forms need to be carefully designed for clear information and quick decisions. Trustees may need to visit churches to talk face to face and to see the local situation, but this could be integrated into the normal functions of certain trustees – for example, it would make a pleasant change for an archdeacon to visit a parish with a view to giving it a grant rather than to enquire whether it intends to pay its parish share this year.

Of course, the time spent on the DGF is time well spent – it is time on the core business of the diocese and the Christian Church, fulfilling the Great Commission. Too many dioceses have become depressed through spending their time organizing their own retreat, managing their own decline. A well resourced and high-profile DGF will change the whole culture, give hope for the future, encourage those parishes and clergy with a heart for the growth and future of the Church, and help create positive thinking throughout the diocese. Which diocese can afford to be without one?

17

Central funding for the growth of the Church

Devote yourselves to prayer, keeping alert in it with thanksgiving . . .
pray . . . that God will open to us a door for the word. (Colossians 4.2,3
NRSV)

Prayer and precedence

Finally, in this exploration of ways of financing the Church's mission and
ministry, we take a brief look at the significant role of the Church Commissioners. As with so many of the Church of England's financial arrangements,
the way the Church Commissioners' funds are distributed/spent could easily
proceed thoughtlessly without significant change from year to year, the
traditional beneficiaries of the Commissioners' funding receiving their automatic allowances. The forces of old habits, vested interest and established
formulae can be more powerful than those of fresh policy-thinking and
open-minded prayer for future guidance.

The founding documents of the Church Commissioners actually require them
constantly to rethink how their money is best spent. The Ecclesiastical Commissioners Act of 1840 states: 'Additional provision shall be made for the cure
of souls in parishes where such assistance is most required, in such manner as
shall be deemed most conducive to the efficiency of the established church.'[1]
Efficiency in the use of money requires constant attention if it is to be
achieved in a fast changing world. The Commissioners have always from time
to time sought to develop the Church's ministry as well as maintain it, for
example, by their funding of clergy and lay workers in mission areas during
and between the world wars, and their funding of ministry in the new
housing areas developed after the Second World War.

It would seem that the criterion by which efficiency should be judged is
that of the cure of souls – how can money best be disbursed to serve the
mending of broken souls, the saving of straying ones and the discipling of
Christian ones? This is a deeply spiritual ministry that is best guided by prayer
rather than precedence. It is also clear that it is not the job of the Church
Commissioners necessarily to finance the institutional, Christendom parts of

the Church of England on the grounds that national money should finance the national establishment. This should certainly be done if it is deemed to be the most efficient way of spending money on the cure of souls, but it should always be considered alongside other contenders for the efficient use of Commissioners' money. These include the parish mission and ministry that the 1840 Act clearly had in mind, and the fresh expressions required for a mission-shaped cure of souls in the new post-Christendom missionary world the Church of England is fast entering.

The changing use of the Commissioners' money

Between 1993 and 2003 the current spending of the Commissioners rose from £156 million to £171 million. However, within that total, spending on pensions rose from £69 million to £105 million. Non-pension spending therefore went down from £87 million to £66 million. The support given to bishops and cathedral staff has risen in line with costs and earnings during the period, totalling £11 million for bishops and £5 million for cathedrals in 1993, rising to £19 million and £6.5 million respectively by 2003. The Commissioners' own administrative costs have remained constant at £10 million. The amount available for parish mission and ministry support emerges as a residual spend after these and one or two other costs have been met. It fell from £57 million in 1993 to £26 million in 2003.

Thus it will be seen that the amount made available to parishes is not the result of newly considered policy each year but of how much is left once pensions, bishops and cathedral deans and canons have been resourced. Here is not the place to rehearse the history of clergy pensions, simply to record that expenditure on this item is locked in and sacrosanct. It is no bad thing that retired clergy no longer need sink into poverty, and, of course, many continue to offer Christian ministry free to the Church for many years after they cease to draw a stipend, but it is only over their non-pensions spending that there is a degree of freedom of action. Since 1999, the power over the use of the Commissioners' funds has been shared with the Archbishops' Council.

The dwindling total support available to parishes is not the only important issue – equally important is the way in which it is distributed. The formula by which funds are divided between dioceses was changed in 2002 by the Archbishops' Council in an attempt better to reflect their relative need of central subsidy. Some dioceses gained and some lost from the change. However, the change to the allocation formula did not address what is arguably the major problem with the system – that the grants are paid out by the Commissioners without knowing exactly how they will be spent nor whether that spending is in any way 'efficient' for the cure of souls. There is no audit trail through to the end use and no process by which the Commissioners can steer, or even discover, how their money is spent or how much it was needed by the diocese in question. In each diocese it is put into the general diocesan pot out of which stipends and other costs are met. This further limits the ability of the Commissioners to fulfil their function of efficiently targeting help where assistance with the cure of souls is most required. This is particularly so because there is now a large body of evidence and a growing consensus that the Church of England needs to direct some of its spending towards the cure of souls of people who will not be reached by the traditional geographical parish model. The Church needs to fly with two wings, yet what Commissioners' money is available is mainly going into the traditional wing, and they are finding it hard to find any levers of power to change this.

Another major problem with the formula used to allocate the Commissioners' funds between dioceses is that, like many diocesan parish share allocation formulae, it penalizes growth and subsidizes decline. The formula is constructed so that, if a diocese's giving levels per member increase, it does not get penalized through a reduction in grant. This is clearly a good thing, otherwise dioceses would lose the incentive to encourage personal generosity. However, if a diocese's income increases in comparison with other dioceses because of a growth in the number of its members, then it will lose money from the central allocation. Conversely, a diocese whose income declines relative to others because of a fall in membership will be rewarded with extra support. No wonder that dioceses trying to sort their financial problems concentrate on getting existing members to be more generous rather than attracting new ones! A growing diocese will have the financial benefits of growth taken away from it by the Archbishops' Council and given to dioceses that are still shrinking. It would seem that the allocation formula between dioceses needs to be revisited in just the same way as those within dioceses.

The Parish Mission Fund

The first major attempt by the Archbishops' Council and the Commissioners to break out of this straightjacket came in late 2001 with the offer of a £10 million parish mission fund spread across all dioceses over a period of three years 2002–2004. The intention was that the money be spent on developing new church ministry in a changing world. It was the first significant attempt to provide financial fuel and a fuel line for the engine of the fresh expressions wing of the Church. For the first time, dioceses have been asked to report back on how they have spent their grants. The results enable the Council to learn lessons for the future. Some dioceses indeed spent the money in the sort of ways intended, others simply abstracted it for traditional stipends support, and others, as can be seen from the pie chart below, were slow or reluctant to spend it at all:

Figure 17.1 Use of Commissioners' Parish Mission Fund 2002 and 2003

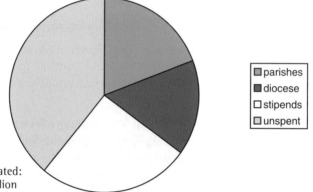

Total allocated:
£6.431 million

The, at best, mixed results of this exercise have been due just as much to the desperation of many dioceses to get their hands on any money to support hard-pressed current stipends as to their lack of vision for doing something new. Dioceses, anyway, do not like having their hands tied, preferring to receive money without strings and restrictions. Some have been reluctant to spend the money because they fear the supply will dry up. If the Archbishops' Council wants to be sure of directing support to the fresh expressions wing of the Church over the long term, then it will need to ring-fence its funding for this and offer assurance of long term continuity of funding.

At the time of writing, the parish mission fund looks set to deliver funding at the rate of around £4 million per annum, divided up between the dioceses, for each of 2005, 2006 and 2007. So there is some promise of continuity, and there is beginning to be more of a culture in some dioceses of spending the money on growing a mission-shaped Church.

The Spending Review Working Group

This group was asked by the Archbishops' Council and the Commissioners to consider the optimal use of the Commissioners' spending for the years 2005–2007, though also looking further into the future than this. It was asked to bear in mind both the *needs* and the *opportunities* for funding the ministry and mission of the Church, implying it had a responsibility for both *maintenance* and *innovation*. The group concluded that money was not always distributed according to needs because every diocese, rich or poor, received the same treatment in relation to its bishops and cathedral. Moreover, virtually all the money was going on maintaining existing ministry rather than innovation, so the balance ought to be corrected if the Commissioners were to contribute towards the future growth of the Church.

The group therefore recommended the creation of a six-year grant scheme directed towards supporting mission initiatives, with at least £9 million a year being on offer by 2010. This would go alongside better targeting of support at poorer dioceses, and be part-funded by a reduction in support for bishops and cathedrals. An annual grant of £9 million a year implies an average per diocese of around £200,000 – coincidentally about the same sum as the current average financial support per bishop. This would be a substantial injection of funds to support the emergence of the fresh expressions of a mission-shaped Church. However, the spending review received a rough ride at the February 2004 General Synod, particularly through opposition to the reduction in support to bishops and cathedrals. The whole future of mission-initiative funding was thereby sent into the long grass, to be picked up by another working group.

The Resourcing Mission Group

This working group, asked to pick up the issue of how the Church's future mission can best be resourced, made an initial report to Synod in July 2005. This emphasized the need for a shift to a dynamic mission emphasis in every aspect of the Church's life, including financial provision. It recommended that the parish ministry and mission support should no longer be the residual items of Commissioners' spending, taking all the cuts in times of financial constraints. The whole budget should be considered afresh each year. The Mission Initiatives funding should become a permanent, and hopefully growing, feature of Commissioners' spending. The historic debate, not just about whether the Commissioners should be allowed to move funding from maintenance of bishops, deans and canons towards mission innovation, but also about the whole future structure of financial arrangements for a mission-shaped Church, will rumble on for some time yet.

The Church Commissioners and the diocesan growth fund

Suppose that a sum of money is made available by the Commissioners via the Archbishops' Council towards the financing of the sorts of fresh expression listed in the report *Mission-shaped Church.*[2] This could simply be a continuation or enlargement of the existing parish mission fund, or a bigger new shift or initiative. What would be the best way of distributing the money? In view of the temptation many dioceses experience to pocket parish mission funding for stipends support, and the difficulty some dioceses have in spending the money at all, the end use of grants needs to be controlled. It is tempting to imagine a system of direct grants straight to parishes, controlled by the Council's and Commissioners' own grant-making body. The Church Urban Fund provides a model for this. However, such a precedent will almost certainly be resisted by dioceses because they, the 'middlemen', are being cut out. It could also be quite expensive to run, requiring a new organization to vet and oversee grant applications and the progress of supported initiatives. However, any system of disbursing money carries its own costs: it can, for example, be quite costly in terms of management time and disruptions to revisit a distribution formula from time to time. Each diocese would itself need to spend some time and money distributing its own part of the fund. The great advantage of the direct grants system is that it immediately puts all the money into the hands of those who have contracted to try to grow the future Church with it.

If, however, this solution is not possible politically, another would be to offer grants only to dioceses that had set up their own 'mission initiatives and growth' fund. The Commissioners' cheque would be paid straight into the bank account of the fund, spending from which would be restricted in the ways suggested in Chapter 16. Dioceses without such a fund would be deemed not to be interested in receiving money for such a purpose. This should encourage every diocese into creating one. An average injection each year of £200,000 would clearly be a major boost to a DGF. Unlike the money generated from within the diocese, this annual grant should be treated as income not capital, as it is itself the result of a financial return on an asset. If dioceses are not sure for how many years the Commissioners will be providing this support, they could hold some back to smooth a transition if it comes.

The trustees of a DGF would determine how the money was spent and make a report to the Council and Commissioners each year as well as to their own synod. In this way, the Commissioners' contribution would be coordinated with that of the diocese in a coherent and joined-up strategy for funding future innovation and growth.

Funding by the centre, the diocese and the local church

If, as argued in Chapter 16, the Church of England is, overall, becoming richer rather than poorer because of the growth in income and giving among local church members, it may be that the greatest potential for funding the emergence of new shapes of Church is to be found locally in the parishes. How does this fit in with the contributions of the centre and the dioceses?

It may be that the most important job of the centre and diocese is to provide the right environment for encouraging the giving of the people for the work of the Church. The creation of a substantial DGF is a means of encouraging that giving. First of all, the fact that the diocese and the centre are willing to offer money to help fund a parish initiative is immensely encouraging to the parish. Innovative churches in the past have often felt rather disapproved of and unsupported. The availability of such a fund changes this atmosphere completely. Second, the DGF would not usually fully fund a project – it would offer to partner the parish in a shared venture. Grants could, for example, be for matched funding so that the partnership is 50–50. Or the percentage of the total cost offered by the fund could be much lower – simply some seedcorn (or start-up) money to encourage the locals to find the bulk of the money themselves. A key priority is to get what funding is available into the hands of those who will use it in mission to grow the Church. At the moment this is not always the case. The offer of matched funding is one way of achieving that aim; central and diocesan funding is then going only to churches that already have a vision and are prepared to part fund it themselves.

This should not, of course, be a rigid procedure that effectively excludes poor or UPA churches from receiving funds. In certain cases, DGFs should be prepared to consider full or nearly full funding. One example of such a church would be a youth church, for these almost always need outside funding.

The other vital element in the provision of a financial environment that encourages local funding of local projects is the parish share system, the future of which was discussed in Chapters 13 and 14. The right environment is provided when the regular money the parish needs to provide to the diocese is not affected either by the parish's own income-generation for development projects or by the growth of the church that results from them. Chapter 14 suggests a better set of financial arrangements with which to replace parish share formulae by providing a more helpful environment for encouraging financial and numerical growth.

The publication and adoption of the report *Mission-shaped Church* in 2004,[3] the obvious enthusiasm of the Archbishop of Canterbury for a future Church that flies with two wings, and the creation by him of 'Fresh Expressions' as a new mission agency with the aim to resource a growing movement of fresh expressions of church, all serve to encourage local churches to produce their own innovations. The spreading of news of good practice, simple exhortation, and the provision of a helpful financial environment all work together to enable and encourage local initiatives and local funding.

A further advantage of a developing partnership through the DGF between the centre, diocese and parish is to change the dynamic of relationships. The new focus on the diocese offering financial and other help to churches to aid their growth and secure their future is an antidote to the old focus on the diocese taking money from the parishes in parish share. It will help focus the minds of diocesan leaders on churches that are growing and developing, as well as on those who can't or won't pay their share. As diocese and parish keep working together on positive initiatives both morale and relationships will inevitably improve. Rather than fighting each other trying to manage decline, it is far more joyful together to fight the decline itself.

The growth cycle

We have now come full circle. Starting with the role of church growth, we have moved through the provision of human resources and of financial resources to show how the various influences on church membership and attendance can become positive rather than negative. There remains but one more task – to face the fundamental question of the inner heart and capacity of the Church of England to change and grow in all these ways that are mechanically possible but only really work in a Church possessing a measure of spiritual health and vitality.

18

The road to growth through spiritual renewal

> Rend your hearts and not your clothing. Return to the Lord, your God . . .
> I will repay you for the years that the swarming locust has eaten . . . You
> shall . . . praise the name of the Lord your God, who has dealt wondrously
> with you . . . I will pour out my spirit . . . then everyone who calls on the
> name of the Lord shall be saved. (Joel 2.13,25,26,28,32 NRSV)

Renewal and growth

For three years, during which *Hope for the Church*[1] was written and this book
begun, my job as research missioner for Springboard was 'to research, develop
and disseminate ways of turning round the numerical decline of the Church
of England'. This task was not to invent ways of growing but to discover the
ways in which churches are already turning from decline to growth. Because it
is God who grows the Church, the job has been to discern what God is doing
in the churches and what he is saying to the churches. So what sounds at one
level like a dry statistical enquiry can also be seen as an enquiry into the very
heart of the spiritual life of the Church. I may have spent too much time
with my calculator and too little time in prayer over this, but my sense from
an extensive enquiry is that there is promise as well as judgement. Within a
declining national Church there is enough spiritual renewal going on to
enable and empower significant church growth. Spiritual renewal is hard
to quantify and measure, but, being at the heart of genuine church growth, it
is time to have a go.

Passion

Lukewarm people will never have the energy and attractiveness to grow the
Church. Churches grow when the people are passionate about their faith and
the business of sharing it. It is more important to reshape and refresh the
people than to reshape and refresh the structures of the Church.

A vicar rang me to ask if I could lead a day conference for his church members on strategies for church growth. 'But we have to get our personal spirituality right first, so the PCC and other leaders are having a day away a month before you come, for our own spiritual renewal, to refresh our own passion and walk with God.' I suddenly became more optimistic about the outcome of my day with such a church.

So how can we rekindle the passion for Jesus that creates the energy for evangelism and growth? For some people this happens through attending inspiring Christian events such as Spring Harvest or a pilgrimage to Walsingham. For some it is through a more personal process such as that offered by Cursillo or work with a spiritual director. For some the passion will come out of encounter or worship within the context of their local church. Some church leaders may wish to adopt a growth strategy that is mainly about finding ways of stimulating their people to be passionate about Jesus and then setting them free to follow where their new energy takes them.

Next we explore how this passion can be re-kindled so as to make a lasting, wide-reaching impact across the country.

Listen to what the Spirit is saying to the churches

Increasingly, Anglicans say to me, 'We live in exciting times.' There seems both a greater sense of God being on the move, and of vision for the future growth of his Church. But there is little sense of a mass people movement or revival. A fragmented culture still moving away from the Church, and a flawed Church not yet ready for profound change, make stony ground for the seeds of new life. Over these years of enquiry I have not heard God promising revival, but I may have heard him say, 'Let my people grow.'

A book by Michael Harper actually entitled *Let my people grow* was published in 1977.[2] Calls for the renewal and reform of the Church of England so that it can start to grow again have been around for a long time, but things have moved on since 1977. There is enough evidence around today to describe the ways in which good practices, changes, fresh expressions and, in this chapter, spiritual renewal *are already* leading to growth across the whole spectrum of the Church of England. These are ways that transcend the different traditions and are open to all. These routes to spiritual renewal are, of course, as old as the Church, though perhaps with a contemporary twist.

Choosing to live differently

The authors of *Mission-shaped Church* identify the present time as a moment of opportunity for the Church to move forward through repentance. 'We have allowed our culture and the Church to drift apart, without our noticing. We need the grace of the Spirit for repentance if we are to receive a fresh baptism of the Spirit for witness.'[3] The report speaks of a spiritual malaise that can only be cured through the renewal of hearts. It is personally heartening to me that my own longing for this inner transformation is shared by so many other Anglicans from all traditions.

However, the spiritual renewal of the Church comes not when the Church realizes it ought to live differently, but when it actually does so. Liturgies and acts of reflection organized and led by the Church's national leaders would, I believe, have enormous significance and may well start restoring the years that the locusts have eaten. A parish, diocese or national Church that undergoes a period of self-examination followed by a formal act of absolution has a chance of a new start, of turning round to live in a new way in the future.

It could also be argued that general awareness of sin and its consequences is at an all time low both in our society, and perhaps in the Church. How realistic is a call to costly change in an age that promotes personal sovereignty, that values being non-judgemental, and that prefers the love of God to the judgement of God? But, as Revelation chapters 2 and 3 point out, a Church that cannot turn around is a Church that will die. Those who are able to do so need to take upon themselves the failings of the Church and then take them to God for forgiveness and new life. Repentance is a potent spiritual force for good, and now is the time to unleash it.

Prayer

The old priest, ordained before the Second World War and now well in his nineties, had lived through decade after decade of numerical decline. His view of the state of the Church was succinct and surprising: 'Church of England's never been in better fettle.' What he meant was that there had never been so many Anglicans who prayed together. In church after church there had been a quiet revolution. It was no longer the priest who prayed and the people who listened, but the people were now meeting to pray together in home groups, cells, prayer groups, in church on Sundays, in pairs and triplets, through the Sunday service prayer rota, praying for each other, for the world and for the Church. Things like healing prayer ministry offered at the end of Sunday services or half nights of prayer that were rare events even in 1977 are now much more normal. The Devil mocks our activism, scoffs at our strategies, sniggers at our synods, laughs at our PCC agendas, rejoices at our divisions, but trembles when we pray. The resurgence of the Church nationally will be underpinned by groups in every place praying their hearts out to God for the strengthening of the local church through the gift of new Christians and the growth of new disciples.

Prayer, however, is not a soft option. Jesus sweated blood as he prayed. If we package the Christian faith to suit consumer society as the Dream Topping on the rich trifle of life, our nights of prayer might be all too cosy. We sing a song or two, we have a drink and a chat, we put on some background music and try to form a couple of thoughts, and we come and go in relays.

The parish church had grown in numbers enormously. The vicar was exceptionally able, but it seemed to me there was something else going on as well, behind the scenes. One day I visited an elderly housebound lady who had not been able to attend a church service for some years. She spent her entire day praying for the church and the people of the parish. The vicar visited her regularly to update her on prayer needs and listen to her wisdom. I couldn't prove a thing, but it seemed to me that this lady's serious, sacrificial prayer was the unseen ingredient in the spectacular growth of her church.

One parish church found it impossible to fill in my questionnaire asking for a list of factors affecting their attendance trends and enquiring whether they used growth-friendly tactics like Alpha courses. 'You see,' said the vicar, 'it's really all down to a group of people many years ago very seriously praying together. That's why we've grown.' The vicar was Sandy Millar and the church was Holy Trinity Brompton.

Clearly, this is not to undervalue the role of leadership strategies, nurture courses and process evangelism but it is about a fresh emphasis on an unseen ministry. Increasingly it is recognized that the main role of clergy in the churches is not to do the ministry of the Church but to prepare and support the lay members in *their* spiritual and practical ministries. The main spiritual ministry is prayer. Gerard Hughes wrote: 'Training in prayer should be the main preoccupation and service given by the bishops and the clergy to the adult members of the Church.'[4] But only praying people can train others in prayer – so the Church's fundamental need is for leaders at all levels who are serious about prayer.

If it is true that the Church that prays together grows together then perhaps there are grounds for optimism today. However, the situation may be more mixed when it comes to the Bible.

Bible

If the Bible is indeed 'the word of the Lord' then hunger for its message will be at the heart of spiritual renewal. Whereas once the Bible was seen as an evangelical's speciality, there does now seem to be a much more widespread concern among church leaders about the erosion of knowledge of and respect for the Bible and the need for all Christians to engage properly with it.

The small, catholic, parish church was going to have to wait a long time for a new priest. The warden decided to do more than simply hold the fort. He did some training himself and then started leading weeknight evening nurture and Bible study courses. He was surprised and delighted by the hunger for them from church members and others alike. At the end of the first course one lady remarked, 'I have been a church–goer here for 25 years. Now I'm a Christian.' Such is the power of the written word when studied together.

On the other hand, some evangelicals fear that the Bible is actually losing ground in their tradition. There may be more Bibles in the pews today, but fewer people bring their own Bible to church. There may be more cells and other small groups in churches than there used to be, but fewer of them seem to spend solid hours in the serious study of the written word. There is a greater emphasis in the churches on Christian experience (and therefore on prayer) than there used to be, but in some there is less emphasis on, and confidence in, biblical truth. Sermons have become shorter; children are less likely to learn the Bible at home or school; Christians attend church less regularly; fewer people today memorize Scripture; fewer evangelicals have their daily 'quiet time' any more; fewer have any regular discipline of daily prayer and meditation on Scripture. There is also the nagging fear among those of us who, like Timothy (2 Timothy 3.15), have known the Scriptures from childhood, that today's Christian young people have a much less solid biblical foundation than we had.

In short, the current scene appears more mixed and the trend more uncertain than it is with prayer. Technology and society seem to be moving us into a post-book culture, yet the Christian story, Christian truth, and the sword of the Spirit are all contained in a rather large and hard to read book. Learning methods changed in the schools many years ago, but in most churches biblical teaching is still in lecture form, with no interaction, no questions, no individual exploration. There may be a long way to go in terms of conveying the stories and truths of Scripture for new generations.

Yet there are some ways forward. We worried that our teenage son's new Bible was unopened, and his Bible study notes unread until we discovered him using the Church Army's 'Word on the Web' on his laptop.[5] Some churches are including interactive Bible study groups as part of their main worship event. The 'sermon' becomes the introduction to the passage the groups will study later. In some churches there is new power in the reading of the Scriptures when handed over to the church drama group and a dramatized version of the Bible. Data projectors are able to keep the words of Scripture before the congregation's eyes and allow them to sink in. In a previous 'non-book' culture, people learnt the Bible stories from mystery plays and stained glass windows. There is scope today for the flourishing of many art forms as means of communicating biblical truth.

For others the problem is more profound. The hermeneutical uncertainties and disagreements in relation to the issues of the day rob the Bible in some minds of its unambiguous authority. In what sense is the Scripture reading in church 'the word of the Lord'? Growing churches tend to have a confidence in their own life that comes from a confidence in God that comes in part from a confidence in the Bible as the word of God. Maybe this loss of confidence is partly about the spirit of the age – prayer is thought to be about experience and Bible is thought to be about the making of truth claims on which even biblical scholars can't agree. So there is more confidence today in prayer than Bible. If so, then the counter-cultural Church needs confidence in the truths of God found in 'the word of the Lord' as well as the experience of God found through lives of prayer.

It is also possible that the Bible is being misunderstood, or at least its potential impact minimized and undersold. It may bring knowledge of God but it also brings experience of God. Meditating on Scripture, perhaps using one of the contemplative methods, or a regular pattern of daily Bible readings, often speaks directly to personal situations. So do exegetical sermons, homilies, times of personal study, Ignatian retreats and so on. The Bible transports the reader into God's strange new world – it lives and breathes, and it changes us. So perhaps we should work at emphasizing the Bible less as the book that makes truth claims about God and humans, and more as the book that enables us to experience God in our lives.

Love

God is love. Love is the only new commandment Jesus gave us. To be loved is the deepest human need. To love God and others is all we have to do. The liberation theologians were right all along – God is more interested in ortho-praxis than orthodoxy. His ultimate aim for us is right behaviour rather than right belief. Nevertheless, it is our *belonging* to the Church and our *believing* in the faith that lead to our *behaving* as Jesus' followers.

The love and integrity of the Church have never been more important. Fewer churchgoers have a private view of religion. Not so many people attend church out of habit or duty. Far more are trying to belong to a Christian community, and Christian community is what happens when Christians start loving one another. In today's world love is a bigger magnet than truth but, when Christians lose their Christian integrity through scandal or internal dispute or cold heartedness, more people are turned away from the faith in such a world. There are too many former church members who have been turned off church by the behaviour of Christians. Some of these may be attracted back through the loving behaviour of other Christians.

The Church of England is no longer automatically respected because it is part of the Establishment. The Church has to earn the respect, interest and allegiance of the people. As Mother Teresa so vividly demonstrated, this is best achieved by love – love for the poor, love for each other, love for God's world, love for God. Many people today are initially more interested in whether the Christian faith works than in whether it is true. It works if it is transforming Christians into people who love. In a postmodern privatized hedonistic world the counter-cultural Christian community reaching out in love will be irresistible.

And there are some signs of renewal. Not so many years ago the evangelical churches did not, by and large, touch 'social work' type projects. They left that sort of thing to the liberals. Now all strands of the Church have realized that it is 'social gospel or no gospel', that only a full expression of love for the whole human being, body and soul, is good enough for reflecting God's love in Christ. Helped by the creation of the Church Urban Fund, increasing numbers of Anglican churches are engaged in social projects projecting the love of God into their local communities. Sacred spaces, once used for a few hours only on Sundays, have been opened up to local communities for myriad uses during the week.

The churches are undoubtedly showing greater love and care towards local communities, but is there a greater level of love and care within church fellowships than there used to be? I do not know the answer to this, for who has experience of the inside of enough communities over a long enough period of time to tell? But where there is, the Church tends to grow.

Saph was diagnosed with cancer and given months to live. Two Christians spent time with her, went on holiday with her, cried with her, cared for her, laughed with her, sustained her, prayed for her, loved her. Responding to their love, Saph sought out the source of it through an Alpha course. There she met the source of love – God himself – and became a Christian. Sustained by faith, love and prayer Saph lived on for several years. As I took her funeral I rejoiced in the power for good contained in the love of the Christian community.

One stumbling block to the growth of the Church today is its national image – the picture painted of a shrinking, ageing, irrelevant, divided organization, the perception of its hypocrisy, and the publicity given to its sins. Many people have a better image of their own local church than they have of the Church nationally. Local church leaders cannot change the perceived national backdrop, but they can take the lead in their own local churches, remembering that love cannot be taught unless it is modelled.

Encounter

A commonly cited cause of church growth is church services that act as vehicles for religious experience. Where genuine encounter with the living God is expected and experienced, congregations tend to grow. The transformation of a weekly service, whatever its format, whatever the tradition of the church, into a series of unique, moving encounters with the divine must lie at the heart of any spiritual renewal that will draw people into the Christian community. Such a transformation does not necessarily need an alteration in the outward ordering of things but rather a renewing of the inner spirit of the worshippers. God made accessible in Christ by the Spirit through the Church, whatever the worship style, is the ultimate church growth draw.

The Holy Spirit, of course, is not some tame budgerigar whistled in by command of some superspiritual vicar in order to draw a crowd. He is a free and wild dove, flying where he wills, dancing to no human tune. So God may not be interested in manifesting himself to a Church that wants him to show up for an hour on Sunday, and then puts him back in the box until next time – the 'Andy Pandy' God. Yet he is accessible to those who sincerely seek him for the whole of life. We have the full authority of the oft-quoted words of Jesus for that: 'Where two or three are gathered in my name, I am there among them'.[6] We are not trying to persuade Jesus to turn up with us, we are tuning in to the Jesus who is already there with us. When we take communion in memory of Jesus, the echo of his broken body and shed blood is already present in the bread and wine. We do not put him in it, he comes to us through it. It is a means of grace.

Rituals and buildings designed to help people encounter the numinous mystery of God are clearly one plank of renewal for growth but they need a constant fresh eye upon them if they are not to become impenetrable imports from the past. Are we doing things this way because this is our tradition or because it is genuinely helping today's congregation encounter God afresh?

The use of silence, a hushed and holy stillness with life's background chatter switched off, enables people to hear the still small voice of God within. The use of older spiritualities, of candles and contemplation, can stir stressed and busy contemporary Christians to new spiritual depths. Christians have been encouraged to meet God through the emotions of a new style of singing – love songs *to* God rather than theology-hymns *about* God. The songs may seem to some trite and limited, but at their best they are vehicles for enabling worshippers to feel in touch with the God they love. The use of interview and testimony in the services enables the whole congregation to encounter God at work in the lives of others. The offer of prayer ministry at the end of services or of healing prayer at the communion rail gives people the chance to encounter the God who heals as well as saves. The warmth of fellowship over a drink at the end of the formal event enables people to meet God in each other and in the love of the whole community. The encouragement from the leaders to expect to encounter God in daily life and private prayer over the next seven days gives people the confidence to ascribe their personal religious experience to God rather than their own imagination. This of course carries the danger of encouraging people to see the hand of God in inappropriate ways but there is greater danger in encouraging Christians to ignore or deny the hand of God on their daily lives. Churches that keep God locked up inside their own buildings, or inside the pages of the Bible, or trapped inside their liturgies or doctrines, or reduced to a nice idea, will not satisfy the longings of the crowds. When a church is about helping people to live their lives in the ever-presence of God, it attracts the spiritually searching, and usually grows.

These outward changes to a church service are not, of course, the content of spiritual renewal, they are only the vehicles for it. It may also be that church leaders seeking spiritual renewal for their churches may need to pray the old prayer 'Lord renew your church and begin with me.' Leaders may only be able to take congregations to waters from which they themselves have drunk, but the faith of the leader that 'this morning we are going to encounter the living God' can be infectious.

All this, of course, chimes in with the age of experience. The question 'is it true?' may best be answered by a sermon, the question 'is it real?' is answered by encounter. That is why the Holy Spirit weekend is so important to the Alpha course – a course designed simply to answer questions about God without being a vehicle to ride to meet with God has limited appeal today. 'Alpha News' contains little by way of teaching or apologetics, but is stuffed full of gripping human stories.

So one way of renewing the Church for growth is to evolve the nature of the services with an eye to giving more opportunity for personal and corporate encounter with the living God. Alternatively, the real breakthrough may come in small groups where people feel freer to express themselves and may have more time in which to make meaningful contact with God. Another approach is to appoint one or two people with a sensitive manner or journalistic flair to interview church members for their personal stories. These should be recorded in some way or other – perhaps written down or videoed – and then circulated. The aim is to enable the people of the church to share their experiences of God with each other and so to encourage each other, raising levels of expectations of future encounters.

Another advantage may be to uncover the wide range of ways in which people encounter God. Some church leaders seem to assume that, because I encounter God in this particular way, that is how all encounters happen. My spirituality is the real one. But people's spiritualities vary enormously. A charismatic family service congregation may be housing one or two natural contemplatives who have got there by accident, or people whose spirituality has developed in that direction, and are being made to feel second-class because they don't feel the presence of God in the noise of celebration as the others seem to. It is important to find ways of enabling, honouring and acknowledging the whole range of ways in which different personalities and individuals encounter the living God. If people are on spirituality searches, then churches that encompass a wider range of Christian spiritualities are likely to contact and nurture a wider range of people.

Stories and testimonies can be repeated in church services on the data projector or in person. The power, reality and diversity of their own stories will astonish many church communities, and the church will be learning through the exercise not just to encourage one another but also to communicate their Christian stories with others. As we both encourage and discover the reality of encounter with God, then we both renew and grow the Church.

Testimony and story gain in power if Christians live story-rich lives. It is the job of church leaders not just to tease the stories out of individuals but also to provoke a church into leading a story-rich life. The story of a church and its people, collectively and individually, may be enriched by social encounter and a passion for justice in the back streets of the parish. It may be enriched by the youth fellowship trip to an African country to work in an orphanage for a few weeks. The key to a story-rich life is, in Ann Morisy's phrase, to 'journey out' from the internal safety of the church community to encounter and serve the world outside it.[7]

Contemporary spirituality tends to emphasize the role of the sacred space. Churches that are open during the week and have suitable places for private prayer can be very popular. Insurance advice is increasingly to keep churches unlocked to avoid the cost of putting right break-in damage. Thieves sometimes erroneously believe that, if a church is locked, it must be hiding something of value that is stealable. There may increasingly be an opportunity for many more church buildings to act as places of encounter for people with God in private at a time of their own choosing. Such private encounters may lead on to contact with the visible church community. Open, welcoming church buildings, striking the right spirituality chords, could play a significant future role.

The last century has been the age of encounter, as witnessed by the rise of the Pentecostal strand of Christianity. If authority for the evangelical comes from the truths of Scripture and for the catholic from the tradition of the Church, for the charismatic it comes from encounter with the Holy Spirit. Yet there are limits to the fashion for encounter with God, for religious experience, as the core of the Christian life. We are to be in love not with the gifts, feelings or experiences God gives us but with God himself. 'Encounter' Christians, for whom Church is a conduit of God's blessings, can be fair-weather Christians, losing their faith when suffering comes or the blessings cease to flow. We cannot build churches out of fair-weather Christians because the weather, like life, is not always fair. Solid, reliable church growth happens with Christians capable of echoing Job: 'The Lord gave, and the Lord has taken away; blessed be the name of the Lord.'[8] Christians who will be around for the long term, through thick and thin, need to be firmly rooted in the spiritual disciplines of prayer and Bible, and firmly locked into the love of the Christian community.

A different road?

In the book of Acts and in the worldwide twenty-century history of the Christian church, growth has normally come about through sacrifice, suffering, persecution, and martyrdom. It has resulted from healings, miraculous signs and outpourings of the Holy Spirit. It has been conveyed through apostles, disciples and missionaries who have laid down their entire lives in order to share the good news with others. When considering the courage and supreme sacrifices required to birth the Church, where does that leave a book primarily devoted to the apparently much more superficial idea that a national Church can grow again through reform of the institution and a quickening of its inner life? Would we not do better by ignoring or leaving the institution and just concentrating on God, asking for fire to fall from heaven and hearts to be set aflame?

In the economy of God there are times and seasons. At this time and in this national Church the sense is that reform and renewal is where God is taking us. The road to growth is an unglamorous road. The gradient is undulating and the view ahead winds only slightly uphill. It is a long road, not for the impatient quick fix merchants. Not many of us are athletes – we may be spiritually fit enough to walk, but we are a bit arthritic for running. We are dragging heavy weights of institutional and heritage burdens, of creaking organizational systems and world-weariness behind us. We have been ridiculed and written off. We squabble among ourselves about the direction we should take. Yet, miraculously, we remain in every place, and are gaining ground in many. The survival of the Church of England in every locality, and its moving forward in many, is living proof of the existence and power of God. Left to our own devices we would have folded years ago. God has not given up on us. He has given us the internal resources and the social climate in which renewing growth can become the new normality. As we faithfully serve this vision, who knows what God can do with us!

Notes

Chapter 1 Building hope

1. Bob Jackson, *Hope for the Church*, Church House Publishing, 2002.

Chapter 2 The genesis of the exodus of numbers

1. The Clergy Stipends Review Group, *Generosity and Sacrifice*, Church House Publishing, 2001.

Chapter 3 Self-inflicted wounds

1. The English Church Census is conducted periodically (1989, 1998, 2005) by the independent company 'Christian Research'.
2. The Centre for Youth Ministry colleges are Ridley Hall, St John's College Nottingham, Oxford Youth Works and Bristol Baptist College.

Chapter 4 Church growth – the main solution

1. Matthew 6.33 (NRSV).

Chapter 5 Church growth through good practices

1. Matthew 16.18 (NRSV).
2. 1 Corinthians 3.6 (NRSV).
3. *Hope for the Church*, 2002.
4. See note 1, Chapter 3, above.
5. *Hope for the Church*, 2002, p. 160.
6. From an unpublished paper by Carol Roberts, Mandy Robbins and Leslie Francis, 'The ordination of women and the Church of England today: Two integrities but one pattern of decline', Welsh National Centre for Religious Education, 2005.
7. Reported in *Hope for the Church*, 2002, Chapter 13.
8. See *Hope for the Church*, 2002, Chapter 8, p. 80.
9. See *Hope for the Church*, 2002, Chapter 1, p. 6.

Chapter 6 Church growth through change

1. From 'Abide with me' by H. F. Lyte, 1793–1847.
2. See *Hope for the Church*, Chapter 12.
3. Proverbs 17.22 (NRSV).
4. Ephesians 4.12 (NRSV).

5. See Christian A. Schwarz, *Natural Church Development Handbook*, BCGA, 1996.
6. Matthew 6.28 (NRSV).
7. John Henry Newman (1801–1890) citing Dr Scott.
8. For an interesting critique of this see Mark Ireland and Mike Booker, *Evangelism: Which way now?* Church House Publishing, 2003.
9. *Natural Church Development Handbook*, third edn, BCGA, 1998 and how to conduct an exercise in your own church in *Natural Church Development Implementation Manual*, BCGA, 1998.
10. Robert Warren, *The Healthy Churches' Handbook*, Church House Publishing, 2004.

Chapter 7 Growing the Church through fresh expressions

1. I am indebted to Pete Ward for introducing the very helpful descriptive term 'liquid church'.
2. Matthew 18.20 (NRSV).
3. *Mission-shaped Church*, Church House Publishing, 2004.
4. Luke 22.19 (NRSV).
5. There is a useful chapter on cell church in Mark Ireland and Mike Booker, *Evangelism: Which way now?* Church House Publishing, 2003.
6. Matthew 11.28 (NRSV).
7. See *Hope for the Church*, 2002, Chapter 12.
8. See *Hope for the Church*, 2002, Chapter 10.
9. More information is available at: www.encountersontheedge.org.uk; www.freshexpressions.org.uk and www.acpi.org.uk.

Chapter 8 Growing the Church in practice

1. Romans 1.8 (NRSV).
2. Mentioned in Romans 16.5.
3. Colin Buchanan, in 2002, entitled 'Mission in South-east London'.
4. The report can be found at www.london.anglican.org/CapitalIdea.
5. See *Hope for the Church*, 2002, Chapter 11, p. 121.
6. From the New Wine Networks web site: www.new-wine.org.

Chapter 9 Clergy training and selection for a missionary Church

1. *Crockford's Clerical Directory 2004–2005*, Church House Publishing, 2003.
2. From the Church of England Ministry Division's guidance notes for candidates.

Chapter 10 Deploying and equipping the clergy

1. Christian Schwarz, *Natural Church Development Handbook*, BCGA, 1996.
2. John 8.32 (NRSV).

Chapter 12 A time of transition

1. See especially Book 5, Chapter 1, Part 3, Article 3D found on page 847 of the Modern Library Paperback edition, 2000.

2. First Royal Charter of Queen Anne's Bounty, 1704.
3. For an explanation of this, see Peter Brierley, *Act on the facts*, Marc Europe, 1992.

Chapter 16 *Delivering the financial resources for growth*

1. See *Hope for the Church*, 2002, chapter 14.

Chapter 17 *Central funding for the growth of the Church*

1. Section 67 of the Ecclesiastical Commissioners Act 1840.
2. *Mission-shaped Church*, Church House Publishing, 2004.
3. *Mission-shaped Church*, 2004.

Chapter 18 *The road to growth through spiritual renewal*

1. *Hope for the Church*, 2002.
2. Michael Harper, *Let my people grow*, Hodder & Stoughton, 1977.
3. *Mission-shaped Church*, Church House Publishing, 2004, p.13.
4. Gerald Hughes, *The God of Surprises*, Darton, Longman & Todd, 1985, p. 22.
5. See www.word-on-the-web.co.uk.
6. Matthew 18.20 (NRSV).
7. Ann Morisy, *Journeying Out*, Morehouse, 2004.
8. Job 1.21 (NRSV).

Appendix 1

Kensington Clergy Conference 2004

Q1:   Name:

Q2:   Name of benefice and church:

Q3:   Could you describe your area? (e.g. posh, poor, ethnicity)

Q4:   Could you describe your church? (e.g. style of church life, types of people involved)

Q5:   Are you the incumbent or another role? How long in post?

Q6:   About what per cent of your adult members are under 45?

Q7:   Do you use process evangelism courses? (ring as appropriate)

Alpha   Other (e.g. Emmaus)   None

Q8:   What (if any) special provision do you make for teenagers? (e.g. Youth Fellowship, specialist youth worship, paid leadership)

Q9:   Please estimate average Sunday attendance of:

Adults	Children (under 16)
In 2002:	
In 2003:	
In 2004 so far:	

Q10:   Please indicate your service pattern? (use ticks)

Service	Attendance trend			
	falling	steady	rising	no sevice
Early Communion				
Main Sun Morning				
Other Sun Morning				
Sunday Evening				
Midweek				
Other regular				

Q11: What have been the main changes to your church services and church life over the last three years? (if no major changes, please reply 'none')

Q12: What are the main factors affecting your current attendance trends?

Q13: How can the diocese or area help your church to thrive and grow?

Appendix 2

The Diocese of Lichfield's growth fund application form, guidance notes and explanatory letter from the Bishop

Diocese of Lichfield Growth Funds   **Application Form**

Church, Deanery or other body making the application:

Section 1 – How we can contact you

Details of the contact person:

Name:	
Address:	

Post Town:		Post Code:	
Day Time Tel No:		Evening Tel No:	
Email:			

Position in Organisation:

Section 2 – About your Growth Initiative/project

What is the aim or objective of your proposed initiative?

Please describe your proposal and indicate how it might result in growing the number of worshipping Christians:

How does this fit with your overall strategy or Mission Action Plan?

Who will be responsible for delivering the initiative and spending the money?

How do you propose to monitor implementation and measure success?

Describe the support or partnership you have from the wider church for your proposal (if possible attach endorsements to this application form):

If the project is time limited how long will the project last?

When do you wish to start?

Section 3 – Financing the project

Please provide a budget for your project. A suggested format is attached. Be accurate with your costings as we will not be able to increase any grant that we may make.

How much will your project cost?

	Year 1	Year 2	Year 3	Total
	£	£	£	£
How much do you already have?	£	£	£	£

How much are you seeking from the Growth Fund?

	Year 1	Year 2	Year 3	Total
£	£	£	£

The Growth Fund grant will normally be for up to 50% of the proposal's cost. How will you raise the rest of the money?

Probable sources of funding

	Year 1	Year 2	Year 3	Total
	£	£	£	£
	£	£	£	£
	£	£	£	£
	£	£	£	£
	£	£	£	£

Possible sources of funding

	Year 1	Year 2	Year 3	Total
	£	£	£	£
	£	£	£	£
	£	£	£	£
	£	£	£	£
	£	£	£	£

It is unlikely that the Fund will be able to continue assisting ongoing projects for longer than three years. If you envisage a long-term project, how will you plug the funding gap in three years' time?

Section 4 – Staffing the Project

If you propose employing someone please give or append a job description:

Section 5 – Your Parish Share

Are you up to date with your Parish Share payments?   Yes: [   ]   No: [   ]

If not, please describe the arrangements for getting up to date:

What percentage of your Parish Share is paid by regular monthly amount?   [   ] %

Section 6 – Bank Account Details

Grants will be made by BACS transfer. Please provide details of the account to which the money should be paid:

Account Name: [   ]
Account No: [   ]   Sort Code: [   ]

Who are the signatories on this account?

Name: **Position:**

Appendix 2

Signature of Applicant:

Position in Organisation:

Date:

Please send your application to:

by post:	by email:
Ven Bob Jackson	archdeacon.Walsall@lichfield.anglican.org
Archdeacon of Walsall	

Do not forget to attach the budget for your initiative/project.

For internal use:
Date received:
Grants Panel Date:
Grant approved: Yes: No:
Date Applicant informed:

Grant-making criteria – guidance notes

1   Grants from the Growth Funds will be made for initiatives in evangelism, the numerical growth of the Christian Church, and fresh expressions of church.

2   Grants are available for one-off costs and for annual costs, including staff costs, for up to three years.

3   Grants are not available towards major building works or projects that are primarily social in nature. If you are in any doubt about the eligibility of your project please check with a member of the grant-making group.

4   Grants will normally be made for up to 50% of the total cost, up to a limit of £15,000 per annum. The minimum grant application considered will be £250.

5   Projects should normally involve initiatives that relate to people in their twenties or thirties, families, teenagers or children – the generations that the churches have been losing and need to re-connect with.

6   Any unit of the Diocese of Lichfield may apply for a grant – parishes, teams, clusters, deaneries, fresh expressions, areas, or divisions.

7   The application form asks how much of your Parish Share is paid by regular monthly amount. This is a serious question – we can only set aside money for the Growth Funds if Parish Share payments come in reliably and regularly. Please show your support for the Growth Fund by increasing the proportion of your Share paid by regular monthly amount.

8   In order to become eligible for a grant, Parishes with Share arrears will need to show how their arrears are being dealt with.

9   It will be helpful if larger applications show some evidence of wider support from within the diocese, e.g. a parish should show some level of support from their deanery or cluster.

10   The following examples of eligible projects are given simply to stimulate ideas – applicants are invited to use their God-given imaginations in finding creative ways of growing the twenty-first century church:

  • Start up funding for a new congregation meeting in a school hall – musical instruments, data projector, initial rental, etc.

  • Training and equipment needs for a team of Children's Group Leaders for newly improved Sunday groups.

  • Salary costs for a youth or children's minister, a families worker, an alpha group co-ordinator, an evangelist, a church planter, a young adults networker.

  • A mix of start up and staffing costs for a new deanery post for a pioneer fresh expression such as a young-adult network church.

  • Start up and initial running costs for an after-school congregation.

  • Costs of an evangelistic mission.

All applications will need to pass five tests:

1   Relevance – that your application comes within the indicated criteria.

2   Competence – that you have filled in your form and answered any supplementary

questions in such a way as to convince the grant-making group that you have a fair chance of delivering your project competently.

3   Plausibility – that you establish a plausible route by which your proposal could result in the growth of the church.

4   Comprehensiveness – that you have answered all the questions on the form (plus any supplementaries) in such a way as to give the grant-making group a clear and full picture of your intentions.

5   Sustainability – that the larger, longer term projects show how you might keep the project going once our funding has finished or personnel have moved on.

The presumption is that any application passing all five tests will be awarded a grant, subject to funds being available. If applications exceed funds available then the grant-makers reserve the right to decide whether to award small grants to all, or larger grants to some and none to others.

Please feel free to contact the Chair of the group if you would like help with framing your proposal or filling in your form. He may be able to put you in touch with someone who can assist you. Remember – small applications will not need as much detail as large ones.

Members with a personal interest in a proposal will withdraw from the meeting while it is being discussed.

The Group will meet to consider applications on the following dates:

Tuesday _ _ July 20_ _

Wednesday _ _ October 20_ _

Thursday _ _ January 20_ _

Thursday _ _ April 20_ _

All completed applications forms should be sent to the Chair and must arrive at least ten days before the date of the next meeting in order to be considered at it. Early applications are advised where possible in order to give time for the group to obtain any clarifications that it needs before the meeting. In complicated cases a member of the group may arrange to visit you prior to the grant-making meeting. Applicants will be notified of the outcome as soon as possible after each meeting.

Letter from the Bishop of Lichfield

From the Bishop of Lichfield

Dear friends,

'Seek first God's Kingdom and his righteousness,' said Jesus, 'and all the other things you need will be given to you.' Ever since I arrived I have felt the need for a fund for the Diocese to enable people to take new initiatives, and I give thanks to God that we can now launch the fund – and you can apply for grants from it.

Some creative initiatives cost very little. I think of the priest who provided hot-cross buns on Good Friday this year, and the congregation for the Good Friday service doubled; or the parish that gave out Easter cards to its congregations and suggested they invite friends, with the result that this Easter the numbers trebled. The best ideas come from praying together, where those responsible for a congregation or a division wait on God for his promptings.

Some initiatives, however, cost serious money. If you want to hire a hall for that new congregation or employ a children's and families' worker you will need to trust God for large sums. In this kind of situation the diocese can help you prime the pump for the first few years.

Of course almost all our diocesan budget will continue to go straight back to the parishes for the stipends of the clergy. The good news is that more parishes have started to pay their Share regularly each month and this means that we are keeping up with our stringent financial strategy. A big thank you if you are one of those parishes who have started to pay regularly in this way. The Church Commissioners have provided some new money specifically for growth and we have identified some old Diocesan funds which can also be used for this Fund. One or two individuals are directing their giving for the Fund too. The result is that from July we will have over a quarter of a million pounds to spend each year on backing imaginative new schemes. We trust that this will be an encouragement to those who are gripped by missionary zeal, church-planting zest or enthusiasm for a new after-school club.

The enclosed papers show you how to apply for support. The grant-making meetings will meet every three months. So the money will not have run out if you are not ready for a while yet.

Letter from the Bishop of Lichfield

I have been impressed by the numbers of churches in the diocese who are dreaming new dreams together. May God use this new Growth and Opportunities Fund to help you turn your God-inspired dreams into reality!

Yours in the service of Christ,

Index